W9-CHR-009

always up to date

The law changes, but Nolo is on top of it! We offer several
ways to make sure you and your Nolo products are up to date:

1 **Nolo's Legal Updater**
We'll send you an email whenever a new edition of this book is
published! Sign up at **www.nolo.com/legalupdater**.

2 **Updates @ Nolo.com**
Check **www.nolo.com/update** to find recent changes
in the law that affect the current edition of your book.

3 **Nolo Customer Service**
To make sure that this edition of the book is the most
recent one, call us at **800-728-3555** and ask one of
our friendly customer service representatives.
Or find out at **www.nolo.com**.

please note

We believe accurate, plain-English legal information should help
you solve many of your own legal problems. But this text is not a
substitute for personalized advice from a knowledgeable lawyer.
If you want the help of a trained professional—and we'll always
point out situations in which we think that's a good idea—consult
an attorney licensed to practice in your state.

9th Edition

Nolo's Guide to
California Law

**by Attorneys Lisa Guerin &
Patricia Gima & Nolo Editors**

NINTH EDITION   JUNE 2006
Editor   EMILY DOSKOW
Book Design   JACKIE MANCUSO
Proofreading   SARA TOLCHIN
Index   PATRICIA DEMINNA
Printing   DELTA PRINTING SOLUTIONS, INC.

ISSN 1546-7279
ISBN 1-4133-0491-5

Quantity sales: For information on bulk purchases or corporate premium sales, please contact the Special
Sales department. For academic sales or textbook adoptions, ask for Academic Sales. 800-955-4775, Nolo,
950 Parker Street, Berkeley, CA 94710.

ACKNOWLEDGMENTS

Thanks to all of the editors at Nolo, whose specialized legal knowledge and ongoing vigilance make this book possible.

I'd also like to thank Jake Warner, Mary Randolph, and Lisa Guerin for creating the first edition and all the inspiration for this tiny wonder of a book.

And a special thanks to Shae Irving for her patience and great editorial and organizational skills.

— Patricia Gima

This book represents the hard work of many people. I owe special thanks to:

All the editors at Nolo, who not only wrote much of this book but also edited, kibbitzed, researched, and nurtured me through the writing process.

My editors Jake Warner and Mary Randolph, who had the idea for the book. Thank you for your tireless efforts to take the lawyer out of my writing and for having confidence in me.

Barbara Kate Repa, who began my career at Nolo with the most cryptic response to a resume I've ever received and has continued to delight and amuse me at work.

Stephanie Harolde, for her skillful handling of a messy manuscript and her many helpful comments.

Jackie Mancuso for her wonderful book design.

Deanne Loonin, for her patient explanations of government benefits and other legal intricacies, and for sitting next to me on that first day of law school—I can't imagine what it would have been like otherwise.

— Lisa Guerin

Contents

About This Book

As citizens, we are presumed to know the law. Ignorance—as many of us learn the hard way—is no excuse. But how do we learn about the laws that affect our dealings with neighbors, family members, landlords, employers, or creditors? Most schools and lawyers' organizations make little effort to teach us even the basics.

Trying to read up on our own is often a frustrating experience. Most books about law are written for lawyers and stay tucked away on law library shelves. Even if we do manage to get our hands on them, we find they are filled with nearly impenetrable jargon.

This book gathers key legal rules into a readable, affordable book that you can keep on your reference shelf. When you have questions about the state laws that affect Californians on a day-to-day basis, you'll have the information you need at your fingertips.

WHAT THE BOOK COVERS

We have covered the legal topics likely to affect most people in the ordinary course of their lives: consumers' rights, divorce, traffic tickets, real estate, adoption, and so on. We've also included a few basic topics covered by federal law, such as Social Security and bankruptcy. Obviously, no one book can cover all points of California law. So we opted not to discuss criminal law (except traffic violations) or such specialized topics as environmental regulations or banking laws.

HOW THE BOOK IS ORGANIZED

To make it easy to find the information you need, we have grouped laws into broad categories: Relationships, Landlords and Tenants, Real Estate, Wills and Inheritance, and Consumers' Rights, for example. The Table of Contents lists them all.

At the beginning of each section, you will find a list of the topics covered there (they're arranged alphabetically), plus a list of related topics covered elsewhere in the book. You may need to look at several entries to find the information you need, especially if your question doesn't fit neatly into any one category. Check the index for keywords that interest you.

ADDITIONAL RESOURCES

Each section of the book also contains a list of additional resources. These include books, pamphlets, organizations, and websites that can give you more information about a particular subject. For example, under "Children," we list several books and groups that help adoptive parents. Because Nolo is by far the state's largest publisher of self-help law materials, inevitably some of our referrals are to other Nolo publications. But we have done our best to include the most helpful legal materials, whether or not we publish them.

KEEPING UP TO DATE

The law changes constantly as the state legislature passes new bills and courts hand down their rulings. We will publish new, revised editions of this book periodically, but it will never be perfectly current. It's always your responsibility to be sure a law is current before you rely on it. For updates four times a year, check the "Updates" section of the Nolo website at www. nolo.com. You can get updates via email by subscribing to our online newsletter, *Nolo Briefs*.

LEGAL CITATIONS

This book summarizes most laws of general interest. There may be times, however, when you will want to go further and read the full text of a statute. For this reason, citations to California and federal statutes (and, occasionally, crucial court cases) appear throughout the book. The section on "Looking Up the Law" at the front of the book explains how to use these citations to find the laws you need.

Looking Up the Law

Nolo's Guide to California Law not only summarizes many laws but also serves as a way to find the text of any law you want to read word for word. And once you find the law, you'll probably also find references to articles and court cases that discuss the law.

This brief discussion tells you how to use a reference from this book to look up a state or federal statute or a court decision. Until recently, a law library was the only place to do legal research. Now it is increasingly possible to find useful information online. First, we offer some tips on using a law library. Then, we provide some pointers on finding California law using your own personal computer.

FINDING A LAW LIBRARY

To look up state or federal statutes or court decisions, go to your county law library (usually in or near the county courthouse) or the library of a law school funded by the state, such as the University of California at Berkeley, Davis, or Los Angeles; or Hastings College of the Law in San Francisco. Some, but not all, large public libraries also have collections of state or federal statutes; call before you go to make sure.

If it's a local (city or county) ordinance you're curious about, you can probably find it at the main branch of your local public library. Or call the city or county attorney's office and ask how you can get a copy.

FINDING STATUTES

When you go to look up a statute, try to use what is called an "annotated" version of the statutes. Annotated statutes include not only the text of the statutes themselves but also brief summaries of court cases that have discussed each statute. After you find a relevant statute, you may want to scan the case summaries—and even read some of the cases in their entirety—to see how courts have construed the language of the statute.

Federal statutes. Federal statutes are organized by subject in a set of books called the *United States Code* (U.S.C.). An annotated version of this code is available in virtually every law library. If you know the statute's common name or its citation, you should be able to find it easily.

EXAMPLE: *You want to read some of the provisions of the Fair Credit Reporting Act, 15 U.S.C. §§ 1681 and following. You would look in Title 15 of the United States Code Annotated (the numbers are on the spine of the books) and find section 1681. The statute begins with section 1681 and covers many sections.*

California statutes. California's statutes, which fill many volumes, are organized into "codes." Each code covers a separate area of law, such as Education or Health & Safety. The codes come in two annotated versions: *West's Annotated Code* and *Deering's Annotated Codes*. If you have a citation to a statute in a particular code, you'll be able to look up the statute easily.

EXAMPLE: *You want to look up the law that's cited as Veh. Code § 541. Checking the table of abbreviations in the front of the book, you see that you want the Vehicle Code (the spine of each volume has the name of a code printed on it). Once you have the volume that contains the Vehicle Code, just look for section 541.*

MAKING SURE YOU HAVE THE MOST RECENT VERSION OF THE STATUTE

Every year, the California legislature and Congress pass hundreds of new laws and change (amend) lots of existing ones. When you look up a statute, it's crucial that you get the most recent version.

To do that, always look for a pamphlet that is inserted in the back of the hardcover volume of statutes. It's called a "pocket part," and it contains any changes made to the statutes since the hardcover book was printed. Pocket parts are updated and replaced every year—it's much cheaper than producing a whole new hardcover volume every year.

Look up the statutes again in the pocket part. If there's no entry, that means the statute hasn't been changed as of the date the pocket part was printed. If there is an entry, it will show you what language in the statute has been changed.

To check for changes that are even more recent—made since the pocket part was printed—you can check something called the Advance Legislative Service. It's a series of paperback pamphlets that contain the very latest statutory changes. It may be on the shelf next to the hardcover volumes; if not, ask the law librarian where you can find it.

FINDING CASES

If you want to look up a case (court decision) and you have the citation (either from this book or from an annotated code), all you need to do is decipher those strange numbers and abbreviations.

Let's take a hypothetical citation:

Smith v. Jones, 175 Cal. App. 3d 88 (1984).

The names at the beginning are the names of the parties to the lawsuit. The date at the end is the year the case was decided.

"Cal. App. 3d" stands for California Appellate Reports, 3rd series, the book in which the case is printed. California cases are printed in four different sets of books: California Reports ("Cal.") covers cases from the California Supreme Court; Cal. App. publishes appellate court cases; the California Reporter ("Cal. Rptr.") includes both Supreme and appellate court cases; and the Pacific Reporter ("P.") publishes Supreme and pre-1960 appellate court cases, along with cases from the other Western states.

The number following the volume title is the series in which the case can be found. There are several series of each of these sets of books; the series with the highest number contains the most recent cases.

To find our case, you would locate the shelf space devoted to the 3rd series of Cal. App. and select volume 175. The case begins on page 88.

MAKING SURE THE CASE IS STILL GOOD LAW

Judges don't go back and change their earlier decisions, like legislatures amend old statutes, but cases can still be profoundly affected by later court decisions. For example, the California Supreme Court has the power to overrule a decision of a California Court of Appeal. If it does, the Court of Appeal's written decision no longer has any legal effect.

There are several ways to find out whether a case still represents valid law. The most common is to use a collection of books called *Shepard's*, which lets you compile a list of all later cases that mention the case you're interested in. Unfortunately, the *Shepard's* system is too complicated to explain here. If it's important to you, consult one of the legal research tools mentioned below.

MORE LEGAL RESEARCH

Legal research is a subject that can (and does) easily fill a whole book of its own.

For a thorough, how-to approach to finding answers to your legal questions, see *Legal Research: How to Find & Understand the Law*, by Stephen R. Elias and Susan Levinkind (Nolo).

ONLINE LEGAL RESEARCH

It is increasingly possible to do basic legal research from your home computer. With access to the Internet, you'll have a wealth of legal information at your fingertips. For example, the Web offers direct access to such important legal resource materials as:

- federal statutes and regulations
- state and federal appellate court cases
- California statutes
- California Supreme Court and appellate court case opinions
- pending and recent legislation, and
- state agency rules and regulations.

You can find these legal sources on many different websites. You can visit our site, www.nolo.com, to find statutes and cases from every state. Or you can use an online catalog known as Findlaw, at www.findlaw.com, to look up state laws and cases.

The California court system has its own website, www.courtinfo.ca.gov. You can find recent California Supreme Court and appellate court decisions here, as well as helpful information on the entire court system. You can also find older cases on the Internet, but you will probably have to pay a private company for access to its database. Versuslaw, at www.versuslaw. com, maintains an excellent library of older state court cases. You can do unlimited research here for a reasonable monthly fee.

Westlaw, at www.westlaw.com, and Lexis, at www.lexis.com, are the largest electronic legal databases. Although subscriptions to these services are pricey, both offer some free and some fee-based services to nonsubscribers.

Abbreviations Used in This Book

CALIFORNIA CODES

Bus. & Prof.	Business & Professions
Civ.	Civil
Civ. Proc.	Civil Procedure
Corp.	Corporations
Educ.	Education
Elect.	Elections
Fam.	Family
Fin.	Financial
Gov't.	Government
H & S	Health and Safety
Harb. & Nav.	Harbors & Navigation
Ins.	Insurance
Lab.	Labor
Mil. & Vet.	Military & Veterans
Pen.	Penal
Pub. Res.	Public Resources
Rev. & Tax.	Revenue & Taxation
Unemp. Ins.	Unemployment Insurance
Unif. Comm.	Uniform Commercial
Veh.	Vehicle
Welf. & Inst.	Welfare & Institutions

FEDERAL LAWS

C.F.R.	Code of Federal Regulations
I.R.C.	Internal Revenue Code
Stat.	United States Statutes at Large
U.S.C.	United States Code

CASES

Cal. App.	California Court of Appeal Reports
Cal.	California Supreme Court Reports
F.2d	Federal Reporter, 2nd Series (United States Court of Appeal)
F.3d	Federal Reporter, 3rd Series (United States Court of Appeal)
U.S.	United States Supreme Court Reports
S.Ct.	United States Supreme Court Reporter

Children

Although the law usually lets parents decide how to raise their children, in certain circumstances the state gets involved in the relationship between parents, children, and those who are otherwise responsible for the care and education of children. The law regulates some methods of having a child, such as artificial insemination and adoption, as well as controlling what happens to children when parents divorce or die. Children whose parents are unable to care for them may be removed from their home and put in alternative living arrangements. The law also grants children rights in school, in the courtroom, and at home.

TOPICS

Adoption
Age of Majority
Birth Certificates
Breastfeeding
Child Abuse and Neglect
Child Support
Children Born to Unmarried Parents
Custody
Donor Insemination
Education
Emancipated Minors
Foster Care
Gay and Lesbian Parents
Grandparents' Rights
Guardianships
Housing Discrimination
Juvenile Court
Parental Kidnapping and Custodial Interference
Parents' Liability for Their Children's Acts

> **Safety**
> **Students and Teachers**
> **Visitation**

RELATED TOPICS
> **Employees' Rights**
>> Child Labor
>> Family and Medical Leave
>
> **Government Benefits**
>> Aid to Families With Dependent Children
>
> **Inheritance and Wills**
>> Inheritance by Minor Children
>
> **Traffic and Vehicle Laws**
>> Seatbelt and Child Restraint Requirements
>
> **Landlords and Tenants**
>> Discrimination
>
> **Relationships**

ADDITIONAL RESOURCES

Legal Services for Children, Inc., 1254 Market Street, 3rd Floor, San Francisco, CA 94102, 415-863-3762, www.lsc-sf.org, gives information, referrals, and legal assistance to minors.

Do Your Own California Adoption: Nolo's Guide for Stepparents & Domestic Partners, by Frank Zagone and Emily Doskow (Nolo), provides step-by-step instructions and all the forms necessary to complete an uncontested stepparent or domestic partner adoption in California.

Adopting in California: How to Adopt Within One Year, by Randall Hicks (Wordslinger Press), explains all types of adoption procedures in California.

The Essential Adoption Handbook, by Colleen Alexander-Roberts (Taylor Pub.), covers domestic, international, and open adoptions.

The Adoption Resource Book, by Lois Gilman (Harper Collins), explains independent, interstate, and foreign adoptions.

Families Adopting Children Everywhere (FACE) National Helpline, 410-488-2656, www.faceadoptioninfo.org, provides referrals to local specialist groups and conducts training courses for adoptive parents.

North American Council on Adoptable Children, 970 Raymond Avenue, Suite 106, St. Paul, MN 55114-1149, 651-644-3036 (direct), 651-644-9848 (fax), www.nacac.org, is a coalition of adoptive parent support groups that makes referrals to local organizations.

International Vital Records Handbook, by Thomas Jay Kemp (Genealogical Publishing Co., Inc.), gives information on how to get a birth certificate from any country. Order forms are included.

How to Change Your Name in California, by Lisa Sedano and Emily Doskow (Nolo), includes information on birth certificates.

California Divorce Helpline, 800-359-7004, gives legal information about child support, charging $10 for your call and $5 per minute, and can also run a computerized support calculation program to determine child support payments for about $75. See www.divorcehelp.com for more services and information.

Divorce Without Court: A Guide to Mediation & Collaborative Divorce, by Katherine E. Stoner (Nolo), explains child custody, divorce mediation, and collaborative law, including what to expect from the process and how to work out the best arrangements with a former spouse.

Building a Parenting Agreement That Works: How to Put Your Kids First When Your Marriage Doesn't Last, by Mimi Lyster (Nolo), shows separating or divorcing parents how to create win-win custody agreements.

National Center for Lesbian Rights, 870 Market Street, Suite 370, San Francisco, CA 94102, 415-392-6257, www.nclrights.org, provides legal information, referrals, and assistance to lesbian and gay parents and publishes *Lesbians Choosing Motherhood: Legal Implications of Alternative Insemination and Reproductive Technologies*.

A comprehensive website for gay and lesbian parents—and those considering parenting—is www.familypride.org.

The Guardianship Book for California: How to Become a Child's Legal Guardian, by David Brown and Emily Doskow (Nolo), contains all forms and instructions necessary to become a child's guardian.

Law in the School, Crime and Violence Prevention Center, 1300 I Street, Suite 1150, Sacramento, CA 95814, 916-324-7863, www.safestate.org, gives detailed information about the rights of students and teachers in California schools.

ADOPTION

Adoption is a court procedure by which an adult legally becomes the parent of someone who is not his or her biological child. Adopting parents assume legal responsibility for the child—including the duty to provide support—and the child inherits from the adoptive parents as if they were birth parents. The birth parents' legal relationship to the child is terminated unless there is a legal contract allowing them to retain or share some rights (as in a stepparent or domestic partner adoption).

Consent of the Birth Parents

The child's natural parents each have the right to be notified of a proposed adoption and to object to it. Each parent's rights depend on the degree to which he or she has been involved in raising and caring for the child.

A man is presumed to be the child's natural father and is entitled to notice of adoption proceedings regarding the child if any of the following is true:

- He was married to the mother when the child was born, or was married to the mother before the child's birth and the child was born within 300 days of the end of the couple's marriage by divorce, legal separation, annulment, or death.
- He attempted to marry the mother, but the marriage was not valid for some technical reason.
- He married the child's mother after the child was born (even if the marriage was later annulled), and he was willingly named on the birth certificate as father, or he paid child support under a written promise or court order.
- While the child was a minor, he welcomed the child into his home and openly held the child out to be his natural child. (Fam. Code § 7611.)

A woman does not need to take any special steps to be presumed the natural mother.

A natural (or presumed) parent must give consent for an adoption to take place, unless his or her parental rights have been terminated for some reason, such as abandonment or unfitness. A parent's rights can be terminated if the parent has willfully failed to communicate with or financially support the child for at least one year.

Types of Adoption

- **Stepparent adoption** occurs when a parent with custody of a child marries or registers with a domestic partner, and the new spouse adopts the child. Consent of the child's other parent may be necessary (see above). The natural parent and the new spouse or registered domestic partner must file a petition in superior court, after which a social worker will conduct an investigation and write a report for the judge. If the report is favorable, the judge is likely to grant the adoption.

- **Domestic partner adoption** is like a stepparent adoption in that the registered domestic partner of a legal or biological parent may adopt that parent's child. Domestic partner registration is available only to same-sex couples in California, so heterosexual partners must either marry to take advantage of stepparent adoption rules or complete a second parent adoption, described below.

- **Second parent adoption** is an independent adoption (see definition below) by an unmarried partner in a heterosexual or same-sex relationship, where the partner becomes a legal parent while the child's parent retains parental rights (the same as in a stepparent or domestic partner adoption). Second parent adoption would be available to same-sex couples who aren't eligible for domestic partner registration because they do not live together or are in the process of terminating a previous domestic partnership, for example, and to heterosexual couples who are parenting together but do not wish to marry.

- **Agency adoption** occurs when a licensed public or private adoption agency places a child in the home of adopting parents. The agency will make sure that the birth parents' rights have been terminated before the placement. The adopting parents must file a petition, submit to an investigation by a social worker, and be approved by a judge.

  Adoption agencies are usually extremely selective because they have long waiting lists of prospective parents. Agencies usually charge between $1,000 and $6,000 for placing young children and up to $10,000 for placing newborns.

- **County adoption** occurs when the county has custody of a child because the parents have abused, neglected, or abandoned the child, or the child has been declared beyond the parents' control. These children are usually placed in foster homes while efforts are made to reunite the family; typically, parents must agree to attend parenting classes or counseling and must meet other conditions imposed by the judge. If, after 18 months, the parents have not met the conditions for reunification, the judge terminates their parental rights and frees the child for adoption. These children are sometimes adopted by their foster parents.

- **Independent adoption**, also called private adoption, occurs when birth parents consent to place a child directly with the adoptive parents, without any agency participation. Although it is illegal in California for adoptive parents to advertise that they are looking for a baby to adopt (Fam. Code § 8609), few other state laws regulate independent adoption. In some counties—such as Los Angeles— local law requires that the birth mother and adoptive parents meet in person. The adoptive parents may pay the medical, legal, and other necessary living expenses of the mother. However, if the birth mother decides not to go through with the adoption, the adoptive parents are not entitled to get their money back.

  As in other kinds of adoption, in an independent adoption the adoptive parents must file a petition in superior court, be investigated by a county social worker, and be approved by a judge. The adoption becomes final about six months after the birth parents agree to give up their parental rights.

- **Intercountry or international adoptions** occurs when parents adopt a child from outside the U.S. Adoptive parents may (and sometimes must, depending on the country) readopt the child in California. The advantage to doing so is that a new California birth certificate will be issued. (Fam. Code § 8904.)

AGE OF MAJORITY

Every state designates children as minors until they reach a certain age: the age of majority. In California, that age is 18. (Fam. Code § 6501.)

A minor may not give legally binding consent in many situations. (Fam. Code §§ 6700, 6701, 6920, 6921, 6925, 7050.) Specifically, a minor may not:

- enter into a contract relating to real estate or the sale of personal property not in the immediate possession of the minor
- buy or sell property, including real estate and stock
- get married without the written consent of parents or guardian and a judge
- sue or be sued in his or her own name (except in a personal injury lawsuit)
- compromise, settle, or arbitrate a claim
- make or revoke a will, or
- inherit property outright—it must be supervised by an adult.

However, a minor in California may:

- donate blood if he or she is at least 17 years old, or if he or she is at least 15 years old and has the written consent of parents or guardian and a doctor (H & S Code § 1607.5.)
- consent to his or her own hospital, medical, or surgical care if he or she is legally married or on active duty in the armed services (Fam. Code §§ 7002, 7050.)
- consent to his or her own mental health treatment or counseling on an outpatient basis or participate in a decision to consent to residential shelter services if he or she is at least 12 years old, is determined to be sufficiently mature to consent to residential shelter services, or is otherwise emancipated. (Fam. Code §§ 6920, 6921, 6924.)
- consent to pregnancy treatment, treatment for a communicable disease, treatment after a sexual assault, and drug or alcohol treatment. (Fam. Code §§ 6925, 6926, 6927, 6929.)

BIRTH CERTIFICATES

A birth certificate is a document that officially records the birth of a child. Birth certificates give the child's name and sex, the names of the child's parents, and when and where the birth took place. Birth certificates are usually completed by hospital personnel or the person delivering the baby.

How to Get a Copy of a Birth Certificate

To obtain a certified copy of a birth certificate from the Office of Vital Records, mail your request to the California Department of Health Services, Office of Vital Records, M.S. 5103, P.O. Box 997410, Sacramento, CA 95899-7410. You can check procedures for obtaining records at the Office of Vital Records website at www.dhs.ca.gov/hisp/chs/OVR/ordercert. htm. You can get copies more quickly by going to the county recorder in the county where the birth took place or, if the birth was within the last two years, to the county health department in that county. Another good resource for getting a birth certificate or other similar documents is www. vitalcheck.com.

Unmarried Parents

If the parents of a child are not legally married, the father's name will not be added to the birth certificate unless he:

- signs a voluntary Declaration of Paternity in the hospital, or
- signs the form later or legally establishes paternity and pays to amend the birth certificate. (H & S Code § 102425.)

Amendments to a Birth Certificate

Birth certificates may be amended in certain situations. The amendment is attached to the birth certificate and becomes an official part of the birth record. Amendments are allowed only to:

- **Reflect a court-ordered name change and/or gender change.** If you obtained a name change from any court in the United States or territory, you may add this name to your birth certificate. (H & S Code §§ 103400.)
- **Add a parent's new name to a child's birth certificate.** If a parent's name is changed by usage or court order, an attachment may be added showing the parent's new name. The attachment indicates that the parent is "AKA" (also known as) and gives the new name.

- **Add the father's name to the birth certificate.** For unmarried parents, the father's name may be added to the birth certificate after the father signs a voluntary Declaration of Paternity or paternity is otherwise legally established. (H & S Code §§ 102766.)
- **Correct minor typographical errors or omissions on the original birth certificate.** Minor errors or missing information may be corrected by amendment. There is no charge for correcting errors to a birth certificate if the change is made within one year of a child's birth. (H & S Code §§ 103225-103255.)

  If the incorrect sex is listed and the birth was recent, a hospital official should complete an affidavit (sworn statement) indicating the error. This affidavit should be sent with the application to amend.

  If the wrong father was listed on the birth certificate, an attachment cannot be used to correct either the certificate or the child's last name, regardless of the explanation.

How to Get a New Birth Certificate

When a new birth certificate is issued, the old one is sealed, and no one can look at it without a special court order. A new California birth certificate is issued only in these circumstances:

- **Acknowledgment of paternity.** If a birth certificate omits a child's father, or the father is listed but the child's last name is different from the father's, a new birth certificate is available. (H & S Code §§ 102750-102765.) The mother and father acknowledging paternity both must sign statements under penalty of perjury confirming that they are the natural parents and requesting changes to the birth certificate. The child's name may also be changed to reflect the father's last name.
- **Judicial decree of paternity (court order required).** If a court in the United States finds that a man is the father of a child and issues an order stating this fact—often referred to as a "judicial decree of paternity" or "adjudication of paternity"—a new birth certificate may be issued. Information about the father may be included on the birth certificate, and the child's last name may be changed to that of the father. (H & S Code §§ 102725-102735.)

- **Adoption (court order required).** A new birth certificate may be issued for the child in the name of the new parents (including same-sex adoptive parents). (H & S Code § 102635.) The court clerk (or agency, if the adoption was outside of California) must send notice of the adoption to the Office of Vital Records within five days after the adoption is finalized. (H & S Code § 102625.)
- **Sex change operation (court order required).** People born in California who have undergone a surgical sex change operation may obtain a new birth certificate reflecting their new name and sex. They must first go to court and obtain an order that affirms both the sex change and the new name. (H & S Code §§ 103425-103445.)
- **Offensive racial description.** Upon request, a new birth certificate will be issued if the original contains a derogatory, demeaning, or colloquial racial description and the person prefers a different racial description. (H & S Code §§ 103260, 103350-75.)

BREASTFEEDING

A mother may breastfeed her child in any location, public or private, where the mother and child are otherwise authorized to be present, except in the private home or residence of another who objects. (Civ. Code § 43.3.)

CHILD ABUSE AND NEGLECT

Child abuse is any physical injury or mental suffering inflicted on a child by other than accidental means. Child abuse may be sexual in nature: touching a child's genitals or other private parts for sexual gratification, masturbating in front of a child, or filming or photographing a child participating in actual or simulated sex acts. Child abuse is a felony punishable by up to six years in state prison for a first offense. (Pen. Code §§ 273a, 11165.1, 11165.6.)

Child neglect is the mistreatment or negligent (unreasonably careless) treatment of a child by a person responsible for the child's welfare, in circumstances that threaten or cause harm to the child. Failure to provide necessary food, clothing, shelter, supervision, or medical care (except in the case of treatment by spiritual means) all constitute neglect. Neglect is a misdemeanor, punishable by up to one year in the county jail, a fine of up to $2,000, or both. (Pen. Code §§ 270, 11165.2.)

When a report of suspected child abuse or neglect is made, Child Protective Services (a branch of the California Department of Social Services) must immediately assess the child's safety. A child in serious danger will be removed from the home at once. Then a case plan will be developed, with the ultimate goal of safely reuniting the child with his or her family. In some cases, the state may require counseling or parenting classes. If the child cannot return home safely, the child will stay in foster care and eventually be freed for adoption. (Welf. & Inst. Code §§ 16500 and following.)

Reporting Requirements

Teachers, administrators, camp counselors, clergy members (priests, ministers, rabbis), foster parents, and others whose job responsibilities include direct supervision of children have a legal duty to report suspected child abuse or neglect to a police or sheriff's department, a county probation department, or a county welfare department. These people must report their suspicions immediately by phone and submit a written report within 36 hours. Similarly, any commercial film or photographic print processor who sees a depiction of a child under 16 engaged in sexual acts must telephone and submit a written report, including a copy of the material in question, to the local law enforcement agency within 36 hours. (Pen. Code § 11166.)

If, upon further investigation, it appears that the person making the child abuse report was mistaken, that person cannot be held liable for the mistake as long as it was honest; this encourages reporting. However, someone who makes what he or she knows or should know to be a false report of child abuse is liable for any damages caused by that report. (Pen. Code § 11172.)

Lawsuits for Sexual Abuse

Some people who suffered sexual abuse as children don't remember the abuse until much later in their lives. When these memories surface, some want to sue their abusers. Formerly, these lawsuits were barred by statutes of limitation, which prevent personal injury suits that aren't brought within a certain time following the injury. However, in California, lawsuits based on sexual abuse suffered as a child can be brought until the person reaches age 26, or until three years have passed since the person discovered or reasonably should have discovered that their injuries were related to childhood sexual abuse. If suit is brought after the person turns 26, his or her attorney and a licensed medical health practitioner must file statements with the court asserting that they believe the lawsuit has merit. (Code of Civ. Proc. § 340.1.) Some other rules may apply in specific circumstances, so look carefully at the statute and consult a lawyer if you have any questions about these time limits.

CHILD SUPPORT

Parents are legally obligated to support their children until the children turn 18. The obligation may continue until age 19 if the children are attending high school full-time and aren't self-supporting. Parents may have to support a child beyond age 19 if the child is disabled and can't support himself or herself.

The actual amount of support owed a child is usually set in court orders issued in divorce or paternity actions. Typically, the noncustodial or "absent" parent is required to contribute his or her share of the support directly to the custodial parent, who uses it for the benefit of the children.

How the Amount Is Determined

The amount of child support owed by a parent is based on the net monthly income of each parent, the amount of time each parent spends with the children, and the number of children to whom support is owed. The actual figure is determined using an algebraic formula that is so complex that virtually all judges and divorce lawyers rely on computers to get it right.

Generally, the higher a noncustodial parent's income, the higher his or her support payments will be, especially if the custodial parent's income is significantly lower. However, the more time a noncustodial parent spends with the children, the greater the amount the court will presume he or she spends on the children—so a noncustodial parent with very little visitation will have higher payments than a noncustodial parent with equal custody.

When an initial figure is determined, it is adjusted to account for the number of children receiving support. Then, that figure will usually be increased by:

- a percentage of any necessary child care costs incurred by the custodial parent (at least one-half but possibly more if the noncustodial parent's income allows), and
- uninsured health care costs incurred by the children.

In addition, the judge may increase the child support obligation if any of the following is true:

- The noncustodial parent has remarried or has a live-in partner, and the new spouse or partner contributes enough to their joint living expenses to free up additional money for support (but only in extraordinary circumstances and not more than 20% of the new spouse or partner's income).
- The custodial parent has or anticipates having uninsured health care costs for herself.
- The custodial parent suffers "extreme financial hardship" because of uninsured catastrophic losses.
- The custodial parent is supporting either natural or adopted children from other marriages or relationships.
- A child needs to attend private school or has other special needs that require additional support.
- The custodial parent has transportation expenses made necessary by the noncustodial parent's visits with the child.

Judges also have authority to change the formula amount if they conclude, in writing, that its application would be unjust or inappropriate due to special circumstances in the particular case.

Finally, judges may depart from amounts produced by the formula if any of the following is true:

- The parents agree to something else.
- Sale of the family home is postponed by the court, and the custodial parent and children are allowed to stay there for some specified period of time to protect the emotional condition of the children.
- Either parent has remarried or has a new nonmarital partner who is helping with basic living expenses.
- The noncustodial parent has such an extraordinarily high income that the amount produced by the formula is more than the children need.

- The noncustodial parent is not contributing to the needs of the children at a level commensurate with each parent's custodial time.
- The noncustodial parent has a net monthly income of less than $1,000.

Modifying Child Support

Once child support is established, it can always be modified if circumstances change. Changes that lead to modification most often involve sudden decreases in income because of job loss, disability, or medical emergencies. But a significant change in the cost of living over time or an important change in the child support laws can also result in a modification.

Enforcement of Child Support

Child support obligations can be enforced in many different ways. The most effective technique is to use a court order called a wage attachment that automatically deducts money from the noncustodial parent's paycheck. Other enforcement techniques a judge can order include:

- intercepting federal and state tax refunds and lottery winnings
- suspending professional, business, and commercial drivers' licenses
- requiring the noncustodial parent to deposit a year's worth of child support payments in a special security fund
- requiring the noncustodial parent to post sufficient assets with the court to cover two years of support
- requiring an unemployed or underemployed parent to prove he or she is looking for a job and to undergo job training if necessary, and
- filing an action against a nonpaying parent for contempt of court.

Once a child support obligation becomes due, it cannot later be cancelled by court order or bankruptcy. This means that any missed child support payments will be considered arrearages that can be collected using the techniques described above or through a court judgment. Because of the rule that child support arrearages are never cancelled, it is very important for a noncustodial parent to seek a modification promptly if he or she is unable to make the payments required by a child support order.

Using a Computer Program to Determine Support

The best way to calculate child support payments is to use a computer program. In fact, virtually all judges require such a computer determination to be made before they will set child support.

Most judges and divorce lawyers use either DissoMaster (CFLR) or Support Tax (Thomson West). Other websites offer affordable programs designed specifically for nonlawyers.

If you want to calculate your child support by computer, you can:

- call the Divorce Help Line, 800-359-7004, which will compute your probable payment level for a charge of $75

- find an online support calculator and make the calculations yourself

- contact a divorce typing service or a community-based women's center, some of which offer this service for as little as $10, or

- ask the judge to make a computer run for you in the courtroom when the child support hearing is held; many will do so.

CHILDREN BORN TO UNMARRIED PARENTS

Children whose parents are not married, or were not married at the time of the children's birth, have all the same rights as children of married parents, including the right to support from both parents. (Fam. Code § 7602.) These children are also entitled to Social Security or private insurance benefits if a parent becomes disabled or dies, provided that parentage can be proven.

Parental Rights

Sometimes the rights of the parents depend on whether or not they have treated the child as their own and supported the child. For example, a parent cannot inherit from a child born out of wedlock unless the parent or a relative of the parent has acknowledged the parent-child relationship and contributed to the child's support. (Probate Code § 6452).

More important, if the father of a child born out of wedlock doesn't acknowledge his child (sign a paternity statement or welcome the child into his home) or assume the role of a parent (support and visit the child), a court can limit or end his parental role—for example, allow the child to be adopted despite the father's opposition.

Inheritance

For purposes of inheritance, a child of unmarried parents is treated the same as a child whose parents are married. For example, if a parent dies without leaving a will, all children of that parent inherit equally under the state law that determines inheritance. And if a parent's will leaves property to "my children," this group includes all children, whether born within or outside of marriage. (Probate Code § 6450.)

CUSTODY

One of the most important issues when couples split up is who gets custody of their minor children. Custody has two components: Legal custody is the right and responsibility of child-rearing, including the right to make decisions affecting the child's life. Physical custody is providing a home for the child and having actual physical control over the child.

When parents share custody, it is called joint custody. Joint custody may be joint legal custody, joint physical custody, or both.

How Custody Is Determined

A judge ultimately decides who gets custody, although if the parents reach a custody agreement between themselves, the judge is likely to follow it. The judge's decision must be based on the child's best interests. California no longer has a statutory preference for joint custody (shared legal or physical custody). Joint custody, however, is still presumed to be in the child's best interests if the parents choose it. (Fam. Code §§ 3002-3004, 3006, 3007, 3011, 3080-3089.) Even if joint custody is not considered appropriate by the parents or the judge, the judge will try to make sure that the child has frequent contact with both parents. The parent who is more likely to allow frequent contact between the other parent and the children is usually favored in a custody dispute.

The court cannot consider the race or sex of a parent in determining custody, nor can the court award custody based on which parent has more money. If the child is old enough to have a reasonable preference about custody, the court must consider this preference.

In those rare situations when neither parent is fit for custody and the judge decides that parental custody would be harmful to the child, the judge can award custody to someone else, preferably to a person who has already been providing the child a stable environment. If the child has not been living with such a person, the judge can award custody to any person found suitable and able to provide proper care and guidance for the child.

Disputing Custody

If parents can't agree about custody, mediation is mandatory before the dispute can be resolved by a judge. The court-appointed mediator tries to help the parents agree on custody after explaining possible arrangements that might make sense for the family. Mediation sessions are private and are often conducted without lawyers. If there is any history of domestic violence, the mediator may meet with the parents separately. (Fam. Code §§ 3160, 3162, 3170, 3173, 3176-3177, 3181.) The mediator will also meet with the children, if they are old enough.

If the parents still can't agree, the mediator makes a recommendation to the judge, based on what the mediator thinks is best for the children. Absent a history of abuse of the child, the mediator will usually suggest an arrangement that lets the child stay in a familiar school and neighborhood, continue to see relatives, and maintain the closest possible relationship with both parents. Courts almost always adopt mediators' recommendations.

Modifying Custody Orders

The court can modify custody and visitation if a parent with joint custody shows that there has been a significant change in circumstances since the previous order, or shows that his or her right to custody or visitation has been interfered with. As with the original custody decision, the question is referred to mediation before a judge rules on it. However, a parent with sole physical custody who wishes to move and take the child along no longer needs to prove that the move was "necessary" for employment or financial reasons. The custodial parent can move for more personal reasons, such as convenience, unless the noncustodial parent can persuade the court that a hearing is required to determine whether the move would be harmful to the child. (*Brown v. Yana*, 37 Cal. 4th 947 (2006).) The law in this area is in flux, so if you are contemplating a move, or have an ex-spouse who is, consult an attorney about your rights.

Taxes and Child Custody

Each year, only one parent can claim the child as a dependent on his or her income tax return. This is true even if parents have joint custody. If the custodial parent will not claim the exemption, he or she must sign a declaration waiving her right. Each parent can deduct the amount that parent spent on a child's medical expenses, regardless of who takes the dependent deduction.

Interstate and International Child Custody Disputes

To avoid conflicting custody decrees—which arise if one parent is awarded custody in one state and the other parent is awarded custody in a different state—every state has adopted the Uniform Child Custody Jurisdiction Act. (Fam. Code §§ 340 and following.) The Act requires that a state meet at least one of the tests below before its courts may make or modify a custody award. These tests are listed in order of preference. If there is a conflict between the courts of two states, the state meeting the higher test is usually given priority.

1. The state is the child's home state. This means that the child has resided in the state for a least six consecutive months, or was residing there for six consecutive months but is now absent because a parent is outside the state, and a parent or person acting as a parent continues to live in the state.
2. The child and at least one parent have significant connections with the state, and there is substantial evidence in the state regarding the child's care, protection, training, and personal relationships.
3. The child is physically present in the state and either has been abandoned or is in danger of being abused or neglected if returned to the other parent.
4. No other state can meet one of the above three tests, or another state that can meet at least one of the tests has declined to make a custody award when provided an opportunity to do so.

The Act also applies in international disputes. California courts will enforce properly made custody decrees from other countries and will refuse to make a custody award when a child has been snatched and brought to the U.S., unless the child is in danger. In addition, a parent who lives in the U.S. and has a valid custody order can deliver a copy of the order to the U.S. State Department's Passport Issuance Office. The State Department will either revoke any passport already issued for the child or make sure that no passport is issued for the child if one is requested by someone other than the custodial parent.

The U.S. signed an international treaty, the 1988 Hague Convention on Civil Aspects of International Child Abduction, to help parents involved in international custody battles. Countries that sign the treaty pledge to help each other when evidence of international child abductions is brought to the government.

DONOR INSEMINATION

Donor insemination (also called artificial or alternative insemination) is a procedure by which a woman is impregnated by a means other than sexual intercourse. If the semen came from her husband (called homologous artificial insemination), the father is treated the same as any other father of a child conceived during the marriage.

If a woman is married, and the semen came from a man other than her husband (called artificial insemination by donor or heterologous artificial insemination), the husband is treated as if he were the natural father of the child only if he consented in writing to the insemination, and the insemination was performed under the supervision of a licensed physician. (Fam. Code § 7613.) He has all the rights and responsibilities of fatherhood, including the duty to support the child. (Pen. Code § 270.)

If an unmarried woman is inseminated under the supervision of a physician, the semen donor is not considered the father of the child. Donors who provide semen to licensed physicians for use in artificial insemination of a woman other than the donor's wife have no parental rights. (Fam. Code § 7613.) However, if a woman is inseminated without a physician's help and the donor asserts his fatherhood, he is entitled to full parental rights and responsibilities. (*Jhordan C. v. Mary K.*, 179 Cal. App. 3d 386 (1986).)

EDUCATION

California law requires every child between the ages of six and 18 to attend school or continuation school full time unless he or she has graduated from high school or passed a basic skills proficiency test given by the State Department of Education. (Educ. Code §§ 48200, 48400 and following.) This used to be interpreted as requiring public school attendance by every child, but that is no longer the case. Private school, tutoring, and independent study programs can all fulfill the mandatory education requirement.

Home Schooling

Parents may teach their own children at home instead of sending them to school. Home schools used to be a relatively rare phenomenon; today, however, it is estimated that over one million children are being educated at home by their parents. In California, no specific law allows or prohibits home schools.

Parents who wish to educate their children at home typically choose one of the following options:

- **Tutoring.** A parent can be the child's private tutor. The parent must be qualified to teach under the state's guidelines. State certification is also required.
- **Independent study program.** A parent can teach the child using the same curriculum used by the public schools in that county or using a curriculum provided by a private school. This requires consultation with the principals of local public or private schools, but no special skills are required of instructors.
- **Private school.** A parent can form a private school at home, following the guidelines in the Education Code. This requires following some administrative procedures, such as keeping attendance records. Teachers must be "competent," but no test or certification is required.

Parents who wish to start a home school should talk to the principal of their local public school and other parents who have taught their children at home. You can also contact the California Homeschool Network by calling 800-327-5339, or on the Web at www.cahomeschoolnet.org. CHN provides resources and information about homeschooling, in addition to seminars and local contacts for parents interested in educating their children at home.

EMANCIPATED MINORS

An emancipated minor is a person under age 18 who has achieved legal adult status by demonstrating freedom from parental control. To be emancipated, the minor must do one of the following:

- **Marry.** Parental consent and court approval are required, and the court will require premarital counseling. (Fam. Code §§ 302, 304.)
- **Join the armed services.** Parental consent or a court order is required. (Fam. Code §§ 6950, 7002.)
- **Get a court emancipation order.** Minors who are at least 14 years old, live apart from their parents, and lawfully support themselves financially can ask the court for a declaration of emancipation. (Fam. Code §§ 7120-7123.)

Emancipated minors have most of the same rights as adults, including the right to:

- consent to medical treatment
- enter into binding contracts
- buy and sell real estate
- sue and be sued
- make a will or trust
- decide where to live
- apply for welfare, and
- apply for a work permit.

If the law establishes an age other than 18 for certain activities (such as 16 to get a driver's license and 21 to drink), an emancipated minor must reach that age before legally engaging in that activity.

FOSTER CARE

Foster parents are licensed by the state to provide a temporary home for children who are abused or neglected by their parents. Foster care can consist of an emergency placement for a few days, or it can last for years.

If a child is abused, neglected, or beyond parental control, the Child Protective Services of the California Department of Social Services usually tries to have the child removed from the home, but also tries to work out a plan for eventual reunification. If the parents don't agree to such a plan, they will have a formal hearing before a juvenile court judge. If the judge orders the children removed from the home, the judge will also establish reunification conditions, such as parenting classes or drug treatment.

Children taken away from their parents are usually put into foster homes, though some are placed in juvenile centers. If the parents do not fulfill the court's conditions for reunification within about 18 months, the judge may order permanent foster care or guardianship, which gives the parents the right to stay in touch with the children. The court may also order the natural parents' rights terminated, freeing the child to be adopted by the foster parents or someone else.

Foster Parents

Foster homes must be licensed by state-operated or private agencies. Prospective foster parents must fill out an application and be interviewed by an employee of the agency. Single people as well as married couples can get licenses to be foster parents, and openly gay households can get licensed in some large cities.

Prospective foster parents will be visited in their homes by an agency social worker. The applicants should have a separate room for the child, and if they're asking for placement of a young child, they must show that they have time to care for the child or have arranged for child care. The agency will also require a medical exam and fingerprints; ex-felons and sex offenders aren't eligible for foster care licenses.

The state pays foster parents a monthly amount for support of each foster child. The amount varies among counties.

GAY AND LESBIAN PARENTS

No law prevents lesbians and gay men from becoming parents. However, some courts and government agencies may try to discourage gay men and lesbians from adopting children or having custody of their children.

Independent and Agency Adoption by Same-Sex Couples

A gay or lesbian couple is not legally barred from adopting a child simply because of their sexual orientation. Nothing in the adoption statutes prevents adoptions by same-sex parents, and many courts have allowed same-sex couples to adopt children through both public and private agencies.

The Department of Social Services used to be prohibited, by administrative rules, from recommending gay and lesbian parents for adoption. Although this restriction has been lifted, it may still be more difficult, as a practical matter, for gay and lesbian couples to adopt than for married couples. Public and private agencies, as well as individuals putting their children up for private adoption, may see gay men and lesbians as less desirable parents and refuse to place children with them.

Domestic Partner Adoption and Second Parent Adoption by Same-Sex Couples

With the enactment of AB 205 in January 2005, domestic partners gained new rights relative to children born into the partnership. Such children are now considered the legal children of both domestic partners if they are born after the partners register with the state. Both parents' names can be shown on the birth certificate without the necessity of an adoption by the nonbiological parent. However, domestic partner adoptions are still necessary in order to provide federal and out-of-state recognition of the parent-child relationship between the second parent and the child. And if lesbian parents conceive through donor insemination with a donor who is known to them, and don't use a physician for the insemination, there are competing presumptions of parentage between the donor and the second parent, which must be resolved through the adoption mechanism.

If you don't meet the criteria for domestic partnership, but you still want to adopt your partner's child, you can do so under second parent adoption procedures. Second parent adoption is an independent adoption where the partner becomes a legal parent while the child's parent retains parental rights (the same as in a stepparent or domestic partner adoption). The procedure is more expensive and complicated and takes longer, but it can be done.

Custody

When there is a dispute between two legal parents (biological or adoptive) over custody of a child, courts are required to award custody based on the best interests of the child. California courts have ruled that a parent's sexual orientation does not, in itself, go against the child's best interests. However, some judges do have a bias against gay and lesbian parents. If you are involved in a custody dispute where your sexual orientation is an issue, consult an attorney.

GRANDPARENTS' RIGHTS

Grandparents have no legal rights to see grandchildren as long as the grandchildren's parents are still married and living. If the child's parents divorce or die or a child is placed for adoption, however, the child's grandparents have certain rights.

Visitation

If the parents of a minor child divorce, the grandparents may seek visitation rights in superior court. The court will grant visitation if it would be in the child's best interest. If the parents disagree about grandparent visitation rights, the issue may be referred to mediation. (Fam. Code §§ 3100, 3103-3104, 3160, 3180, 3182, 3183.)

If a parent of a minor child dies, the grandparents may seek visitation rights in superior court. The court will grant visitation if it would be in the child's best interest. (Fam. Code § 3102.)

Notice of Adoption

Before a court terminates parental rights to free a child for adoption, the agency seeking the termination (usually a public or private agency facilitating the adoption) must notify the parents that termination of their parental rights is being sought, give them the date and time of the hearing, and specify that they have the right to attend. If a parent's address is unknown, the agency must give the same notification to the grandparents, adult siblings, adult aunts and uncles, and adult first cousins of the child. (Fam. Code §§ 7881, 7882.)

GUARDIANSHIPS

A guardian is an adult who is appointed by a court to be responsible for a minor (someone under age 18). A guardian is rarely necessary unless a child's parents die or are unable or unfit to care for the child. Often, parents who die have named a guardian in their wills, and that person is confirmed by the court.

There are three categories of guardians:

- **A guardian of the person** has legal custody of the child and responsibility for the child's well-being. The guardian provides food, shelter, and health care, and may handle relatively small financial matters, such as government benefits, on behalf of the child.

- **A guardian of the estate** manages the child's money, real estate, or other assets; provides accounts to the court; and obtains court approval before handling anything but simple day-to-day financial matters. The guardian uses the child's money to provide support, maintenance, and education for the child. (Probate Code § 2420.)
- **A guardian of the person and estate** takes care of both the child's personal needs and financial assets.

To become a guardian, an adult (or the child, if he or she is at least 12 years old) must file documents with a court, notify the child's living parents and close relatives, and attend a court hearing. A court investigator will review the file and meet with everyone involved. If no one objects, the court will probably appoint the person who is petitioning to be guardian.

A custodial parent who is terminally ill may seek court approval to appoint someone to be a joint guardian until his or her death. After the custodial parent's death, the court-appointed joint guardian will automatically have legal custody of the child. (Probate Code § 2105.)

A guardian serves until released from his or her duties by the court or until the minor reaches age 18, is adopted, marries, or achieves legal adult status by court emancipation order.

Alternatives to Guardianships

A legal guardianship isn't necessary in every situation when an adult cares for a child. Other options include:

- **Caregiver's Authorization Affidavit.** Adults who are caring for minors living with them may enroll the minors in school and make school-related medical decisions. Certain close relatives, including stepparents, grandparents, aunts, uncles, and siblings, may make all medical decisions. Caregivers must complete a statutory Caregiver's Authorization Affidavit form. (Fam. Code §§ 6550, 6552.)
- **Informal arrangements.** If the child's parents are alive but temporarily unable to take care of their child (because, for example, they are on a lengthy trip), a friend or relative can take care of the child without a guardianship. Parents should write a letter authorizing the arrangement that the caretaker can show to school officials, doctors, and so on.

- **Adoption.** This court-ordered measure permanently changes the adult-child relationship; the adopting adult legally becomes the parent of the child. The natural parent (if living) loses all parental rights and obligations, except in a second parent, stepparent, or domestic partner adoption.

- **Foster care.** Foster parents are licensed to care for children who have been removed from their biological parents' home by a court. If foster parents want to become legal guardians, the local social services agency and county counsel handle the guardianship. (Welf. & Inst. Code § 366.26.)

- **Mental health conservatorship.** This proceeding is used instead of a guardianship for children who are severely disabled because of a mental disorder or chronic alcoholism. A conservator of the person, who takes care of the personal needs of the child, assures that the child is given individualized mental health treatment and services. (Welf. & Inst. Code §§ 5000-5550.) These children are often hospitalized in mental health treatment facilities.

- **Conservatorship of the person.** For minors who are married or divorced, a conservator of the person, rather than a guardian, must be appointed. This is merely a technical difference.

- **Custodianship under the California Uniform Transfers to Minors Act.** The Probate Code allows for the transfer of property to a designated custodian to be held and used for the minor's benefit. Custodianships terminate at age 18, at which point the custodian must distribute the remaining property to the minor unless the document setting up the custodianship says that distribution is to occur later (usually when the minor turns 21, and in some instances at age 25). The custodian has a fiduciary duty to the minor with regard to the funds but is not supervised by the court. (Prob. Code §§ 3900-3925.)

- **Trusts.** Property may be held in a trust and managed by a trustee for a minor's benefit. The trust can specify what expenditures the trustee should make from trust funds for the minor's benefit and when trust funds are to be directly distributed to the minor.

HOUSING DISCRIMINATION

California law contains several provisions designed to ensure that all persons, regardless of their age or family status, have access to housing.

Families With Children

It is illegal to discriminate against families with children in the sale, lease, or rental of real estate, or in the terms or conditions of the tenancy. The only exception is for housing units that qualify as senior housing, which can legally be reserved for senior citizens, their family members, and their health care assistants. (42 U.S.C. §§ 3607(b) and following; Civ. Code §§ 51-51.4; *Marina Point Ltd. v. Wolfson*, 30 Cal. 3d 721 (1982).)

As a rule of thumb, California landlords must allow two people per bedroom, plus one more. But some landlords try to avoid renting to families with children by enforcing more restrictive space-to-people ratios, ostensibly to prevent crowding. These limits are illegal unless they are related to a reasonable business need. For example, a landlord may be able to limit the number of occupants to fewer than two people per bedroom if the building's infrastructure (plumbing or wiring) cannot support higher numbers. (*Pfaff v. U.S. Dept. of Housing and Urban Development*, 88 F. 3d 739 (1996).)

Seniors

Housing that is specially designed to meet the physical and social needs of senior citizens will not violate the ban on discrimination against families with children as long as it meets both of the following tests:

- The housing complex is restricted to occupancy by at least one person per unit who is age 62 or older.
- All other residents in the complex are "qualified permanent residents" (defined below) or are health care workers who live in the same unit with the senior citizen and are paid to take care of him or her.

A "qualified permanent resident" is someone who meets three requirements:

- The resident lived with the senior prior to the senior's death, hospitalization, or "other prolonged absence," or prior to a divorce from the senior.

- The resident was at least age 45, or was a spouse or cohabitant providing primary economic or physical support to the senior.
- The resident has or expects an ownership interest in the housing (that is, the unit is jointly owned, or the other resident is named as the inheritor of the unit in the senior citizen's will). (Civ. Code §§ 51.3 and 51.4.)

Special rules apply to Riverside County (Civ. Code §§ 51.10 and 51.11.)

Senior Citizen Housing Development

The minimum age of 62 drops to 55 for residential developments that are developed, substantially rehabilitated, or substantially renovated for senior citizens, and that meet any of the following size requirements:

- at least 70 units built prior to January 1, 1996; or at least 150 units built on or after January 1, 1996 in a densely populated metropolitan
- area
- at least 100 units in a smaller metropolitan area, or
- at least 35 units in a nonmetropolitan area. (Civ. Code § 51.3(c)(3).)

Requirements as to other residents in the development apply as described above.

Housing constructed before February 8, 1982 that was not specially designed or remodeled to meet the housing needs of seniors could be reserved for seniors as a "senior citizen housing development" through January 1, 2000, if it met two additional requirements:

- The housing is in an area where it is not practicable to require that senior housing be specially designed to meet the specific needs of seniors.
- The housing units are necessary to provide important housing opportunities for seniors.

Any resident who occupied this type of housing prior to January 1, 1990 may continue to live in it after the year 2000. (Civ. Code § 51.4.)

Riverside County note: Requirements for qualifying residents and housing are less stringent in Riverside County than in other parts of the state. (Civ. Code §§ 51.2 (c), 51.3 (j), 51.4 (c), 51.10, 51.11, and 51.12.)

JUVENILE COURT

Juvenile court is a special branch of the court system designated to deal with problems affecting children. The goal of juvenile court is to protect and rehabilitate children. Matters handled in juvenile court include:

- **Child neglect.** Parents who do not or cannot provide their children with adequate food, shelter, clothing, or other necessities may be found guilty of child neglect. The children may be removed from their parents' care and temporarily placed in a foster home. They may also be put up for adoption through a dependency action in juvenile court. (Welf. & Inst. Code § 300.) In rare cases, if a parent's behavior is deliberate and particularly offensive, the case may be prosecuted as a misdemeanor or felony in the criminal courts as well. (Pen. Code § 273a.)

- **Status offenses.** Minors who won't obey their parents but haven't committed a crime are considered "incorrigible." Typically, they have run away from home, are chronically truant from school, have violated a city's curfew ordinance, or are endangering their own or another's health or morals. (Welf. & Inst. Code § 601.) Sometimes these children are allowed to remain in their homes under the supervision of a probation officer; probation conditions may include regular school attendance, drug or alcohol rehabilitation, or family counseling. Children may also be removed from the home and put into foster care or a state institution for minors. Children who are brought under the control of the juvenile court for status offenses are not considered to have committed a crime.

- **Criminal offenses.** Minors who are charged with crimes typically face charges in juvenile court. If the judge decides that the minor has violated a criminal law, the minor can be given probation or sent to a reform institution operated by the California Youth Authority (CYA). If the child's case is handled completely in juvenile court, the child is not considered to have a criminal conviction. But not all juvenile offenses remain in juvenile court. If the minor is between 16 and 18 when the crime is committed, and if the judge decides after a "fitness" hearing that juvenile court proceedings aren't appropriate (such as for particularly violent crimes or frequent offenders), the minor can be charged and sentenced as an adult. (Welf. & Inst. Code

§§ 602 and 707.01.) If the minor is given a prison sentence, he or she may be confined in a CYA institution and, upon reaching the age of 16, can be sent to county jail or state prison to finish his or her sentence (CYA can also choose to keep the offender until the age of 25). Moreover, a juvenile who was only 14 years of age at the time of the offense can be charged as an adult if the minor is deemed unamenable to treatment as a juvenile and is charged with murder or certain other very serious felonies. (Welf. & Inst. Code §§ 707.01.)

A number of agencies participate in juvenile court cases, including the Department of Social Services and/or the Probation Department.

PARENTAL KIDNAPPING AND CUSTODIAL INTERFERENCE

A parent can be prosecuted for kidnapping his or her own child or otherwise interfering with the custody or visitation rights of the other parent. It doesn't matter which parent has legal custody; if a parent conceals his or her child with the intent of depriving the other parent of custody or visitation rights, he or she can be prosecuted for a crime.

If there is no court order determining custody and visitation rights—such as an order issued during divorce proceedings—a parent who conceals his or her child from the other parent can also be prosecuted. However, the parent can defend his or her action by showing that the child was in immediate danger of physical injury or emotional harm. A parent who takes a child under these circumstances must file a request for custody within a reasonable time in the jurisdiction where the child had been living, explaining the basis for the parent's fear that the child would be harmed. (Pen. Code § 278.7.)

A kidnapping parent can be prosecuted for a misdemeanor (imprisonment in a county jail for up to one year; a fine of $1,000; or both) or a felony (imprisonment in a state prison for up to four years; a fine of up to $10,000; or both). The penalties listed above apply regardless of who has custody or when the kidnapping occurs. (Pen. Code § 278.)

A child can be placed in protective custody by a police officer when the officer investigates a report of an alleged instance of child concealment or kidnapping by a parent and concludes that a parent may flee the jurisdiction with the child. (Pen. Code § 279.6.)

PARENTS' LIABILITY FOR THEIR CHILDREN'S ACTS

Normally, parents aren't financially liable for the negligent or clumsy acts of their children. Courts seem to recognize that parents cannot prevent most accidents and mishaps of childhood. However, parents may be liable if the injured person can show that the parent's failure to supervise the child directly caused the injury.

In addition, state statutes make parents liable for:

- Willful misconduct—including defacement of property with paint or a similar substance—up to $25,000 for each incident. (Civ. Code § 1714.1.) If the child injures someone, liability is limited to medical, dental, and hospital expenses, up to $25,000. The maximum liability figure increases every two years, based on the rise of the annual average of the California Consumer Price Index. Parents' insurance companies are not liable for conduct attributed to the parents beyond $10,000.
- Any injury inflicted with a gun that a parent let the child have or left where the child could get it, up to $30,000 for the death of or injury to one person or his property, or $60,000 for the deaths of or injuries to more than one person. (Civ. Code § 1714.3.)
- Willful misconduct that results in injury to school employees, other pupils, or volunteers; or damage to school property or to personal property belonging to school employees. Parents must pay up to $10,000 in damages and may also have to pay up to $10,000 as a reward to the person who reported the child. Parents are also liable for any school property loaned to a student but not returned. Grades, diplomas, and transcripts may be withheld until any damage is paid for. (Educ. Code § 48904.)
- Stealing merchandise from merchants, or books or materials from libraries. Parents are liable to a merchant or a library facility for damages of $50 to $500, plus the retail value of the merchandise or fair market value of the books or materials, plus costs. The total damages may not exceed $500. (Pen. Code § 490.5.)

A parent may also be financially responsible for graffiti created by his or her child. The city or county where the graffiti is located may even place a lien against the property of the child's parent or guardian in order to recover its cleanup costs. (Gov't. Code § 38772.)

Suing Children

People who have been harmed by the carelessness of a child usually sue the child's parents because the child has no money. However, children can be sued for their own careless acts in a personal injury lawsuit. A child will be held liable for his or her action only if the court determines that he or she was capable of knowing that it was wrong at the time. Also, the court will take the child's age into account when determining liability; what may be unreasonable carelessness for a teenager may be acceptable behavior for a preschooler.

SAFETY

Children are subject to several safety requirements not imposed on adults.

Bicycle Helmets for Children

All bicycle riders under the age of 18, and all bicycle passengers (including those who ride in an attached restraining seat or in a trailer towed by the bicycle), must wear an approved bicycle helmet. Your first violation will get you a warning. Subsequent violations carry a $25 fine. Parents are liable for their children's violations. (Veh. Code § 21212.)

Life Jackets for Children in Boats

Children six years of age or younger must wear a Coast Guard-approved life jacket if they are on the deck of a boat under 26 feet long unless it's moored, anchored, or aground. (Harb. & Nav. Code § 658.3.)

Child Restraint Requirements for Motor Vehicles

See Traffic and Vehicle Laws, Seatbelt and Child Restraint Requirements.

STUDENTS AND TEACHERS

Public schools are allowed a good measure of control over pupils, in order to provide a safe learning environment. In addition, teachers are responsible for ensuring the safety of students during school hours. However, students have certain rights.

Student Rights

Public school students don't leave all their constitutional rights at the schoolhouse door (although enforcing those rights might prove difficult.) Some students' rights issues that arise commonly in school include:

- **Prayers and pledges.** Public schools must maintain the same separation of church and state that is required of the government. Prayers cannot be recited in public schools, even if students are not required to attend. Similarly, moments of silence intended for religious contemplation are prohibited.

    A student cannot be required to salute the flag or recite the pledge of allegiance and cannot be disciplined for failing to do so.

- **Dress codes.** A public school can impose a dress code to prevent disruption or ensure student safety. Some schools prohibit gang colors for this reason. However, if a school prohibits clothing bearing only certain slogans, this may violate the students' right to free speech.

- **Free speech.** Students' right to freedom of speech is guaranteed by Educ. Code § 48907. Public school officials cannot censor the content of student speech—in a school paper, for example—unless the statements are obscene, libelous, or slanderous; will cause an immediate danger of inciting students to break the law or a school rule; or will otherwise substantially disrupt the school's operations. This gives schools considerable discretion in banning controversial speech.

    In addition, school officials may regulate the time, place, and manner of student statements, as long as the regulations are reasonable, apply equally to all kinds of speech, and are not intended merely to prohibit speech. For example, a public school can prohibit students from distributing written materials during class, or limit student speeches to recess.

- **Discrimination.** School officials cannot discriminate on the basis of a student's race, national origin, sex, religion, or physical disability. However, this does not require that all students participate in the same activities. Some examples:

— **Athletic teams.** Public schools and private schools receiving federal money must provide equal opportunity for both boys and girls to participate in team sports and use athletic facilities, which includes parity of coaching pay, scheduling game and practice times, and locker rooms. This does not require schools to allow competition between boys and girls. If the school does not offer a girls' team in a noncontact sport, girls may try out for the boys' team, but schools are free to prohibit girls from trying out for boys' teams in contact sports.

— **Bilingual education.** The U.S. Supreme Court has ruled that public school students who cannot benefit from instruction solely in English are entitled to transitional bilingual education, designed to increase their mastery of the English language. In 1998, California voters passed Proposition 227, which generally limits bilingual education to no more than one year. (Educ. Code §§ 300 and following.)

Discipline and Student Safety

School officials have a responsibility to provide safe schools. However, officials' efforts to discipline students are subject to these rules:

- **Corporal punishment** is prohibited in California schools. (Educ. Code § 49001.)
- **Suspension** is to be used only as a last resort. A student can be suspended from school only for the following behavior:
  - threatening or causing physical injury to another, or trying to injure another
  - possessing, selling, or using a dangerous weapon
  - possessing, selling, or using alcohol or drugs, or selling anything that the student claims is alcohol or drugs
  - committing or attempting to commit robbery or extortion
  - possessing or selling drug paraphernalia
  - smoking cigarettes or possessing or using other tobacco products
  - damaging or attempting to damage school or private property
  - habitually using profanity or engaging in obscene acts
  - disrupting school activities or deliberately defying school authorities
  - knowingly receiving stolen property,

— engaging in sexual assault or hate violence, or

— engaging in harassment, threats, or intimidation directed against another student or students so as to disrupt classwork and create an intimidating or hostile educational environment (grades 4–12 only). (Educ. Code §§ 48900–48900.4.)

Only the first four of these behaviors are grounds for suspension following a first offense, unless the principal determines that the student poses a danger to other students or property or will disrupt the educational process. In addition, suspension (and expulsion) can be imposed only for actions that are related to school activity or attendance, including events that happen at school, while the student is going to or coming from school, during recess or lunch periods, or during school-sponsored activities.

- **Expulsion** must be recommended by a school principal for any student who commits the following acts, unless the circumstances render expulsion inappropriate:

  — causing serious physical injury to another, except in self-defense

  — possessing a firearm, knife, or explosive at school

  — selling a controlled substance, except for a first offense of selling less than an ounce of marijuana

  — robbery or extortion

  — committing or attempting to commit a sexual assault or sexual battery

  — harassing, threatening, or intimidating a pupil who is a witness in a school disciplinary proceeding

  — causing or attempting to cause damage to school or private property

  — stealing or attempting to steal school or private property, or

  — possessing or using tobacco products.

  In addition, a student can be expelled for committing any of the acts for which suspension would be appropriate, if other means of correction are not feasible or have failed, or if the presence of the student poses a danger to the safety of other students. (Educ. Code §§ 48900, 48915.) A student can be "emergency expelled" if officials reasonably believe the student is a threat.

  Students are entitled to a hearing within 30 school days of the date that the principal has determined that the student has committed an act warranting expulsion. (Educ. Code § 48918.)

Searches, Detentions, and Arrests

Schools cannot search or detain students freely; they must follow state rules designed to protect students' rights. However, they do have a good deal of leeway.

- **Searches.** A school official who wants to search a student must have a reasonable suspicion that the search will turn up evidence that the student has engaged in illegal activity or has violated school rules. A school official may not search a student's locker or backpack based on curiosity, rumor, or a hunch. A suspicion must be based on reasonably reliable facts, and must be directed specifically at the students involved; searching the whole student body is not allowed. (*In re William G.*, 40 Cal. 3d 550 (1985).) In addition, the scope of the search must be reasonably related to the object of the search and cannot be overly intrusive. Body cavity searches ("strip searches") and removing or rearranging clothing to permit visual inspection of a student's underclothing, breasts, buttocks, or genitals are never allowed. (Educ. Code § 49050.) Metal detector searches of a random sampling of high school students may be allowable if the searches are not too intrusive, the school has a written policy for such searches, the students chosen to be searched are chosen using neutral criteria, and parents and students are periodically notified about the policy. (*In re Latasha W.*, 60 Cal. App. 4th 1524 (1998).) With regard to student athletes in public schools, however, unannounced urinalysis drug testing is allowed pursuant to a U.S. Supreme Court decision. (*Vernonia School District 47J v. Wayne Acton*, 115 S. Ct. 2386 (1995).) The court suggested that such testing is acceptable if all student athletes on a given team are tested and none are singled out for unequal treatment.

- **Detentions and arrests.** School officials or security guards have the right to detain students for their own safety, to wait for police to arrive if there has been some wrongdoing, or even based on a general suspicion, if the detention is not arbitrary, capricious, or harassing. (*In re Randy G.*, 26 Cal. 4th 556 (2001).) School officials or security guards can also make arrests, but their power to act is limited to school personnel, students, or property, and to offenses occurring on or near school premises. (Educ. Code § 38000; 58 Opinions of the Attorney General 363, 5-9-75.)

School officials can call in police to help them conduct searches, quell disturbances, or provide other assistance. School officials may notify police if a student has violated a law, including:
— menacing or attacking a school employee
— committing an assault with a deadly weapon
— possessing a weapon at school, or
— possessing or selling a controlled substance at school.

Police can enter school grounds at any time to perform their duties. They do not have to be invited by school officials, nor can the school prevent the police from coming on campus.

Teacher Liability

The state constitution guarantees all students the right to safe schools, and teachers have a duty to use reasonable care to protect students from reasonably foreseeable injuries, including injuries from other students. (Educ. Code § 44807, Cal. Const. Art. 1, § 28.) This doesn't mean that a teacher must constantly supervise students or prevent all but the safest activities. Teachers must act reasonably to protect students in light of the students' ages, how dangerous the activity is, the skill level of the students, the number of other supervisors, and so on. If a teacher fails to fulfill this duty and a student is injured as a result, the school district, and possibly the teacher, may be liable for the injury. (Educ. Code § 44807; *Dailey v. Los Angeles Unified School District*, 2 Cal. 3d 741 (1970); *Bartell v. Palos Verdes Peninsula School District*, 83 Cal. App. 3d 492 (1978); *Iverson v. Muroc Unified School District*, 32 Cal. App. 4th 218 (1995).)

VISITATION

When one parent is awarded physical custody of a child, the other parent is usually given the right to visit the child, unless visitation would not be in the child's best interests. (Fam. Code § 3100.) Courts want both parents to have as much contact with their children as possible and sometimes award custody to the parent more likely to allow the other frequent contact with the child.

Visitation Disputes

Mediation is mandatory whenever custody or visitation are disputed. (Fam. Code §§ 3162, 3170-3176.) (For a discussion of the mediation process, see Custody, above.)

Modifying Visitation Orders

The court can change visitation rights at any time. A parent must request the change and show that there has been a significant change in circumstances since the previous visitation order, or show that his or her visitation rights have been frustrated by the custodial parent. A parent whose visitation rights have been violated by the other parent may also be entitled to payment from the custodial parent, to make up for time lost with his or her children. As with original visitation decisions, the question is referred to mediation before a judge rules on it.

Limited, Supervised, and Denied Visitation

Normally, a judge denies visitation only if a parent has a history of dangerous or illicit conduct, such as drug or alcohol abuse, prostitution, or domestic violence. Instead of denying visitation altogether, the court may order supervised visitation, which requires that an adult acceptable to the court be present when the dangerous parent sees the child. A court may not order unsupervised visitation to a parent convicted of abusing the child, unless the court finds no significant risk to the child. (Fam. Code § 3030.) But even if a parent is obviously unfit to take care of children over a long period, courts usually try to allow some limited contact.

Religious differences between parents are not ordinarily a sufficient reason to deny or limit visitation, unless the tension created is clearly harmful to the child.

Visitation and Child Support

A parent cannot refuse to pay child support even if the custodial parent interferes with his or her visitation rights. The parent must continue to make the payments regardless of the custodial parent's behavior. (Fam. Code § 3556.) However, if a custodial parent deliberately conceals a child from the noncustodial parent, and then many years later reveals the child's location and tries to collect the child support unpaid all those years, a court may agree that the noncustodial parent need not pay. ■

Citizens' Rights

State and federal laws try to make the government accountable and open to citizens. These laws guarantee that all adults can vote on public officials and ballot measures and can attend certain meetings held by their elected officials. This section discusses citizenship and some of the basic rights and responsibilities it gives people.

TOPICS

California Citizenship and Residency
Immigrating to the United States
Local Government Meetings
United States Citizenship
Voting

RELATED TOPICS

Courts and Lawsuits
   Jury Duty
Employees' Rights
   Immigrant Workers
Government Benefits

ADDITIONAL RESOURCES

Becoming a U.S. Citizen: A Guide to the Law, Exam & Interview, by Ilona Bray (Nolo), explains how immigrants with green cards can apply to naturalize.

U.S. Immigration Made Easy, by Ilona Bray (Nolo), includes instructions on how to secure visas and green cards.

Fiancé and Marriage Visas: A Couple's Guide to U.S. Immigration, by Ilona Bray (Nolo), helps guide couples through the process of immigrating on a marriage visa.

The websites of the U.S. Citizenship and Immigration Service (www.uscis.gov) and the U.S. State Department (www.state.gov) contain lots of information on visas, green cards, and immigration.

CALIFORNIA CITIZENSHIP AND RESIDENCY

You are a California citizen if either of the following is true:

- You were born in California and reside here, unless your parents were "transient aliens" (not citizens of the United States, foreign ministers, or consuls).
- You were born out of state, but are a U.S. citizen and California resident. (Gov't. Code § 241.)

Residency

Your residence is the state in which you live when not called elsewhere for work or some other temporary purpose. The California statute quaintly defines it as the place where a person "returns in seasons of repose." You can be a resident of only one state at a time. You must not only live there, but also intend for that state to be your residence. (Gov't. Code § 244.)

Many state benefits, such as most welfare payments, are available only to California residents. In addition, residents may receive other benefits, such as lower tuition at state universities. The catch is that you must not only be a resident, but also be able to prove your residency.

Proving California Residency

To prove you are a California resident, take the following steps:

- Establish a permanent home mailing address in California.
- Register to vote in California.
- Get a California driver's license and California license plates for your car, and have insurance issued to you at your California mailing address.
- Open bank accounts, take out memberships, and get a local library card or any other tangible evidence that you live in the state and intend to stay here.

IMMIGRATING TO THE UNITED STATES

There are two main ways that a noncitizen can live in the United States legally: get a green card, which gives permanent resident status; or get a visa, which allows a limited stay in the U.S. for a specified purpose, such as doing business, attending school, or traveling.

Green Cards

A green card—formally known as an Alien Registration Receipt Card—is a means of identifying yourself as a permanent legal resident. It gives you the right to work and live in the U.S.

Only people who fit into one of the eligibility categories established by Congress can get a green card. Even eligible people often have to wait a long time for a green card to become available, because of yearly limits on both the number of people who can be admitted within any one category and the number of people who can be admitted from any given country.

Broadly speaking, the categories of people who are eligible for green cards include:

- family members of U.S. citizens and permanent residents
- those who have been offered jobs in the U.S. for which no U.S. workers can be found—particularly jobs requiring specialized skills
- those who invest large amounts of capital in U.S. companies
- people who have been granted refuge or asylum in the U.S., or
- a number of specially recognized immigrants, such as religious workers.

But you'll need to look further into the numerous technical requirements for each category and restrictions on who qualifies as, for example, a relative or an investor. (8 U.S.C. § 1151.)

Nonimmigrant Visas

A nonimmigrant visa gives its holder the right to stay temporarily in the United States to pursue a specific activity. The visa authorizes only that activity—so, for example, a student visa may authorize studying at a university but does not authorize full-time employment. How long you can stay in the U.S. using your nonimmigrant visa depends on the purpose for which the visa was issued—look for the exact date on the I-94 card you're given when entering the United States.

Among the many nonimmigrant visa categories are:
- ambassadors, diplomats, and representatives of foreign governments
- business visitors
- tourists
- students
- fiancés and fiancées of U.S. citizens who are coming to the U.S. to get married
- artists, entertainers, and athletes coming to the U.S. to perform, and
- religious workers. (8 U.S.C. § 1184.)

LOCAL GOVERNMENT MEETINGS

Most local governments in California are required by law to hold open meetings, except under very limited circumstances. (Gov't. Code §§ 54950 and following.) An open meeting means that any member of the public can attend and comment on the issues being discussed. However, the agency can limit overall speaking time and the time allotted for each speaker.

People who attend cannot be forced to identify themselves or sign something. They can tape open meetings by video or audio recording, unless taping would be disruptive. Some meetings may be conducted by teleconference, as long as the teleconference location is stated in the notice and agenda of the meeting. (Gov't. Code §§ 54953.3, 54953.5.)

What Meetings Must Be Open

All regular meetings of the legislative body of a local agency—such as a county board of supervisors, city or town council, school board, or municipal corporation board of directors—must be open and public, unless an exception applies. (Gov't. Code § 54953.) Exceptions include performance evaluations of public employees, security threats to public buildings or facilities, and similarly sensitive issues. (Gov't. Code § 54957.)

Notice and Agendas

If the meeting is one that is regularly scheduled, the legislative body must publicly post an agenda for the meeting at least 72 hours before it is to be held. Disabled persons can request the agenda in an alternate format, including information on how to request disability-based accommodations in order to attend the meeting.

Items not on the agenda can be discussed only if an emergency arises, if the need to discuss the item arose after the agenda was posted, or if the item was continued from a prior meeting held not more than five days before. For special meetings (that is, meetings that are not regularly scheduled), a notice must be posted at least 24 hours in advance in a location that is freely accessible to the public. (Gov't. Code §§ 54954.2, 54956.)

Emergency meetings can be called to deal with threatened or actual disruption of public facilities, such as might be caused by work stoppages or disasters. Although no notice to the public is required, the legislative body must make an effort to notify local newspapers, radio stations, and television stations that have requested mailed notice of meetings. (Gov't. Code § 54956.5.)

If you want to receive advance copies of the meeting agendas, you must file a written request. You may have to pay a fee for this mailing. The request is valid for the calendar year in which it is filed. It must be renewed after January 1 of each year. (Gov't. Code § 54954.1.)

UNITED STATES CITIZENSHIP

There are several ways to become a U.S. citizen. If you were born in the U.S., you are automatically a citizen. If you were born outside the U.S., you may be a citizen if one or both of your parents were U.S. citizens when you were born. Also, you may become a U.S. citizen if you were a lawful permanent resident of the U.S. when your parents were naturalized, or if you apply to naturalize on your own.

Naturalization

Naturalization is a process by which immigrants can become U.S. citizens. You must meet five requirements to qualify for naturalization:

- You must be at least 18 years old.
- You must have a green card (giving you permanent legal resident status).
- Since becoming a permanent resident, you must have lived continuously in the U.S. for five years (occasional short trips outside the U.S. don't count), and in the state where you will apply for citizenship for three months. These time requirements are shorter for spouses of U.S. citizens and refugees.

- You must have good moral character, as determined by the U.S. Citizenship and Immigration Services (USCIS).
- You must not have broken any immigration laws or been asked to leave the U.S. at any time.

If you meet these requirements, you can apply to the USCIS for naturalization. You will be interviewed, which serves three purposes: to verify the information on your application; to test your ability to speak, read, and write basic English; and to test your knowledge of American government and history. You must pass these tests to be approved for citizenship.

When your application is approved, you will be sworn in at a ceremony. You must take an oath to defend the U.S. and to relinquish your allegiance to your former country (although you can retain dual citizenship if your home country allows it).

Rights of Citizenship

Once you become a citizen through naturalization, you have almost all the same rights as native-born citizens, including the right to register to vote, the right to get a U.S. passport, and the right to run for most public offices. However, you may not run for president or vice president of the United States.

You can stop reporting your status to the USCIS, and you can no longer be deported if, for example, you are convicted of a crime.

VOTING

You can vote in California if you have registered and you are:

- a United States citizen
- a resident of California
- mentally competent
- at least 18 years old, and
- not in prison or on parole for a felony conviction. (Const. Art. II, §§ 2, 4; Elect. Code §§ 2000 and following.)

Registration

To register to vote, you must submit a signed application to the county clerk, the Department of Motor Vehicles, or other designated public agency at least 15 days before the election in which you want to vote. Applications will be accepted as long as they are postmarked on or before the 15th day before the election.

Absentee Voting

Any registered voter can request, in writing, an absentee ballot between the 29th and 7th day before the election. The clerk mails the ballot to the voter; there is no fee for the service. The voter must return the ballot, in person or by mail, before the close of the polls on election day. It may be returned to the official who sent it or dropped off at any polling place. Once the voter receives an absentee ballot, the voter can vote at polls only after surrendering the absentee ballot to the precinct board. (Elect. Code §§ 3000 and following.)

The website of the California Secretary of State contains more information about voting procedures, as well as downloads of certain forms. See www.ss.ca.gov. Click "Elections and Voter Information." ■

Consumers' Rights

When you purchase a product or a service, both California and federal law protect you not only from outright rip-offs but also from misleading advertisements, overbearing salespeople who come to your home, and products that don't work as promised.

TOPICS

Advertising

Cancelling Contracts

Car Rentals

Car Repairs

Car Sales

Contractors

Deliveries and Service Calls

Do-Not-Call List

Gift Certificates

Health Insurance

Layaway Purchases

Mail Order and Internet Merchandise

Privacy

Refunds and Exchanges

Sales Tax

Spam (see Advertising)

Warranties

RELATED TOPICS

Debts, Loans, and Credit

Dogs

Pet Stores

Real Estate

Buying and Selling a House

Traffic and Vehicle Laws

Car Insurance Requirements

Registration and Smog Checks

ADDITIONAL RESOURCES

Return to Sender: Getting a Refund or Replacement for Your Lemon Car, by Nancy Barron (National Consumer Law Center), summarizes each state's lemon law. To order, contact NCLC at www.consumerlaw.org or 617-542-9595.

California Department of Consumer Affairs (DCA), Consumer Information Center, 800- 952-5210 (TDD: 800-326-2297, 916-322-1700), www .dca.ca.gov, can help consumers resolve disputes, including those with mechanics. The DCA also provides a multitude of free consumer information publications.

Department of Motor Vehicles, New Motor Vehicle Board, 1507 21st Street, Suite 330, Sacramento, CA 95814, 916-445-1888, www.nmvb.ca.gov, takes complaints about cars that are lemons, helps customers deal with car dealers and manufacturers, and makes sure that customers follow the proper procedures to get a refund.

U.S. Department of Transportation Auto Safety Hotline, 888-327-4236, www.nhtsa.dot.gov, tells consumers which cars are currently being recalled or investigated for safety problems.

California Contractor's State License Board, P.O. Box 26000, Sacramento, CA 95826, 800-321-2752, www.clsb.ca.gov, can give information about a contractor's license and complaints filed against a contractor. The Board also takes complaints about licensed contractors.

The Federal Trade Commission, 600 Pennsylvania Avenue, NW, Washington, DC 20850, 877-382-4357, www.ftc.gov, publishes free pamphlets on consumer issues, including *Door-to-Door Sales*, *Layaway Purchase Plans*, *Shopping by Mail*, *Shopping by Phone and Mail*, *Warranties*, *A Businessperson's Guide to Federal Warranty Law*, and *Facts for Consumers—Service Contracts*. You can also call either California office at 415-356-5270 (San Francisco) or 310-824-4300 (Los Angeles), or visit the FTC online at www.ftc.gov.

California Department of Insurance, Consumer Services Division, 300 S. Spring Street, South Tower, Los Angeles, CA 90013, 800-927-HELP (800-927-4357), www.insurance.ca.gov, publishes consumer information on and takes complaints about providers of auto insurance, homeowners insurance, title insurance, bail bonds and other forms of insurance products.

ADVERTISING

California law prohibits advertisers from making false or misleading statements about products or services that they are trying to sell or lease. An advertiser who makes such statements knowing that they are false, or without taking reasonable steps to make sure that they are true, can be fined up to $2,500, sentenced to up to six months in the county jail, or both. (Bus. & Prof. Code § 17500.)

Furthermore, an advertiser cannot solicit buyers by mail using any symbol or language that falsely implies or states that the advertiser is connected to or has the endorsement of the federal government or any state or local government. (39 U.S.C. § 3001(h); Bus. & Prof. Code § 17533.6.)

Price

An advertisement cannot compare its prices with a "former price" unless that former price was actually the prevailing market price within three months before the ad ran, or the ad clearly and conspicuously specifies when the former price was in effect. (Bus. & Prof. Code § 17501.)

If a retail seller sells its consumer product or service in multiple units only, it must advertise the price of the minimum number of units in which the product or service is offered. For example, a company that sells razor blades in packages of 12 must advertise the package price. As long as the company advertises the package price, it can also advertise a single unit price, but the single unit price must not be displayed in a larger or more conspicuous typeface than the multiple unit price. (Bus. & Prof. Code § 17504.)

If a manufacturer's cash rebate requires the buyer to send in a coupon, the merchant's advertisements must state the price the buyer must actually pay the merchant for the product. The merchant may not simply advertise the price of the product after the rebate. (Bus. & Prof. Code § 17701.5.)

Availability

Unless stores advertise that there are only limited quantities of a particular item available, they must let customers buy as many as they want. If the store refuses to sell this amount, the customer can sue for any losses suffered as a result, plus a $50 penalty. (Bus. & Prof. Code § 17500.5). Also, a store may not intentionally have a limited supply of an advertised item on hand unless the ad states a limitation. (Civ. Code § 1770 (a)(10).)

"Bait and switch" advertising is illegal. That means a store cannot advertise a product that it has no intention of selling. For example, a store may not advertise a low-priced product—which turns out to be unavailable or defective—simply to lure customers into the store to sell a higher-priced product. (Bus. & Prof. Code § 17500; Civ. Code § 1770(a)(9).)

Quality of Goods

An advertisement cannot state that goods are original or new if they are in fact used, previously owned, altered, or deteriorated. (Bus. & Prof. Code § 17531; Civ. Code § 1770(a)(6).) In addition, an advertisement can't claim that goods are of a particular standard, grade, or style if they are not, and can't falsely claim that a product has been endorsed or sponsored by a person or group if it has not. (Civ. Code §§ 1770(a)(5), (7).)

A product cannot be marked "Made in USA" if the product or any part of it is partially or substantially manufactured or produced outside the United States. (Bus. & Prof. Code § 17533.7.)

Email Advertising

State law prohibits the sending of "unsolicited commercial email" advertisements to or from a California email address. It also prohibits:

- the collection of email addresses or registering multiple email addresses in order to send unsolicited commercial email advertisements to or from a California email address
- sending a commercial email advertisement that is false or misleading, and
- using an electronic mail service provider's equipment in California to send unsolicited email advertisements in violation of the provider's policy.

The recipient, the electronic mail service provider, or the attorney general may sue the sender for damages and penalties. (Bus. & Prof. Code §§ 17529-17529.9, 17538.45.)

Tobacco Advertising

State law prohibits the advertising of tobacco products on any outdoor billboard located within 1,000 feet of any public or private elementary school, junior high school, high school, or public playground. (Bus. & Prof. Code § 22961.) Local laws may provide standards that are even more restrictive. Displays that oppose the use of tobacco products are not prohibited by California law.

Contest Advertising
Sweepstakes solicitation materials may not misrepresent that the recipient is a prize winner. These materials must state prominently that no purchase is necessary to enter the sweepstakes and must include official rules for the sweepstakes. Sweepstakes entries not accompanied by an order for products or services may not be disadvantaged in the selection process as compared to entries accompanied by orders. (Bus. & Prof. Code § 17539.15.)

Violation of Advertising Laws
Any person or entity that violates any of the laws discussed in this section is subject to a civil penalty of up to $2,500 per violation in an action by the Attorney General or a district attorney; this penalty is split between the state and county where the violation occurred; it is not paid to the victims of the unlawful practices. (Bus. & Prof. Code §§ 17206, 17536.) However, victims can sue to recover their actual losses, and for an injunction to prevent the person or entity from continuing the unlawful practice.
If the victim of the unlawful advertising practice is a senior citizen or disabled person, then an additional penalty of up to $2,500 may be added. (Bus. & Prof. Code § 17206.1.)

CANCELLING CONTRACTS
Even after you sign on the dotted line, the law gives you a chance to back out of certain kinds of contracts if you have second thoughts.

The Three Day Cooling-Off Rule: Door-to-Door Sales
Federal law (16 C.F.R. § 429.1) gives consumers the right to cancel contracts for the purchase or lease of consumer goods costing $25 or more until midnight of the third business day after the contract was signed. This cancellation right applies to:
- door-to-door sales
- sales made anywhere other than the seller's normal place of business—for instance, at a hotel or restaurant, outdoor exhibit, computer show, fairgrounds, or trade show.

The Three-Day Cooling-Off Rule: Home Loans

The federal Truth in Lending Act (15 U.S.C. § 1635) lets consumers cancel home improvement loans, second mortgages, or other loans where you pledge your home as security (except a first mortgage or first deed of trust) until midnight of the third business day after the lender gives you the required loan disclosures and notice of your cancellation rights, or after you sign the contract, whichever occurs first.

California has a similar law. (Civ. Code §§ 1689.5–1659.14).

The truth in lending laws require sellers to make certain disclosures (about, for example, the terms of the loan, the total cost of the loan to you, the interest rate, and any applicable fees) to you before credit is extended. For most home mortgage transactions, the lender must give you good faith estimates of these disclosures within three business days after receiving your loan application. If the loan is not being used to finance the purchase of a house (for example, if the loan is a second mortgage to finance home improvements), the lender must also give you notice of your right to cancel the loan within three business days after you sign the loan documents. This "cooling-off period" can be even longer if the lender does not give you the required notice.

How to Cancel a Contract

To cancel a contract, call the seller within the cooling off period and say you want to cancel. Then sign and date the cancellation form or, if you were not given a form, write your own letter telling the seller that you are canceling the contract. Keep a copy for yourself. It must be postmarked (or fax-marked) by midnight of the last business day on which you are entitled to cancel. If you hand deliver it, get a signed, dated receipt from the business. The seller must refund your money within ten days, then either pick up the items purchased or reimburse you within 20 days for the cost of mailing the goods back. If the seller doesn't come for the goods or make an arrangement for you to mail them back, you can keep them. (Civ. Code §§ 1689.7, 1689.10, 1689.11.)

Other Contracts You Can Cancel

California law gives you the right to cancel many consumer purchase contracts within certain time limits. Some common contracts consumers may cancel include (see the complete list at www.dca.ca.gov/legal/k-6.html):

- dance lessons, within 180 days, but you must pay for lessons received (Civ. Code § 1812.54)
- dating service contracts, within three business days (Civ. Code § 1694.1)
- purchase contracts for houses sold immediately before a foreclosure sale, within five business days or until 8 a.m. on the day of the sale, whichever is first (Civ. Code § 1695.4)
- contracts with prepaid job listing service firms, within three business days (Civ. Code § 1812.516(a))
- contracts for seller-assisted marketing plans, within three business days (Civ. Code § 1812.209)
- seminar sales, within three business days (Civ. Code § 1689.20)
- contracts for weight loss services, within three business days (Civ. Code § 1694.6)
- home solicitation contracts for a personal emergency response unit, within seven business days (Civ. Code § 1689.6(b))
- home improvement work following a national, state, or local disaster, within seven business days (Civ. Code § 1689.6(c))
- membership camping contracts, within three business days if buyer visits site and within ten business days if buyer does not visit site (Civ. Code §§ 1812.303–1812.304)
- purchase contracts for time-share properties, within three days (Bus. & Prof. Code § 11024)
- dental services, within three business days, but you must pay for treatments received (Civ. Code § 1689.3)
- health studio services, within three business days (Civ. Code § 1812.85)
- discount buying clubs, within three days (Civ. Code § 1812.118), and
- most contracts that were negotiated in the following languages, if no translation was provided before the buyer signed: Spanish, Chinese, Tagalog, Vietnamese, or Korean (Civ. Code § 1632).

Even if there is no cooling-off period, you still might be able to cancel a contract if you agreed to the contract under certain unfair circumstances. Courts may allow you to cancel a contract if you can show:

- **Incapacity.** A contract is invalid if you did not have the necessary mental capacity, because of your age or mental disability, to understand and agree to its terms.

- **Duress.** You may be able to cancel a contract if you were coerced or threatened into signing it.
- **Fraudulent misrepresentation.** A contract may be cancelled if the seller fraudulently misrepresented critical terms of the contract, and you relied on the seller's claims when you decided to sign the contract.
- **Unconscionability.** Courts sometimes allow you to cancel a contract because the terms are so one-sided that they "shock the conscience" or because the bargaining process was extremely unfair.

CAR RENTALS

The driver of a rental car, not the owner, is responsible for producing evidence of the car's registration upon demand by a police officer. A California Highway Patrol officer who stops you for expired registration will issue the citation to you unless you have the name of the rental agency manager, so you should always write the manager's name on the rental contract.

The renter is responsible for all collision damage to a rented vehicle, even if someone else caused the damage or the cause is unknown. The renter is liable for the cost of repair up to the value of the vehicle, as well as loss of use and towing, storage, and impound fees. However, the rental company may not try to recover for damage or loss by charging, debiting, or blocking the renter's credit card without approval. The cost may be paid:

- by the renter's own auto insurance policy
- through certain automatic credit card coverage—but credit card companies have been cutting back coverage, so call first before assuming your card will protect you, or
- by any collision damage waiver (CDW) coverage the driver purchased from the car rental company.

If the rental car company recovers from someone else (for example, the person who caused the accident if it was not the renter), they cannot recover from the renter as well. (Civ. Code § 1936(d)(5).)

Collision Damage Waivers

A collision damage waiver (CDW) is a form of liability protection sold by most car rental companies. The law regulates industry practices regarding CDWs, and other optional goods or services, as follows:

- A rental company cannot require the purchase of optional insurance (such as CDW), goods, or services.
- A rental company cannot charge more than $9 a day for CDW for "economy" or "compact" cars, or more than $15 a day for other cars.
- A rental company cannot engage in any unfair, deceptive, or coercive conduct to induce a renter to purchase optional services such as CDW.
- A rental company cannot debit or block the renter's credit card account as a deposit if the renter declines to purchase optional services such as CDW. (Civ. Code § 1936.)

CAR REPAIRS

Mechanics must be registered with the Bureau of Automotive Repair. Mechanics must give a written estimate of the cost of proposed repair work before they start work on a car. If they find that more work is necessary, they must get the customer's consent, in writing, over the phone, or by email, before proceeding. Mechanics must provide an invoice itemizing the work done and the parts supplied. The customer is also entitled to all replaced parts, if he or she asks for them when bringing the car in for service. If a mechanic fails to comply with these requirements, a consumer may file a complaint with the Bureau of Automotive Repair, which may in turn file a complaint with the district attorney in the county where the mechanic does business. (Bus. & Prof. Code § 9884.8.) You can check on a mechanic's license at www.smogcheck.ca.gov.

If Your Car Is a Lemon

California's "lemon law" covers vehicles with serious warranty problems that can't be fixed. (Civ. Code § 1793.22.) It applies to vehicles purchased or leased for more than four months for personal, family, or small business use. It also applies to used vehicles sold with the manufacturer's new car warranty, and to demonstration vehicles. It does not apply to the habitation portion of motor homes, or to motorcycles or off-road vehicles.

The lemon law applies during the first 18 months after the vehicle is delivered to the buyer or the first 18,000 miles on its odometer, whichever occurs first. It applies to defects covered by the warranty that substantially reduce the vehicle's use, value, or safety to the buyer.

If your vehicle has one or more substantial warranty defects, you must give the manufacturer or dealer a reasonable opportunity to repair them before you can take advantage of the lemon law. The lemon law creates a presumption that a reasonable number of repair attempts have occurred, and that you are entitled to a replacement vehicle or a refund, if any of the following are true:

- The same warranty defect cannot be repaired by the manufacturer or dealer after four repair attempts during the 18 month/18,000 mile period.
- The vehicle is out of service for a cumulative total of more than 30 days for repair of a combination of warranty defects during the 18 month/18,000 mile period, not counting delays beyond the control of the manufacturer or dealer.
- The vehicle has a warranty defect that might cause death or serious bodily injury that cannot be repaired by the manufacturer or dealer after two attempts during the 18 month/18,000 mile period. (The buyer must directly notify the manufacturer that this kind of defect needs repair.)

In any of these situations, you can file for arbitration and request a refund or replacement. The manufacturer can try to show the arbitrator that you are not entitled to relief because, for example, the problem has been fixed, the defect isn't substantial, or more repair attempts are needed. Going through arbitration may not get you a refund or replacement, but at least you should finally get the car fixed right. The manufacturer is bound by the arbitrator's decision if you accept it. You still may sue the manufacturer if you are dissatisfied with the outcome. (For more information on the lemon law and certified arbitration programs, go to www.dca.ca.gov/acp.)

CAR SALES

California law includes several provisions intended to protect consumers when they buy new or used cars.

New Cars

When you buy a new car, you have no automatic right to cancel the contract later. The sales contract for both new and used cars must contain a notice informing you that California law does not provide a "cooling off" or other cancellation period for vehicle sales. After you sign the contract, you must have the seller's agreement in order to cancel it, unless you have legal cause, such as fraud. (Civ. Code § 2982.)

If the dealer knows of any "material" (significant) damage to a new or previously unregistered vehicle that's been repaired, the dealer must tell you in writing before you sign a contract. If the car had damage that was unknown when the contract was signed, or suffers damage after you sign the contract but before delivery, the dealer must tell you about it before you take delivery, if the car is not repaired. Material damage means damage that:

- exceeds 3% of the manufacturer's suggested price or $500, whichever is greater
- occurred in connection with theft of the vehicle
- is to the frame or drive train, or
- is to the suspension, requiring repairs other than wheel balancing or alignment.

Damage to components that are bolted or attached to the vehicle, such as bumpers, tires, and glass, is exempt from this disclosure requirement only if replaced with identical new, original manufacturer's components—unless the repairs exceed 10% of the manufacturer's suggested price. (Veh. Code §§ 9990 and following.)

New car dealers' demonstrator cars are legally considered used cars, so these disclosure laws don't apply—even if the dealer gives a new car warranty. (Veh. Code § 665.)

Used Cars

All dealers selling used cars must post a large sticker in the car window stating whether the car is being sold "as is" or with a warranty. (16 C.F.R. § 455.2; Civ. Code §1792.4). Most used car dealers try to sell cars "as is," but this is not always legal. For example, dealers can't sell a car "as is" if they give you a written warranty. (15 U.S.C. §2308(a); Civ. Code § 1793.)

If a dealer sells a used vehicle that it or the manufacturer reacquired because the lemon law required that it be replaced for the original buyer, the manufacturer must:

- retitle the vehicle in the manufacturer's name
- request the DMV to place a "lemon law buyback" notice on the ownership certificate, and
- affix a "lemon law buyback" decal to the left doorframe of the vehicle.

The dealer must:

- give specific notice to the buyer that the vehicle's title is permanently branded
- disclose all problems with the vehicle that lead to the buyback and warranty that the vehicle is free of those problems for one year, and
- obtain the buyer's written acknowledgment. (Civ. Code §§ 1793.23, 1793.24.)

Private sellers do not have to post these stickers, but if the buyer relies on the seller's positive statements about the car and then discovers they were lies, the buyer may be successful in suing the seller in small claims court for the cost of repairs or cancellation of the contract. The seller cannot make positive statements that the buyer relies on and then claim that the car was sold "as is."

As with new cars, there is ordinarily no right to cancel a retail purchase contract for a used car. The purchase contract must, however, contain a notice informing you that California law does not provide a "cooling off" or other cancellation period for vehicle sales. (Civ. Code § 2982.) Certain safety-related features must be working on the car: horn, lights, windshield wipers, tires, and brakes. Also, the smog equipment must be intact. It is illegal to sell a car with smog equipment that has been disconnected or tampered with. The seller must provide a current smog certificate.

Service Contracts

All new cars—and some used cars—come with a written warranty covering repairs and adjustments for specific lengths of time or mileage. When you buy a new car, dealers will also try to sell you a service contract (extended warranty), which is a high-profit item for the dealership. Service contracts cannot merely duplicate coverage offered by the manufacturer's express warranty, although a service contract may run concurrently with or overlap an express warranty. (Civ. Code § 1794.41(a)(3).)

If you change your mind after you buy a service contract, you can cancel it. The dealer must notify you, in writing, of your right to cancel and receive a refund. Your must send written cancellation to the person specified in the contract. (Civ. Code § 1794.41.) The amount of your refund depends on when you cancel. The seller can charge you a limited processing fee to cancel.

Financing

If you have taken possession of an automobile but the dealer cannot get the agreed financing for you, the dealer cannot change the terms of the contract unless you agree. (Civ. Code § 2982(h).) However, you may have little practical choice but to agree to the new terms or return the car to the dealer. If you return the car, you are entitled to get your deposit back as well as any trade-in vehicle you gave to the dealer as part of the transaction. If the trade-in has been sold, you are entitled to its fair market value or the price listed in the contract, whichever is higher. You are not required to buy another car from that dealer. (Civ. Code § 2982.7.)

CONTRACTORS

The legal definition of a contractor is anyone who makes alterations or additions to a structure that become part of the real estate—for example, fixing a roof, building an extra room, or strengthening a house's ability to withstand an earthquake.

Licensing Requirements

Any contractor who does home improvement work worth more than $500 (labor and materials), or who advertises as a contractor, must be licensed by the California Contractors State License Board (CSLB). The license number must be included in all advertisements, bids, and contracts. You need not be licensed to work on your own home as long as the work is done by you or your employees, the employees receive wages as their sole compensation, and the work is not intended for sale. If you buy a house solely to fix it up and sell it, you will probably have to be licensed. (See Bus. & Prof. Code § 7044.) Any contract for home improvements or swimming pool construction costing more than $500 must be in writing.

There are various license classifications depending on the contractor's specialty, such as roofing or plumbing. A general building contractor does framing or carpentry and typically also oversees two or more unrelated building trades (such as plumbing and electrical) on a project.

Unlicensed contractors:

- may be prosecuted by the local district attorney and be subject to a fine or imprisonment
- can't get local building permits, which are required for jobs involving structural work or remodeling, and
- can't sue to get paid for work requiring a license. (Bus. & Prof. Code §§ 7028, 7031.)

Any contractor who bids for typical home improvement projects on residential property with four or fewer units must provide the homeowner with a three-paragraph notice specifying that state law requires contractors to be licensed for jobs of $500 or more. The notice must also state that if you use an unlicensed contractor, CSLB may not assist you with a complaint. Finally, it must explain how to contact CSLB to determine whether a contractor has a license. (Bus. & Prof. Code § 7030.)

Complaints About Licensed Contractors

The CSLB handles complaints about licensed contractors—such as shoddy or incomplete work on a home remodeling project—and may mediate or arbitrate some cases. However, the CSLB has a large backlog of complaints, and getting your problem addressed may be a slow process.

Contractors who are at fault may be fined up to $2,000; be required to make repairs or restitution; or have their licenses suspended or revoked. (Bus. & Prof. Code § 7099.2.)

Checking a Contractor's Record and Insurance

The CSLB will verify that an individual contractor's license is current and valid and will disclose whether or not any legal action has been taken against a contractor for inadequate or unfinished work. However, the CSLB will not disclose the number or details of any complaints filed. Call 800-321-CSLB (800-321-2752) or go to www.cslb.ca.gov to check on licensing and lawsuits.

Contractors must be insured against claims covering workers' compensation and meet the other legal obligations of independent contractors, such as contributing to state and federal benefit programs like unemployment and Social Security and withholding state and federal income taxes.

Deposits

By state law, a contractor cannot require a down payment larger than $200 or 2% of the contract price for swimming pools, or $1,000 or 10% of the contract price for other home improvements (excluding finance charges), whichever is less. (Bus. & Prof. Code § 7159(d).)

Mechanics' Lien

California law allows anyone who furnishes labor or materials to your home to place a "mechanics' lien" against your home if you do not pay. (Civ. Code § 3109 and following.) A mechanics' lien is a legal claim for money owed.

Even if you paid the general contractor, if he did not pay the subcontractors or material suppliers, they can place a lien on your home by recording it at the County Recorder's office. This means you might have to pay a bill twice to remove the lien. To avoid this, you should get a copy of each bill paid by the contractor to a subcontractor or material supplier, marked "paid."

To enforce a mechanics' lien, the contractor must file a lawsuit to foreclose on your home within 90 days of the date the lien was recorded.

DELIVERIES AND SERVICE CALLS

Finally responding to consumers irked by deliveries and repair people that never come, the legislature has put limits on businesses' freedom to make and break these promises.

Merchandise Deliveries

Retailers employing 25 or more people must specify a four-hour time period within which any delivery or service call will be made, if they require you to be home to receive the delivery or while the service is rendered. (Civ. Code § 1722.)

Home Services

Utility and cable TV companies are also covered by the four-hour requirement. These companies must inform you of your right to have service begin during a four-hour connection or repair period (if your presence is required) before the date of service or repair. (Civ. Code § 1722.)

Late Deliveries and Service Calls

If the merchandise or covered service is not delivered or begun within the specified four-hour period, you can sue in small claims court for lost wages, expenses actually incurred, or other actual damages up to $600. However, the retailer, utility, or cable company is not liable if the delay was caused by unforeseen or unavoidable events beyond its control or if you were not home. (Civ. Code § 1722.)

Do-Not-Call Registry

Consumers can add their home and cell telephone numbers to the National Do-Not-Call Registry to cut down on the number of unsolicited telemarketing phone calls they receive. The Do-Not-Call Registry is part of the federal Telemarketing and Consumer Fraud and Abuse Prevention Act (15 U.S.C. §§ 6101 and following), which also requires telemarketers to transmit caller ID information when they make solicitation phone calls.

To add a telephone number to the Do-Not-Call Registry, call 888-382-1222 (TTY 1-866-290-4236) from the phone number you want to block or register online at www.donotcall.gov. Within 31 days after registration, most telemarketing calls will stop, although you may still get calls from: political organizations, charities, telephone surveyors, companies with whom you have done business within the last 18 months, and companies you've given permission to call.

If you registered with the Do-Not-Call Registry at least 31 days ago and a telemarketer calls, you can file a complaint with the Federal Trade Commission, either online at www.ftc.gov or by calling 888-382-1222 (TTY1-866-290-4236).

GIFT CERTIFICATES

California law prohibits a merchant from selling a gift certificate containing an expiration date or a service fee for nonuse. Any gift certificate containing an expiration date may be redeemed for cash or replaced with a new gift certificate at the issuer's discretion, at no cost to the purchaser or holder. This law does not apply to the following, as long as the expiration date appears in capital letters in at least 10-point font on the front of the certificate:

- gift certificates issued as part of an award, loyalty reward, or promotion without money or another thing of value being exchanged
- gift certificates sold below face value at a volume discount to employers or to nonprofit or charitable organizations for fundraising purposes, so long as the expiration date is not later than 30 days after the sale, and
- gift certificates issued for a food product, such as a grocery item.

A service fee may be charged on gift cards with a remaining value of $5 or less that have been inactive for 24 consecutive months. (Civil Code § 1749.5.)

HEALTH INSURANCE

Health insurance pays some or all of the costs of treating specified medical problems. If you pay your premiums, you are entitled to coverage under the terms of your policy.

Employers Required to Provide Health Insurance

A new law requires large employers to provide health insurance for their California employees according to the following schedule:

- Employers with 200 or more employees must provide insurance to workers and dependents beginning January 1, 2006.
- Employers with 50-199 employees must provide insurance to workers (but not dependents) beginning January 1, 2007.
- Most employers with fewer than 50 employees are exempt. (Health and Safety Code § 1357.20 and following; Ins. Code § 10760 and following; Lab. Code § 2120 and following.)

For more information about health insurance through your employer, see Employees' Rights, Health Insurance.

Insurance Requirements

There are no rules for insurance policies regarding what injuries or illnesses must be insured, but your policy must clearly spell out what is covered and what is excluded.

California law requires your insurer to pay any covered bill within 30 days. However, there is no penalty against insurance companies that don't meet the deadline, so the law has no real teeth.

Health care service plan contracts and disability insurance policies issued, renewed, amended, or delivered on or after January 1, 1999 must allow female patients direct access to their obstetrician's and gynecologist's services. (H & S Code § 1367.695; Ins. Code § 10123.84.) Thanks to the Newborns' and Mothers' Health Act of 1997, health care service plan contracts and disability insurance policies may not restrict inpatient hospital care for mothers having babies to less than 48 hours following a vaginal delivery or less than 96 hours following a delivery by caesarean section, unless the mother and her physician agree to a shorter hospital stay and a follow-up visit is allowed by the insurer. (H & S Code § 1367.62; Ins. Code § 10123.87.)

If you wish to file a complaint against your health maintenance organization (HMO), you may contact the California Department of Managed Health Care (which regulates HMOs) at 800-HMO-2219 (800-466-2219) or www.dmhc.ca.gov.

LAYAWAY PURCHASES

A layaway agreement is a contract under which you make a deposit on consumer goods that the retailer holds for you until you finish making the payments. If you decide before you finish paying that you no longer want the item, you may be able to get a refund of what you have already paid. Your written layaway agreement will indicate whether or not you are entitled to a refund. If you do receive a refund, the seller may be able to keep a portion of your payments as a service fee. However, this fee should not be more than the cost of storing the goods.

If you complete the layaway payments, you are entitled to a refund if the goods aren't available in the same condition as when you first bought them. (Civ. Code § 1749.)

MAIL ORDER AND INTERNET MERCHANDISE

The federal government puts strict requirements on how mail order companies conduct business.

Delayed Goods

If you order goods by mail, phone, or fax, or on the Internet (except magazine subscriptions other than the first shipment, COD orders, or seeds or plants), the seller must ship within the time promised or, if no time was stated, within 30 days. (Fed. Trade Commission Mail Order Rule, 16 C.F.R. §§ 435.1-435.3.) If the seller cannot ship within that time, it must notify you of a new shipping date and offer you the option of canceling your order and getting a refund.

If you opt for the second deadline and the seller can't meet it, the seller must send you a notice requesting your consent to a third date. If you don't return the second notice, your order must be cancelled and your money refunded. The seller must issue the refund within seven work days if you paid by check or money order, or within one billing cycle if you charged your purchase. California has a similar mail order and Internet purchase rule. (Bus. & Prof. Code § 17538.)

Mail Fraud

If you receive a mailing that you suspect contains false or fraudulent representations, notify the Postal Inspector. You can locate your local postal inspection service office by looking in the "Post Office" listing under "United States Government" in the phone book, or by visiting www.usps. gov. An inspector who agrees the mail is fraudulent will get a court order to intercept the company's mail. The inspector will investigate the company and try to get back any money you sent.

PRIVACY

Every California business is required to take reasonable steps to destroy customer records that contain personal information, once the business no longer plans to use or keep the information. A business can meet this requirement by shredding, erasing, or otherwise making the personal information unreadable and undecipherable. If a customer is harmed by a business's failure to destroy records, the customer can sue for money damages plus a penalty of $500 ($3,000 if the violation was willful, intentional, or reckless) and attorneys' fees. (Civ. Code §§ 1798.80–1798.84.)

Every California business with computerized personal information data that learns that its security system has been breached must tell all those whose unencrypted personal information may have been acquired by an unauthorized person. This notification may be delayed if it would compromise investigation of the breach. (Civ. Code § 1798.82.) State agencies have a similar obligation. (Civ. Code § 1798.29.) If a customer is harmed by the business's failure to notify, the customer may sue for money damages plus a penalty of $500 ($3,000 if the violation was willful, intentional, or reckless) and attorneys' fees.

Beginning July 1, 2004, operators of commercial websites or online services that collect personal information on Californians must post a privacy policy and comply with it. The privacy policy must identify categories of personal information collected and categories of third parties with whom the operator may share the information. (Bus. & Prof. Code §§ 22575–22576.)

REFUNDS AND EXCHANGES

Merchants are not required to give a cash refund or even a store credit for returned merchandise, although many do. However, merchants who do not allow a full cash or credit refund or equal exchange within seven days of purchase, with a receipt, must post the store's refund-credit-exchange policy at each cash register and sales counter, at each public entrance, on tags attached to each item, or on the retailer's order forms. If the merchant doesn't post the policy, you may return the goods, with a receipt, for a full refund, up to 30 days after the purchase. (Civ. Code § 1723.)

A merchant is not required to post a no-return policy for, or accept returns of food; plants; flowers; perishable goods; merchandise marked "as is," "no returns accepted," or "all sales final"; goods used or damaged after purchase; special order goods received as ordered; goods not returned with their original package; and goods that can't be resold due to health considerations.

SALES TAX

Sales tax is assessed on products and services purchased in California, as well as products bought out of state for use in California, in certain circumstances. The state sales tax is 7.25%, and cities and counties may assess an additional sales tax. The amount of tax charged varies by county, 0.125% to 0.50%.

What Can Be Taxed

Almost all products sold are subject to sales tax. Periodicals are subject to sales tax unless they are sold on a subscription basis and delivered by a common carrier. Food products such as the following are not taxed (unless they're sold as meals or in vending machines):
- candy and other confections
- cereals, meats, fish, eggs, vegetables, fruit, and spices
- coffee, tea, cocoa, cocoa products, milk and milk products, and
- food and nonalcoholic drinks sold by nonprofit groups (such as the Boy Scouts or the 4-H Club) at occasional events like fairs and parades. (Rev. and Tax. Code §§ 6359, 6361.)

Prescription medicines are not subject to sales tax. (Rev. and Tax. Code § 6369.)

Products Bought Out of State

If you purchase products from a mail order company based out of state, you may have to pay sales tax. California law requires companies that have a physical presence in California (a store, warehouse, or salesperson, for example), or that have salespeople in California, or that regularly advertise by mail in California, to pay sales tax to the state. (Rev. and Tax Code § 6203.) Some businesses meet this requirement by simply incorporating the tax into their pricing; others include a separate sales tax charge on your bill.

If the company has no physical presence in the state, it does not have to pay sales tax to California.

If you purchase a car in another state, you will have to pay California sales tax (called a "use tax"), or the difference between the tax that you paid in the state where you bought the car and the California state tax, when you register the car in California. You may not be subject to this tax if you can show that the person who sold you the car is a close relative who isn't in the automobile business or that you purchased the car intending to use it in another state, then moved to California unexpectedly. (Veh. Code § 4300.5, Rev. and Tax Code §§ 6285.)

If you buy something in a foreign country, you must pay a use tax on all items brought into the state that are normally subject to sales tax in California. The first $400 worth of purchases are exempt, however. (Rev. & Tax Code § 6405.)

WARRANTIES

A warranty is a promise made by the seller or manufacturer about the quality of goods. Warranties can be express or implied. An express warranty is a statement made by the merchant or manufacturer that promises, for example, that the goods are defect-free or that they will perform as promised for a specified period of time. An express warranty may be written or oral. An implied warranty is one that the law automatically provides.

Express Warranties

A federal law (the Magnuson-Moss Warranty Act, 15 U.S.C. § 2301 and following) governs express warranties. This act does not require manufacturers to give written warranties. If one is given, however, the following rules apply:

- It must be written in ordinary language that is easy to read and understand (if the goods cost more than $15).
- The seller must show you a copy of the warranty before you make a purchase of more than $15, and provide you with a copy when you buy.
- It must be labeled either "full" or "limited" (if the goods cost more than $10).

A full warranty must have these features:

- The product must be repaired or replaced for free during the warranty period.
- The product must be repaired within a reasonable time.
- You don't have to do anything unreasonable—such as return a heavy item—to get warranty service.
- You do not have to return a warranty card for the warranty to be valid.
- Implied full warranties cannot be disclaimed, denied, or limited to a specific length of time.

A limited warranty offers less protection. You still don't have to return the owner registration card to be eligible for the warranty, regardless of what the warranty says. However, you may have to pay for labor or reinstallation, or bring a heavy item in for service. In addition, your implied warranty may expire when your written warranty expires, and you may be entitled to only pro rata refunds or credits, which means you have to pay for the time you used the product.

Implied Warranties

California's Song-Beverly Consumer Warranty Act (Civ. Code §§ 1790 and following) provides an "implied warranty of merchantability" on almost every new product. This means that the manufacturer and seller automatically promise that the product is fit for its ordinary purpose. The Act also provides an "implied warranty of fitness for a specific purpose" when a product is sold or marketed in a context where the specific need or intent of the consumer is known. For instance, if you buy a sleeping bag after telling the sporting goods salesperson that you plan to camp in subzero weather, the sleeping bag must be suitable for very cold temperatures. If the product comes with a written warranty, the implied warranty lasts as long as the written one (but not more than one year). If the written warranty does not state how long it lasts, the implied warranty lasts one year.

Sales of the following items are not covered by the implied warranty:

- food, personal care, or cleaning products
- clothing, including under and outer garments, shoes, and accessories made of woven material, yarn, fiber, leather, or similar fabrics, and

- "as is" sales that have a proper "as is" disclaimer conspicuously attached to the product. A retail seller who gives a written express warranty, however, can't legally get out of an implied warranty.

Implied warranties apply to used products only when a retail seller gives an express warranty, and they last only as long as the written warranty, but no less than 30 days or more than 90 days. Implied warranties on used goods imply that the item will work, given its age and condition.

Servicing a Product Under Warranty

The Song-Beverly Act requires manufacturers who give a written express warranty to maintain service facilities in California reasonably close to all areas where their products are sold. The manufacturer can use retailers or independent repair shops. Repairs must be completed within 30 days, unless a delay is beyond the control of the manufacturer or its representative. While a product that costs more than $50 is being repaired, your written warranty is extended by the amount of time the item is in the shop.

If the product's size and weight or installation make it impossible or very hard for you to return the product, the manufacturer must provide warranty service at your home or arrange to have the malfunctioning product picked up without additional charges for transportation.

Some retailers, particularly those who sell consumer electronics, sell extended warranties on their products. These warranties usually offer service, repair, or replacement of the product for a period of time beyond the regular warranty. The value of these extended warranties is variable, depending on the product, coverage under the regular warranty, and likelihood of malfunction.

The only legal rule governing these warranties is that they cannot merely duplicate coverage offered by the manufacturer's express warranty. (Civ. Code § 1794.41.) ■

Copyrights and Patents

The law of copyrights, patents, and trademarks (called intellectual property law) allows people to protect their creations from unauthorized use by others.

Most of the laws and agencies regulating intellectual property are federal. All patent and copyright lawsuits must be brought in federal court.

TOPICS

Copyrights

Patents

RELATED TOPICS

Courts and Lawsuits

Federal Court System

Small Businesses

Trademarks and Service Marks

ADDITIONAL RESOURCES

The Copyright Handbook: How to Protect & Use Written Works, by Stephen Fishman (Nolo), is a complete guide to the law of copyright and includes forms for registering a copyright.

Getting Permission: How to License & Clear Copyrighted Materials Online & Off, by Richard Stim (Nolo), spells out how to obtain permission to use art, music, writing, or other copyrighted works.

Circular 2: Publications on Copyright is a list of government pamphlets about copyright law. To get a copy, download it from the Copyright Office website at www.copyright.gov.

Patent It Yourself, by David Pressman (Nolo), takes you step-by-step through the process of getting a patent.

Patent, Copyright & Trademark: An Intellectual Property Desk Reference, by Richard Stim (Nolo), defines and explains patent, copyright, trademark, and trade secret law (includes sample nondisclosure agreements and patent, copyright, and trademark forms).

The Inventor's Notebook, by Fred Grissom and David Pressman (Nolo), helps inventors document the invention process to ensure they are entitled to the greatest legal protection available.

Nolo's Patents for Beginners, by David Pressman and Richard Stim (Nolo) provides a straightforward explanation of patent principles and rules for documenting and acquiring patent rights.

The Public Domain: How to Find & Use Copyright-Free Writings, Music, Art & More, by Stephen Fishman (Nolo), explains how to recognize whether or not a creative arts work is in the public domain.

How to Make Patent Drawings, by Jack Lo and David Pressman (Nolo), is a step-by-step guide to creating formal patent drawings that comply with U.S. Patent and Trademark Office rules.

Profit From Your Idea: How to Make Smart Licensing Deals (License Your Invention), by Richard Stim (Nolo), guides the reader through the important process of giving others permission to use, develop, and market an invention.

Patent Pending in 24 Hours, by Richard Stim and David Pressman (Nolo), shows you how to prepare, assemble, and file a provisional patent application—an abbreviated patent application that preserves your priority of invention for 12 months.

What Every Inventor Needs to Know about Business & Taxes, by Stephen Fishman (Nolo), provides information on taxes, starting and running your invention business, and licensing and protecting inventions.

The website of the U.S. Patent and Trademark Office, at www.uspto.gov, provides information and forms on patents.

The website of the Copyright Office, at www.copyright.gov, provides information, forms, and searchable records on copyrights.

Trademark: Legal Care for Your Business & Product Name, by Stephen Elias (Nolo), shows how to choose a distinctive name, conduct a trademark search, and register a mark with the U.S. Patent and Trademark Office.

COPYRIGHTS

Federal copyright law gives someone who creates an original work of expression—a play, song, painting, or book, for example—the right to control how that work is used. A copyright grants a number of specific rights regarding the expression, including the exclusive right to:

- make copies or authorize others to make copies
- make derivative expressions, such as translations or updates
- sell the expression
- perform or display the expression, and
- sue others who violate these rights.

A copyright automatically comes into existence when expression takes a tangible form—when words are written on a page, for example. Copyrights last a long time: For works made after 1977, a copyright lasts for 70 years after the death of the creator. For works created by employees for an employer, a copyright lasts for 95 years from the date of publication (which includes any form of dissemination) or 120 years from the date of creation, whichever comes first. (17 U.S.C. §§ 101 and following.)

The Fair Use Rule

Under the "fair use" rule of copyright law, an author may make limited use of another author's work without asking permission. The fair use privilege is perhaps the most significant limitation on a copyright owner's exclusive rights.

Subject to some general limitations, the following types of uses are usually deemed fair uses:

- criticism and comment—for example, quoting or excerpting a work in a review or criticism for purposes of illustration or comment
- news reporting—for example, summarizing an address or article, with brief quotations, in a news report
- research and scholarship—for example, quoting a short passage in a scholarly, scientific, or technical work for illustration or clarification of the author's observations
- nonprofit educational uses—for example, photocopying of limited portions of written works by teachers for classroom use.

In most other situations, copying is not legally a fair use. Without an author's permission, such a use violates the author's copyright.

Violations often occur when the use is motivated primarily by a desire for commercial gain. The fact that a work is published primarily for private commercial gain weighs against a finding of fair use.

What Can Be Copyrighted

Literary works, computer software, musical arrangements, websites, graphic works, audiovisual works, or compilations of these and other works are all covered by copyright. The work must be in some way original. A copyright does not protect works that are merely clerical or factual, such as a blank form or the phone book. The facts or ideas expressed are not themselves protected by copyright—only the way the creator has expressed those facts or ideas. Anyone, for example, is free to write a book about a subject that other books have already covered. But the author of a new book cannot legally copy language from an earlier book.

Notice of Copyright (©)

A copyright notice tells the world that the creator of the work is claiming a copyright. A complete notice consists of the © symbol or the word "copyright" or "copr.," the year of publication, and the name of the copyright owner. Works published before March 1, 1989 must have a copyright notice to maintain the copyright in the work. For works published after that date, a notice is not required. Even if no notice is required, however, putting a copyright notice on your work serves to warn others that your work is protected and will help you enforce your copyright in court if necessary.

Registration of Copyrights

You can register your copyright with the U.S. Copyright Office at the Library of Congress in Washington, DC (www.copyright.gov). To get the full benefits of registration, you must register within three months of the date of publication, or before an infringement has begun. Registration makes it easier to prove and win an infringement action in federal court and recover enough money to make the lawsuit worthwhile. Also, you must register before you can bring a lawsuit for infringement of copyright.

PATENTS

A patent is the legal right, granted by the U.S. Patent and Trademark Office, to exclude others from making, using, or selling an invention for up to 20 years from the date the application for a patent is filed. The certificate that grants the patent and describes the invention is called a patent deed. If someone infringes on your patent by marketing your invention, you may sue in federal court for the economic loss you suffer as a result.

Types of Patents

There are three types of patents:

- **Utility patents** cover inventions that work in a unique manner to produce a "utilitarian result." Most gadgets that perform a function fall under this category. A utility patent lasts for 20 years from the date of filing.
- **Design patents** cover unique, ornamental, or visible shapes or designs of objects. Inventions that are aesthetic rather than functional—such as the ornamental shape of a truck fender—fall into this category. A design patent lasts for 14 years from the date the patent issues.
- **Plant patents** cover new strains of plants. A plant patent lasts for 20 years from the date it is filed.

Patent Requirements

Not everything can be patented. For example, you can't patent an abstract idea, a purely mental process, or a process that can be simply performed using a pencil and paper. Nor can you patent naturally occurring things. To be patentable, an invention must be a process, a machine, a manufacture, a composition, or an improvement on one of these. Each of these categories includes a wide variety of items, from computer software to genetically engineered bacteria.

An invention must satisfy three additional requirements to be patentable:

- **Novelty.** The invention must be a new idea, physically different in at least some small way from what already exists (known in inventors' circles as the "prior art").

- **Nonobviousness.** The invention must be a new or unexpected development, something that, at the time of its invention, would not be obvious to a person skilled in the technology of that particular field.
- **Usefulness.** The invention must have some positive use or, in the case of a design patent, must be ornamental. This requirement precludes, for example, inventions that have only illegal uses or drugs that have only unsafe uses.

How to Get a Patent

To get a patent, you must submit a detailed application to the U.S. Patent and Trademark Office (www.uspto.gov). You must file your application within one year of the first commercialization of your invention or the first publication of the details of your invention. It generally takes 18 months to two years to get a patent. ■

Courts, Lawsuits, and Mediation

Many people consider taking legal action when faced with a seemingly unresolvable dispute. Almost as many are brought into court unwillingly to defend themselves. For most people, the court system is unfamiliar and intimidating. But there may be easier, faster, and cheaper alternatives to lawsuits, like mediation and arbitration. This chapter discusses all of the available options when you have a legal dispute.

TOPICS

> **Alternatives to Court**
> **Appeals**
> **California Court System**
> **Discovery**
> **Federal Court System**
> **Good Samaritans**
> **Jury Duty**
> **Lawsuits Over Contracts**
> **Lawyers' Fees**
> **Personal Injury Lawsuits**
> **Settling a Lawsuit Out of Court**
> **Small Claims Court**
> **Statutes of Limitation**
> **Victims of Crime**

RELATED TOPICS

> **Children**
>> Juvenile Court
> **Traffic and Vehicle Laws**

ADDITIONAL RESOURCES

Mediate, Don't Litigate: Strategies for Successful Mediation, by Peter Lovenheim and Lisa Guerin (Nolo), shows you how to choose a mediator, prepare a case, and conduct yourself during a mediation.

Represent Yourself in Court: How to Prepare & Try a Winning Case, by Paul Bergman and Sara J. Berman-Barrett (Nolo), explains how to conduct a civil trial without an attorney.

Nolo's Deposition Handbook, by Paul Bergman and Albert Moore (Nolo), explains how to conduct a deposition or attend one as a witness.

How to Win Your Personal Injury Claim, by Joseph Matthews (Nolo), takes the reader through the process of negotiating with an insurance company over a personal injury claim.

Everybody's Guide to Small Claims Court in California, by Ralph Warner (Nolo), explains how to evaluate your case, prepare for court, and convince a judge you're right.

Building a Parenting Agreement That Works: How to Put Your Kids First When Your Marriage Doesn't Last, by Mimi Lyster (Nolo), shows separating or divorcing parents how to create win-win custody agreements.

Divorce Without Court: A Guide to Mediation & Collaborative Divorce, by Katherine E. Stoner (Nolo), is a complete guide to divorce mediation and the new collaborative divorce process.

How to Collect When You Win a Lawsuit in California, by Robin Leonard (Nolo), explains 19 ways to collect after you win a lawsuit in California.

Fight Your Ticket & Win in California, by David Brown (Nolo), shows you how to fight all types of California tickets.

Win Your Lawsuit: A Judge's Guide to Representing Yourself in California Superior Court, by Rod Duncan (Nolo), shows you how to file a case for up to $25,000 in superior court under simplified limited jurisdiction rules.

ALTERNATIVES TO COURT

A lawsuit is not usually the best or only way to resolve a dispute. Non-adversarial approaches can provide a fair, mutually agreeable solution without the typical delay, expense, and hostility of a formal court proceeding.

Because of the expense of lawsuits, many companies (banks, for example) now put a standard clause in their contracts requiring dissatisfied customers to submit their disputes to mediation or arbitration. This is normally a decent approach as long as the mediators are truly neutral (not beholden to one side) and fees are low.

Mediation

Mediation is a structured process in which a neutral third party meets with the people having the disagreement to help them find a mutually agreeable solution. The mediator is chosen by the parties unless a contract or court names a particular person to mediate. The goal of mediation is to allow the disputing parties to reach their own agreement; the mediator has no authority to impose a solution on anyone. Although it's common to think of mediation as consisting of little more than a process by which contending parties meet with a wise friend who will help them arrive at compromise, in fact it's a structured process in which a trained mediator uses a number of proven approaches to guide the parties to a resolution. Although lawyers can participate in mediation, many parties elect to represent themselves, because the process is informal and easy to understand. The fact that no judge or arbitrator can impose an unacceptable solution on the parties helps reduce tension and contributes to an atmosphere of cooperation and trust. Mediation works in all kinds of legal cases, including family law. In fact, in custody disputes, parents are required by the court to mediate the dispute before submitting it to a judge.

To select a mediator, call your local neighborhood mediation or conciliation service. (Many cities and counties offer free or low-cost mediation services.) If yours is a specialized dispute involving, for example, a divorce, business termination, or employment dispute, consider cooperating with your opponent to hire a private mediator. Ask people in the particular field for a recommendation, or look under "Alternative Dispute Resolution" in the Yellow Pages or on the Internet (www.mediate.com is a website that offers mediator referrals).

Arbitration

Arbitration is a more formal proceeding in which the disputing parties agree to submit their problem to a third person (or sometimes a panel of three or more people) and be bound by the decision of the arbitrator(s). The arbitrators are neutral outsiders chosen by the parties to make a decision resolving their dispute. In arbitration, both sides can give evidence and have witnesses testify, and both sides can have a lawyer if they wish. Often, parties to a contract agree in advance to submit any dispute arising under the contract to arbitration. Usually these contract provisions are honored, unless the contract is heavily slanted in one party's favor, as might be the case where a large corporation unfairly buries an arbitration clause in the fine print of consumer contracts. When arbitration is used, it is often possible to agree in advance to limit the arbitrator's decision-making power (for example, "high-low" arbitration sets a minimum and maximum dollar amount that arbitrators can award). Arbitration decisions are almost always final and nonappealable.

You can find an arbitrator and rules for arbitration through the American Arbitration Association (AAA), a nonprofit organization. The AAA can give you the names of arbitrators in your area. You should expect to pay from $750 to $2,000 to arbitrate a relatively simple dispute, depending in part on how much money is at issue. Arbitrating more complicated disputes over significant amounts of money will be more expensive.

APPEALS

An appeal is a rehearing of a court case that has already been decided. When you appeal a case, you are asking a higher court to change the decision of the trial court (the original court that decided your dispute). Appeals are not like trials, in which witnesses can be heard and evidence about the facts in dispute is presented (except small claims court appeals where, in some states, including California, the entire case is reheard). The only role of the appeals court is to decide whether the trial court made an error in interpreting the law. It accepts the factual findings of the trial court (for example, the disputed work was not done according to specifications or the light was green when the plaintiff entered the intersection).

> ### Important Terms
>
> **Appellant.** The person who brings the appeal, who may have been either the plaintiff or the defendant in the original case.
> **Respondent.** The person opposing the appeal.

CALIFORNIA COURT SYSTEM

California state courts are organized in a three-tier system. At the lowest level are the trial courts, which are the first courts to hear disputes for the first time. On the second level are the appellate courts, which decide appeals from the trial courts. And on the highest level is the California Supreme Court, which rules on appeals only in certain, select cases.

Trial Courts

There are two principal types of trial courts in California:

- **Small claims court.** Handles disputes where the amount at stake is $7,500 or less.
- **Superior court.** California's primary trial court. Handles disputes involving more than $7,500, as well as criminal, family (divorce, adoption, and guardianship), and probate cases. Fortunately, simplified procedures are available in limited jurisdiction court for monetary disputes involving $25,000 or less. These procedures, which are far less complicated than those used for larger disputes, allow lawsuits to be prepared and brought to trial in a relatively streamlined and easy-to-understand fashion. For more information, contact your county's superior court. You can locate your local superior court in the government section of the telephone book or by checking the list at www.courtinfo.ca.gov/courts/trial/courtlist.htm.

Appellate Courts

- **Superior court, appellate section.** Hears appeals from small claims court and from the limited jurisdiction superior court (involving claims of $25,000 or less).

- **California Courts of Appeal.** Hear appeals from the superior court, except cases involving $25,000 or less filed in the limited jurisdiction superior court or cases involving the death penalty.

Supreme Court

The California Supreme Court hears death penalty appeals from the superior court and hears appeals in cases of its choosing from the courts of appeal. The supreme court is free to decide what appeals to hear. The court is more likely to hear an appeal if any of the following is true:

- Different courts of appeal are in disagreement over an issue presented in the case, and a Supreme Court decision could provide uniformity in the law.
- The case presents important legal questions that the Supreme Court wants to address.
- The court of appeal didn't have the authority to decide the case.

Where to Bring Your Case

You must bring a case not only in the proper court, but also in the proper location. The rules of "jurisdiction" and "venue" determine the proper location for a particular lawsuit.

Each county in California has a superior court with one or more branches depending on the size of the county. In any dispute, suit can be filed in one of the following counties:

- where the defendant lives
- where the defendant does business, if the defendant is a corporation
- where the damage to property or personal injury occurred, or
- where the real estate that is the subject of the suit is located.
    In certain cases additional counties are also options.

Contract cases (other than an auto sale or a retail installment contract) can also be brought in the county:

- where the contract was entered into or signed
- where the contract was to be performed, or
- where the defendant lived at the start of the action.

Automobile sale or retail installment contracts can also be brought in the county:

- where the buyer signed the contract
- where the buyer lived when the contract was signed

- where the buyer lives when suit is brought, or
- where the car is permanently garaged or the goods are attached to real estate (for example, a heating unit or portable storage shed).

DISCOVERY

After a case is filed, a number of things must happen before trial. One of the most important is called "discovery" or case investigation. In all courts except small claims, this investigation has both informal and formal aspects (small claims court allows informal investigation only). Informal investigation includes all information-gathering that you can do on your own, working with cooperative people or organizations both before and after a lawsuit is filed. Informal discovery encompasses such activities as:

- conducting interviews
- collecting documents
- taking photographs (of damaged property, accident sites, or other relevant objects or locations), and
- finding out about an adversary's insurance coverage.

By contrast, "formal discovery" is a legal process that begins after a case has been filed. Formal discovery involves a number of investigatory tools, including:

- **Interrogatories.** These are written questions directed to the adversary that the adversary must answer in writing and under oath.
- **Depositions.** These are oral in-person questions that the adversary or another person, such as an eyewitness or expert witness, must answer under oath. Depositions, which are recorded by a stenographer and can be videotaped, are often held at an attorney's office.
- **Requests for production of documents.** These are requests for a particular document or class of documents likely to be relevant to your case.
- **Requests for admissions.** These are written statements you serve on an opponent in an effort to get the person to agree that certain facts are true or specific documents are genuine.

If You Are Deposed

In a deposition, a lawyer (or occasionally a self-represented litigant) asks oral questions of the opposing party in the lawsuit or of a potential witness—for example, a pedestrian who saw an auto accident or an expert witness who will testify that a physician or hospital acted negligently.

Although depositions usually take place in an office or conference room with no judge present, they have many of the characteristics of a court trial. For example, the person whose deposition is taken (called the deponent) testifies under oath, and the testimony is recorded by a court reporter and, occasionally, on videotape.

Depositions are a crucial part of the litigation process for several reasons. First, they allow adversaries to learn the facts of the other side's case and, therefore, better prepare for trial. Second, if a witness dies, is unavailable for trial, or changes her story, the deposition answers can be read to the judge or jury. Third and perhaps most important, deposition testimony helps the lawyers and parties assess the dollar value of the case when attempting to work out a pretrial settlement—and because most cases settle, this is important information to have.

If you are subpoenaed to testify at a deposition, you must cooperate or risk being held in contempt of court. However, you can ask to be deposed at a convenient time and place, and you generally cannot be required to travel more than 100 miles from your home or office to be deposed. Unless you are an expert witness, you need only testify to what you directly witnessed and what you directly know. You can refuse to answer certain types of questions, if your answer might implicate you in criminal activity or reveal privileged (confidential) communications between you and your spouse, domestic partner, attorney, physician, or spiritual adviser.

Asking and answering deposition questions is a highly developed legal art form. To learn the basics, take a look at *Nolo's Deposition Handbook,* by Paul Bergman and Albert Moore.

FEDERAL COURT SYSTEM

The federal court system has three tiers, like the California state court system. Federal district courts, the trial courts of the federal system, hear cases for the first time. On the second level are the federal courts of appeals, which hear appeals from the district courts. And on the top level is the United States Supreme Court, which hears appeals in a few select cases of its choosing.

In addition, certain cases are heard in specialized federal courts, such as bankruptcy court or tax court.

Which Cases Can Be Heard in Federal Court

Only certain cases can be brought in a federal court. They are:

- **Cases involving a question of federal law.** Cases that arise under the U.S. Constitution, U.S. statutes, or treaties can be brought in federal court. Examples include free speech and civil rights cases that claim a violation of federal (rather than state) rights.
- **Cases where jurisdiction is granted by statute.** Certain types of cases can be brought in federal court because a statute specifically allows it. Examples include bankruptcy, patent, copyright, and federal antitrust lawsuits.
- **Cases where there is "diversity of parties."** Cases where there is more than $75,000 at stake can be heard in federal court if the opposing parties are from different states, citizens from one state are suing citizens of a foreign country, or a foreign country is suing citizens of a state.

Which Federal Court Is Appropriate

The country is divided up into a number of federal judicial districts. The district in which suit should be brought depends on what kind of suit it is.

- **Federal question.** A suit based on a federal question can be brought in the district where all the defendants live or do business, or in the district where the claim arose.
- **Bankruptcy.** A bankruptcy case must be filed in the judicial district where the person declaring bankruptcy has lived for the six months before filing.
- **Diversity.** A suit based on the diversity of the parties can be brought in the district where all the plaintiffs live, where all the defendants live, or where the claim arose.

GOOD SAMARITANS

The law wants to encourage people to give whatever assistance they can in emergencies. To that end, California law protects people from lawsuits over injuries they inadvertently cause while trying to help someone in an emergency. The law provides that anyone who gives emergency care in good faith and not for compensation is not liable for any losses that result from an act or omission. (H & S Code § 1799.102.)

Anyone who is injured while trying to prevent a crime, catch a criminal, or rescue a person in immediate danger of injury or death may make a claim to the state for his or her losses. If such a Good Samaritan is killed, his or her surviving spouse or dependents may make a claim. (Gov't. Code § 13970.)

JURY DUTY

Jury service is an obligation of most citizens 18 or older, and although it is an important part of the legal system, it can be an onerous duty. Potential jurors spend most of their time waiting to be questioned, and most never get called to sit on a jury. There are only a few narrow exceptions from the duty to serve: You may be disqualified if you have been convicted of a felony, you have little knowledge of English, or you are the subject of a conservatorship.

Potential jurors are randomly selected from lists of names provided by voter registration rolls and the Department of Motor Vehicles' list of licensed drivers. In many California counties, once someone is summoned to appear as a juror, that person is "on duty" for ten weekdays—although the specifics of service vary considerably from courtroom to courtroom. Some counties have adopted a "one day, one jury" system so that jurors are only on call for one day.

Being Excused From Serving

If you are summoned for jury duty, you must attend as directed or respond promptly to court officials and explain why you cannot attend. If you repeatedly fail to cooperate, you may be held in contempt of court and fined (in theory you can also be jailed, but this almost never happens). (Code of Civ. Proc. § 209.)

A judge may excuse a potential juror for health reasons or for extreme hardship, such as being without income during an extended trial as a result of being unable to work. (Code of Civ. Proc. § 204.) California National Guard members on active duty are excused from jury duty. (Mil. & Vet. Code §§ 391, 560.)

When you receive your jury notice, you can contact the court to have jury service postponed for vacations, illnesses, and other valid reasons. And when you appear for jury service, you will have the opportunity to explain why you should be excused—for example, because you will be unable to support yourself or your family if you are required to participate in an extended trial. But once you are seated as a juror in a trial, you must serve until the trial is over—no matter how long it lasts.

Employers' Responsibilities

Employees may not be demoted, fired, or otherwise punished for serving on a jury, but they must give the employer reasonable notice that they will need time off work for jury duty, unless advance notice is not feasible. (Lab. Code § 230(a).) Employers are not required to pay employees for time away from work for jury service, although many do so voluntarily. The court pays most jurors a small sum for each day they serve and reimburses them for some expenses incurred in getting to the courtroom (but not for the trip back home). (Code of Civ. Proc. § 215.)

LAWSUITS OVER CONTRACTS

A contract is an agreement between two people in which each promises to do something for the other. The key to a contract is that each side must promise or do something of value (called "consideration" for the contract). A promise to make a gift does not form a contract, because the person to whom the gift is promised has not done or promised anything in return.

Many everyday transactions are contracts, such as opening a checking account, purchasing goods or services, arranging for utility services, or buying an insurance policy. Common types of contracts include:

- **Promissory notes.** Agreements to lend money to be paid back later.
- **Sales documents.** Agreements to purchase goods or services, and documents recording the terms of a sale.
- **Warranties.** Guarantees about the quality and performance of a product or service.

- **Service contracts.** Arrangements for everything from fixing your TV to remodeling your kitchen.
- **Leases and rental agreements.** Contracts to rent property.

Contracts That Must Be in Writing

In most situations, an oral contract is legally valid and binding (although if one party wants to sue over the contract, it can be very difficult to prove that the contract was ever made or what its terms were).

Certain contracts, however, must be in writing before a court will enforce them. (Civ. Code § 1624.) The goal is to protect both sides from fraud and failing memories. These contracts include:

- Contracts with terms that cannot be completed within one year of the day the agreement was made. If there is any possible way a contract could be completed within a year, even if it's highly unlikely or actually takes longer than one year to perform, it does not have to be in writing. Exceptions exist for certain "qualified financial contracts" between businesses.
- Contracts that by their terms are not to be performed during the lifetime of the person making the promise.
- Contracts for the sale of more than $500 worth of goods. (Unif. Comm. Code § 2201.)
- Contracts for the sale of real estate.
- Contracts of employment with real estate agents.
- Contracts to lend money exceeding $100,000.
- Contracts with lawyers for a contingency fee, or where it is reasonably foreseeable that fees charged a noncorporate client will exceed $1,000. (Bus. & Prof. Code §§ 6147(a), 6148(a).)

When a Contract Is Broken

If one person doesn't keep his or her promise, the contract has been broken ("breached"). The other person can try to negotiate, seek mediation or arbitration to settle the dispute, or take the breaching party to court. The usual legal remedy for a broken contract is for the person who broke the contract to pay an amount equal to what the other person expected to get from the contract. However, the person who is suing must also show that he or she took steps to mitigate (minimize) his losses. For example, a landlord whose tenant breaks a lease cannot simply sue for all the rent owed under the contract; the landlord must try to find a new tenant as soon as possible and will be able to collect only the money actually lost while the place was not rented.

In some situations, such as when the contract involves the sale of a unique item (usually real estate), a court may order both sides to actually go through with the deal.

What Contracts Are Not Enforceable

Courts won't enforce some contracts because they violate public policy or because enforcement is impossible. These contracts include:

- an agreement to do something illegal
- an agreement that is unconscionable—very unfair to one person because of the other person's superior bargaining power (for example, a prenuptial agreement made between an experienced older businessperson and a naive young immigrant), or
- a contract that is so vague that the court cannot determine what the actual agreement was.

LAWYERS' FEES

Many disagreements between lawyers and clients involve fees.

Hourly Fees

Many lawyers do not charge for an initial half-hour or hour consultation. But they do charge for additional hours (or time)—usually between $150 and $350 an hour.

If it is reasonably foreseeable that a client will end up paying more than $1,000 for legal fees and costs, the agreement between lawyer and client must be in writing. (This law doesn't apply if the client is a corporation or has hired the lawyer for similar services before.) The contract must state the hourly rate and other standard fees or costs that may apply, the general nature of the services to be provided, and the responsibilities of both attorney and client (for example, the client may be responsible for paying out-of-pocket court costs as the case progresses). (Bus. & Prof. Code § 6148(a).)

Bills sent by the attorney can't contain just a bare amount due; they must state the rate or other method of arriving at the total. If the client is billed for costs and expenses, the bill must clearly identify them. A client who hasn't gotten a bill in a month may ask for one, and the lawyer must provide it within ten days. (Bus. & Prof. Code § 6148(b).)

Contingency Fees

Under a contingency fee arrangement, a lawyer agrees to handle a case for a fixed percentage of the amount finally recovered in a lawsuit. If the client wins or settles the case, the lawyer's fee comes out of the money awarded or agreed to. If the client loses, neither the client nor the lawyer gets any money. Although there is no set percentage for contingency fees in most types of cases, many lawyers request an amount between 25%-33% if the case settles before trial, 30-40% if the lawyer must try the case, and often more if the case is won only after an appeal. Contingency fees are negotiable, and it definitely pays to shop around.

Contingency fee agreements must be in writing (unless the client is seeking workers' compensation benefits), and the client must receive a signed copy of the contract. The contract must include the contingency fee rate; explain how incidental costs will be paid; and state to what extent, if any, the client might have to pay the lawyer for related matters that aren't covered by the contingency fee contract. The contract must state that the fee is not set by law, but is negotiable. If the lawyer doesn't comply with these requirements, the client can declare the agreement void at any time. In that case, the lawyer is entitled to collect a "reasonable" fee. (Bus. & Prof. Code § 6147.)

In medical malpractice suits, state law limits the amount of contingency fees to 40% of the first $50,000 recovered; $33^1/_3$% of the next $50,000; 25% of the next $500,000; and 15% of any amount over $600,000. (Bus. & Prof. Code § 6146.)

Clients are always free to change lawyers if the relationship between lawyer and client turns sour.

How to File a Complaint About a Lawyer

To complain about any behavior by a lawyer that appears to be deceptive, unethical, or otherwise illegal, call the State Bar of California's toll-free number, 800-843-9053. Or, contact the Bar at 180 Howard Street, San Francisco, CA 94105-1639, 415-538-2000, or at 1149 S. Hill Street, Los Angeles, CA 90015-2299, 213-765-1000. Online, you can visit the Bar at www.calbar. org. If you believe you have been overcharged and your lawyer will not voluntarily lower your bill, contact your county bar association and ask for materials explaining your rights to contest the amount of the fee in an arbitration procedure.

PERSONAL INJURY LAWSUITS

There are as many different kinds of personal injury lawsuits as there are accidents: Car crashes, injuries caused by a dangerous or defective product, dog bites, or a fall on someone else's property are all potential grounds for a lawsuit. However, not all people who suffer an accident and are injured can recover in court. In order to recover money damages, you must show: that you or your property was harmed; that the harm was caused by the actions (or inaction) of the person you're suing (liability; see below); that the person's actions (or inaction) were unreasonably careless (see below); and the amount of your damages.

Liability

Legal responsibility (liability) for an accident is based on a few commonsense rules. Most accidents happen because someone was unreasonably careless (negligent). In most cases, the law requires the person who was negligent to compensate the injured person.

When both (or all) of the people involved in an accident were negligent, a legal rule called "comparative negligence" allows the judge or jury to decide how much of the fault was attributable to each person involved, and award damages accordingly. For example, driver A, who rolled through a stop sign, might be 30% at fault for an intersection collision, whereas driver B, who was speeding, is 70% at fault. Driver A would be entitled to collect 70% of his damages (which typically includes the dollar value of property damage, personal injuries, loss of income, and pain and suffering) from driver B.

Depending on the circumstances, there may be additional legal twists on the rules of liability:

- If the injured person was someplace he or she was not supposed to be (for example, breaking into someone's home), or should have expected the kind of activity that caused the accident (for example, getting hit by a ball at a baseball game), the person who caused the accident may not be liable.
- If an employee causes an accident while working, the employer may also be legally responsible for the accident.
- If an accident or injury happens because property is poorly built or maintained (for example, an inadequately lit parking lot or a broken elevator), the owner of the property may be liable for the injuries caused, even if the owner did not create the dangerous condition.
- If an accident is caused by a defective product, the manufacturer and the seller of the product are liable even if the injured person cannot show how the defect happened or which one was careless. The law presumes liability in these cases. This is referred to as "strict liability."

Joint Liability

Many accidents involve the carelessness of more than one person. For example, an automobile accident may involve several careless drivers. In these cases, all of those who were negligent are responsible for compensating the injured person. If the injured person sues only one person, that person must pay the full amount. The person who was sued can sue the other negligent people and make them pay their shares. However, the law does not allow the injured person to collect the full amount from more than one person.

When to Consult a Lawyer

In many cases, an injured person does not have to sue to be compensated for his or her injuries. If the person who caused the accident has insurance, the injured person can usually make a claim against that policy. Although this is taxing at times, it can often be done without the assistance of a lawyer. Because lawyers typically take a large percentage of any settlement they negotiate or court judgment they win, it is often cheaper to represent yourself.

In certain cases, however, an injured person will need the help of an attorney. These cases include:

- accidents that cause long-term, severe, or disabling injuries
- medical malpractice cases
- cases involving toxic exposure, and
- cases in which the other side contests liability for the accident.

SETTLING A LAWSUIT OUT OF COURT

A settlement is an agreement between two people to end a dispute. Typically, one person agrees to pay money or provide services in exchange for the other person's promise to drop (or not bring) a lawsuit. In some situations where both sides feel wronged, they may mutually agree to drop any claims they may have against each other. A settlement can be entered into at any time, even in the midst of a lawsuit. In fact, most lawsuits are settled without going to trial.

If two people settle after a lawsuit has begun, the one who initially brought the lawsuit has two options: Ask the court to enter a judgment based on the settlement, or ask the court to dismiss the case. If it's possible that one side may not abide by the settlement, it's best to agree (stipulate) to a judgment. Then, if one person doesn't fulfill the agreement, the other person can use collection methods that otherwise would require going to court and winning a lawsuit.

The plaintiff—the person who originally filed a case—can also dismiss the case. This is done by filing a form called a Request for Dismissal. If the dispute has been completely resolved and the settlement agreement fulfilled (all money paid, for example), the plaintiff should indicate on the form that the suit is being dismissed "with prejudice"—meaning that it can't be filed again. But if the defendant hasn't yet fulfilled his promises, it's usually best to keep the lawsuit on file until he does—or insist that the court enter a judgment.

If you are represented by a lawyer, your attorney may recommend that you agree to a settlement offer she has negotiated. Fine, if you agree that it's fair. But if for any reason you don't, it often makes sense to get an informed second opinion by paying a modest fee to another lawyer to review the proposed settlement.

Settlement Tips

Remember that a settlement is a compromise; you should be willing to accept less than what you might have been able to win in court to avoid the delay, uncertainty, and expense of trial.

To negotiate a settlement, first determine how much it would cost to reimburse you for the damage done by the other person. Consider medical bills, property damage, time taken off work, your own genuine pain and suffering, lost business, money you spent to repair poor work or materials, and so on. Then scale this figure back to reflect the possibility that you might lose the lawsuit or be found partially at fault; the likelihood that the other person will be difficult to collect a judgment from, even if you win; and the time and money you will save by avoiding a lawsuit. Yes, this can be a daunting task, but it will be made much easier if you read *How to Win Your Personal Injury Claim,* by Joseph Matthews (Nolo). Once you figure out how much you're willing to settle for, ask for a bit more to give yourself room to maneuver, and begin to negotiate.

If face-to-face, phone, or other negotiations break down, consider mediation. Often the mediation process helps disputants acknowledge and deal with issues that otherwise may prevent settlement.

Be sure that you get all settlement agreements in writing, signed by everyone involved. This will protect you in case you and your opponent later disagree on what was decided, or your opponent suddenly tries to back out of the bargain.

If you have suffered physical injuries, do not settle until you know the full extent of your problem. Often injuries are more serious than they first appear to be, and you should not accept a settlement that does not compensate you adequately.

If your dispute involves substantial personal injury or property damage, you may want to have a lawyer look over your settlement agreement.

SMALL CLAIMS COURT

Small claims court is designed to resolve relatively minor disputes quickly, without lawyers or legal formalities. In addition to the material contained below, you'll find useful information in these three places:

- **California small claims laws.** These are set out in fairly readable fashion in §§ 116.110–116.950 of the California Code of Civil Procedure. This is available online at www.nolo.com/statute/state. cfm (click on "California").
- **State of California small claims information.** Helpful information and answers to common questions about small claims cases are available at www.courtinfo.ca.gov/selfhelp/smallclaims/.
- *Everybody's Guide to Small Claims Court in California,* by Ralph Warner (Nolo). Provides an invaluable guide to winning small claims.

Monetary Limits

In small claims court, you can sue for an amount up to $7,500 for the first two lawsuits you file within a calendar year (except lawsuits filed by businesses, governmental entities, or against guarantors; see below). All additional lawsuits in that calendar year have a $2,500 limit.

Businesses—including corporations, partnerships, and unincorporated associations—may sue for up to $5,000 for the first two lawsuits filed within a calendar year. Additional lawsuits have a $2,500 limit.

Small claims suits against guarantors (for example, companies that write insurance bonds) have a $4,000 limit based on the actions, omissions, or failure to pay of the person taking out the bond. The business is often a contractor or someone else who must be bonded under state law.

Governmental entities such as cities, counties, or school districts may sue for up to $5,000 in small claims court, but they may file as many small claims cases within that limit as they wish.

Who Can Sue?

With a few exceptions, any mentally competent person at least 18 years of age and any business can sue or be sued in small claims court. There are, however, some exceptions and special rules:

- Although attorneys can sue or be sued on their own behalf, no one may be represented by an attorney in small claims court.

- Collection agencies and other assignees (persons who are not the original creditor) cannot sue in small claims court.
- An owner of an unincorporated business must normally file suit and appear in court. However, when the only issue is failure to pay a bill for goods or services provided by the business, a qualified employee with the proper records may substitute. (Code of Civ. Proc. § 116.540(d).) And a corporation, limited liability company, or partnership may be represented either by an officer (president, vice president, secretary, or treasurer) or by a regular employee authorized in writing to act as representative. (Code of Civ. Proc. § 116.540(b).)
- Minors (children under 18) must have a parent or guardian sue for them.
- Contractors must be licensed, and car and TV repair dealers and pest control operators registered, with the appropriate state agency.
- Prisoners, out-of-state landlords, and active duty military personnel transferred out of state after a claim arose (and whose assignment will last at least six months) can submit testimony in writing or authorize someone to appear on their behalf. But prisoners must first take advantage of all procedures within the prison system designed to resolve their grievances and claims. (Code of Civ. Proc. § 116.540.)
- Owners of rental real estate may send a manager who has a contract to manage that property to court on their behalf. (Code of Civ. Proc. § 116.540(h).)
- An out-of-state owner of real property may defend a claim relating to that property without personally appearing in court, either by submitting a written declaration (statement under penalty of perjury), or authorizing another person to appear in court on his behalf, or by both. (Code of Civ. Proc. § 116.540(g).)
- A husband or wife may appear in court on behalf of the other spouse for a joint claim where the absent spouse has given consent and the court agrees. (Code of Civ. Proc. § 116.540(k).)
- A homeowners' or condominium association may be represented by an agent, management company representative, or bookkeeper. (Code of Civ. Proc. § 116.540(i).)

Where Suits Can Be Filed (Jurisdiction and Venue)

Small claims suits can be filed in the local small claims court in the county where the defendant lives or, if a business is being sued, where the business is located. In addition, you can sue:

- where an injury to persons or property occurred
- where a contract was signed or, for nonconsumer (business-to-business) transactions, where the parties agreed in writing it was to be performed
- for consumer transactions, where the buyer lived at the time the contract was signed or where the goods or vehicle in question is permanently installed or kept.

A defendant who has been sued in the wrong place can write to the court, explain the situation, and ask for a change to the correct court. (Code of Civ. Proc. § 116.370.)

Small Claims Court Procedures

Someone who wants to bring a suit in small claims court must first contact the other party and request payment. This demand should be in writing.

When you are ready to sue, the small claims clerk will help you complete a form called Plaintiff's Claim and Order to Defendant. Businesses using a fictitious name must state that they have properly registered their name. The filing fees are as follows:

•$30 for a claim of $1,500 or less if you have not filed more than 12 small claims cases in the previous 12 months

•$50 for a claim of $1,501-$5,000 if you have not filed more than 12 small claims cases in the previous 12 months

•$75 for a claim of $5,001-$7,500 if you have not filed more than 12 small claims cases in the previous 12 months, or

•$100 for a claim of any amount if you have filed more than 12 small claims cases in the previous 12 months.

Plaintiffs who win can recover these fees from the defendant. In some counties, you can file all your paperwork online.

Every person or business sued must receive a copy of the plaintiff's court papers. Usually this must be accomplished at least 15 days before the court hearing (20 days if the hearing is in a county other than where the defendant lives or does business). There are several ways to serve court papers:

- **Certified mail.** The court clerk does the mailing and the party pays a $10 fee. Service is complete if the defendant signs for the mail.
- **Personal service.** Any person age 18 or older, except the person bringing suit, may hand the papers to the defendant. The plaintiff may hire a sheriff, marshal, constable, or private process server to serve the papers.
- **Substituted service.** Where service is difficult, the plaintiff may leave a copy of the papers with a competent member of the defendant's household who is 18 or older (or in the case of a business, with someone apparently in charge) and then mail another copy to the defendant.

The cost of serving papers is recoverable if the plaintiff wins. Some counties require the plaintiff to try the least costly method first in order to collect.

Defending a Small Claims Lawsuit

Defendants need only show up on the appointed day ready to present their side of the story. There are no forms to file or fees to pay unless they want to counter-sue the plaintiff, in which case they must promptly file a Defendant's Claim with the small claims court clerk and pay a filing fee according to the rules above. If the defendant's claim is for more than $7,500, the entire lawsuit may be transferred to superior court.

If a defendant is unable to appear on the appointed day, she should file a written request to postpone the hearing at least ten days before the hearing date, stating the reasons she cannot appear. Use Form SC-110, available from the court clerk or online at www.courtinfo.ca.gov (click on "Forms"). Normally this will result in the case being rescheduled. However, if no written request to postpone is filed and the defendant fails to show up, the small claims court will most likely enter a default judgment in favor of the plaintiff, assuming the plaintiff proves the basics of her case. The case is now over unless the defendant promptly takes steps to set aside the default. The defendant has 30 days in which to file such a request. The judgment will be vacated if the judge finds the defendant had good cause to miss the first hearing. If the default judgment is set aside, the court will either ask for a presentation of the case itself at that time or schedule it for a future date. (Code of Civ. Proc. § 116.730.)

Presenting Your Case in Court

Be prepared to stand and politely tell the judge what happened, when, and where. Start with the facts. ("Your honor, the defendant's car ran a red light and hit my right front fender, causing $2,000 worth of damage.") Once this is done, supply needed background information.

Bring witnesses and evidence (pictures, receipts, letters, and so on) to court to back up your story and the amount of your loss. Don't argue with the other party, but be prepared to refute all likely claims.

Because much depends on your ability to tell your story convincingly, it pays to practice.

Appeal Rights

A plaintiff who loses in small claims court has no right to appeal the judge's decision, except within 30 days to correct a judgment entered as a clear result of a clerical error or legal mistake. However, the party defending a claim (this could be the plaintiff, if a Defendant's Claim is filed) can appeal within 30 days after the mailing or delivery of the Notice of Entry of the Small Claims Judgment. The appeal results in a completely new trial in superior court. This means all claims of all parties who show up at the appeal will be considered from scratch, as though the small claims trial had never occurred. Both sides may have a lawyer on appeal, but this is often considered unnecessary, because rules are still informal. A judge can award up to $150 for attorney fees, as well as up to $150 for actual loss of earnings and transportation and lodging costs for the appeal. If the judge finds that an appeal was not in good faith, but was intended to delay or harass the plaintiff, the court may penalize the defendant up to $1,000 for attorneys' fees actually and reasonably incurred, and up to $1,000 for lodging expenses, transportation expenses, and loss of wages. (Code of Civ. Proc. §§ 116.710-116.795.)

STATUTES OF LIMITATION

A statute of limitation is the deadline for filing a lawsuit. Here are the time limits for some common kinds of disputes:

- **Personal injury.** Two years from the injury, or two years from the date the injury is discovered (if it wasn't immediately discovered).
- **Breach of a written contract.** Four years from the day the contract is broken.
- **Breach of an oral contract.** Two years from the date the contract is broken.
- **Damage to real or personal property.** Three years from the date the damage occurs.
- **Claims against government agencies (like cities or counties).** You must file a claim with the agency within six months of the incident. If this claim is denied, you are then free to bring a lawsuit.
- **Collecting a debt with a court judgment.** Ten years from the date of the judgment.

Other statutes of limitations can be found in Code of Civ. Proc. §§ 312-363.

"Tolling" the Statute

In certain situations, the statute of limitations is suspended (tolled) for a period of time, then begins to run again. If the defendant is out of the state, in prison, insane, or a minor, the statutory "clock" does not run as long as this condition continues. When the condition ends, the clock starts running again.

Death of a Party to the Lawsuit

Some legal claims survive even the death of the person with the right to sue, or the person who can be sued. In these cases, the statute of limitations is extended. If the person who has the right to sue dies before the statute of limitations has run, that person's representatives can sue after the deadline has passed, as long as they bring suit within six months of death or within the limitations period that would have applied if the person had not died, whichever date comes later. (Code of Civ. Proc. § 366.1.) Similarly, if the person who is going to be sued dies before the statute of limitations has run, the person with the right to sue can bring suit after the deadline has passed, as long as suit is brought within one year of death—regardless of the statute of limitations. (Code of Civ. Proc. § 366.2.)

When the Time Limit Runs Out

Once the deadline passes (or the "statute runs," in legal parlance), a legal claim is no longer valid. However, judges don't always notice when a time limit has expired—if you are sued on an old claim, you should point out that the deadline has passed. In rare situations, an old legal claim will give rise to a new legal claim that starts a new statute of limitations. For example, if one person owes a debt to another, and the creditor doesn't bring suit within the deadline, the creditor loses the right to sue. But if the debtor promises again to pay the debt and begins payments after the original deadline passes, these actions create a new legal claim for the debt, with a new statute of limitations.

VICTIMS OF CRIME

Crime victims have certain rights to be notified of important events and to make statements to the judge or parole board. In addition, they may be eligible for compensation for their injuries.

Notice and statements. As a crime victim, you have a right to be notified of the time, date, and place of all felony sentencing proceedings. In addition, you will be notified of the following events, if you request such notice in writing beforehand from the California Department of Corrections and Rehabilitation, Office of Victim and Survivor Services, 1515 S Street, Suite 502, Sacramento, CA 95814 (call 916-323-6001 or visit www.bpt. ca.gov for more information):

- escape of the inmate
- death of the inmate
- placement of the inmate in a re-entry facility, and
- release of the inmate on parole.

You can also be notified of parole suitability hearings for life term inmates, if you request such notice in writing or by phone from the Office of Victim and Survivor Services.

You have the right to make certain statements, including:

- a victim impact statement to the parole board, indicating the effect the crime has had on your life
- a statement before sentencing, indicating any factors the court should consider in deciding what sentence to impose

- an oral statement at the sentencing hearing, and
- a statement before the parole board when it considers parole for a life term inmate.

Before the Trial

Before the trial, you should tell the prosecutor any special concerns you have about the proceedings, including the amount of bail, the possibility of plea bargaining, or the defendant's eligibility for a diversion program. The prosecutor isn't required to follow your recommendations, but may try to do so.

Compensation. You may be able to recover financial losses you suffered as a result of the crime, using one of the following methods:

- **California Victims of Crime Program can provide up to $70,000 in compensation for monetary losses, including medical bills, lost wages, funeral expenses, and mental health counseling**. There are certain eligibility requirements, and you must have filed a criminal complaint. Family members and dependents of crime victims can also seek compensation. For more information, contact the Victim Compensation and Government Claims Board, P.O. Box 3036, Sacramento, CA 95812-3036, 800-777-9229, www.boc.cahwnet.gov.
- **Restitution ordered by the court as part of a sentence, parole requirement, or plea bargain**. If restitution is ordered, be sure to get a certified copy of the criminal minute order or sentencing order from the court clerk. You will need this order to collect your restitution award, which you can do using standard collection techniques such as garnishing the wages or bank account of the defendant. If you would like the court to order restitution, talk to the prosecutor.
- **Civil lawsuits.** Some victims sue their assailants in civil court to recover for property damage or personal injury, but it's usually not worth the effort.

Further information. Contact your local victim assistance center, or call the Office of Victims and Survivor Services at 877-256-OVSS, for more information on your legal rights. ■

Debts, Loans, and Credit

It's not a crime to fail to pay debts—there is no longer any such thing as debtor's prison. However, creditors can use a number of legal tools to find debtors and make them pay what they owe. This section discusses these debt collection methods, as well as legal options for debtors.

Consumer laws regarding credit and other forms of payment are also covered in this section.

TOPICS

Automated Teller Machine (ATM) and Debit Cards
Bankruptcy
Checks
Cosigners' Rights
Credit and Charge Cards
Credit Bureaus
Credit Discrimination
Debt Collection
Liens
Loans
Repossessing Property
Student Loans

RELATED TOPICS

Consumers' Rights
Courts and Lawsuits
   Federal Court System
Landlords and Tenants
   Cosigning Leases and Rental Agreements
Real Estate
   Homesteads
Relationships
   Marital Debts
Small Businesses

ADDITIONAL RESOURCES

Solve Your Money Troubles: Get Debt Collectors Off Your Back & Regain Financial Freedom, by Robin Leonard (Nolo), explains your legal rights and offers practical strategies for dealing with debts.

Credit Repair, by Robin Leonard (Nolo), provides over a dozen strategies for cleaning up your credit file.

How to File for Chapter 7 Bankruptcy, by Stephen Elias, Albin Renauer, and Robin Leonard (Nolo), is a complete guide to choosing and filing for Chapter 7 bankruptcy, including all the forms you need.

Chapter 13 Bankruptcy: Repay Your Debts, by Robin Leonard (Nolo), contains the forms and instructions necessary to file your own Chapter 13 bankruptcy.

The New Bankruptcy: Will It Work for You? By Stephen Elias & Robin Leonard (Nolo) explains the revised bankruptcy laws and contains worksheets to help you figure out if you qualify for bankruptcy under the new laws.

Take Control of Your Student Loan Debt, by Robin Leonard (Nolo), gives you strategies for dealing with loans you took out to get through school.

Stand Up to the IRS, by Frederick W. Daily (Nolo), contains extensive information on dealing with the most feared of all creditors.

Divorce & Money: How to Make the Best Financial Decisions During Divorce, by Violet Woodhouse with Dale Fetherling (Nolo), contains information about dealing with debts during a divorce.

How to Get Out of Debt, Stay Out of Debt, and Live Prosperously, by Jerrold Mundis (Bantam), explains how to live—happily—without credit. The Federal Trade Commission, Consumer Response Center, 600 Pennsylvania Avenue, NW, Room H-130, Washington, DC 20580-0001, 877-FTC-HELP, www.ftc.gov, takes complaints about credit bureaus and collection agencies. It also publishes free pamphlets on debts and credit, including *"Building a Better Credit Record," "Cosigning a Loan," "Equal Credit Opportunity," "Fair Credit Billing," "Your Access to Fair Credit Reports," "Credit Repair: Self-Help May Be Best," "Need a Loan? Think Twice About Using Your Home as Collateral,"* and *"Credit, Debit, & ATM Cards: What to Do if They're Lost or Stolen."*

The Federal Citizen Information Center (FCIC), General Services Administration, Pueblo, CO 81009, 800-333-4636 or 800-688-9889 (recorded information), www.pueblo.gsa.gov, publishes more than 200 free and low-cost federal booklets on a wide variety of consumer topics, and maintains a one-stop federal consumer information website. Many pamphlets on credit topics can be downloaded for free from the website, including *Building a Better Credit Report,*" *"Consumer Handbook to Credit Protection Laws,"* and *"Healthy Credit."*

The Federal Student Aid Information Center, P.O. Box 84, Washington, DC 20044-0084, 800-433-3243, provides information about federal student loan programs. So does the U.S. Department of Education at http://studentaid.ed.gov.

The Department of Health and Human Services, Bureau of Health Professions, P.O. Box 2910, Merrifield, VA 22116, 888-ASK-HRSA (888-275-4772), http://bhpr.hrsa.gov, provides information about federal student loans for health care professionals.

AUTOMATED TELLER MACHINE (ATM) AND DEBIT CARDS

ATM cards are issued by financial institutions (banks, credit unions, and savings and loans) to allow customers to make most of their banking transactions at a terminal, whenever they wish. In some instances, an ATM card serves as a debit card. When you pay for goods or services with an ATM or debit card, the money is automatically deducted from your checking account.

Statement or Receipt Errors

If your bank, credit union, or savings and loan statement or receipt for an ATM or debit transaction includes an error, you have 60 days from the date of the statement or receipt to notify the financial institution. (15 U.S.C. § 1693f.) This 60-day limit can be extended, if circumstances warrant it. If you don't notify the institution within 60 days, it has no obligation to investigate the error. Notify the institution by calling, then follow up with a letter, keeping a copy for your records.

The institution has ten business days from the date of your notification to investigate the problem and tell you the result. If the financial institution needs more time, it can take up to 45 days, but only if it deposits the amount of money in dispute into your account. If the institution later determines that there was no error, it can take the money back, but it first must send you a written explanation.

Lost or Stolen ATM or Debit Cards

If your ATM or debit card is lost or stolen, you are not liable for any money taken out of your account without authorization after you report the card missing. Otherwise, your liability is limited to:

- up to $50, if you notify the financial institution within two business days of realizing the card is missing, or
- up to $500, if you fail to notify the financial institution within two business days of realizing the card is missing (unless you were on extended travel or in the hospital) but do give notice within 60 days of receiving your statement.

If you fail to notify the financial institution within 60 days of receiving your bank statement, you may be liable for any changes or withdrawals. (15 U.S.C. § 1693g.)

If a financial institution violates these rules, you can sue to recover your actual loss (no less than $100 and no more than $1,000), attorneys' fees, and court costs. (15 U.S.C. § 1693m.) In response to consumer complaints about the possibility of unlimited liability, Visa and MasterCard both cap your potential loss at $50. And several banks won't make you pay for any unauthorized charges.

ATM Fees

Financial institutions must disclose any fees for using an ATM card before the transaction is completed. (Fin. Code § 13080.)

BANKRUPTCY

Bankruptcy is a federal court process designed to help consumers and businesses eliminate their debts or repay them under the protection of the bankruptcy court. When you file for bankruptcy, something called an "automatic stay" goes into effect. The automatic stay prohibits most creditors from taking any action to collect the debts you owe them unless the bankruptcy court lifts the stay and lets the creditor proceed with collections. Once your bankruptcy case is over, your old debts are erased (discharged), and creditors are barred forever from trying to collect those debts, unless a particular debt is not discharged during your bankruptcy case.

Types of Bankruptcy

Although there are several types of bankruptcy, the two most popular for individual debtors are Chapter 7 bankruptcy and Chapter 13 bankruptcy, named after where they appear in the Bankruptcy Code.

- **Chapter 7 bankruptcy**, also called "liquidation" bankruptcy, is the most common kind. In Chapter 7 bankruptcy, debtors ask the court to erase their debts. In exchange, debtors must give up any property they own that is not exempt from collection efforts, which will be sold so the proceeds can be distributed among their creditors.
- **Chapter 13 bankruptcy**, sometimes called "reorganization" bankruptcy, allows you to pay off some of your debt over time. In Chapter 13 bankruptcy, you file a repayment plan with the bankruptcy court to pay back some of what you owe. The amount you'll have to repay depends on how much you earn, the amount and types of debt

you owe, and how much property you own. Some creditors must receive 100% of what you owe. Others may receive nothing.

Eligibility Requirements

Until very recently, most debtors were free to choose which type of bankruptcy best met their needs—and the majority chose to file under Chapter 7. Chapter 7 is a popular choice because, unlike Chapter 13, it doesn't require filers to pay back any portion of their debts.

Under the new bankruptcy law that went into effect in October 2005, however, some debtors will be limited to Chapter 13 bankruptcy. The new law uses a fairly complicated formula to determine who can file for Chapter 7. Generally speaking, debtors whose incomes are higher than the median income for a family of their size in their state may not be allowed to file for Chapter 7 bankruptcy if their disposable income, after subtracting certain allowed expenses and required debt payments, would allow them to pay back a portion of their debt over a five-year repayment period.

There are some eligibility requirements for Chapter 13 bankruptcy as well. For example, if you have secured debts of more than $922,975 and unsecured debts of more than $307,675, then you cannot use Chapter 13.

The Bankruptcy Process

To file for bankruptcy, you must complete a packet of forms describing your property, income, debts, expenses, recent financial transactions, and so on. You file these papers, along with a filing fee, with the federal bankruptcy court. Under the new bankruptcy law, you must also file proof that you have completed credit counseling with an authorized agency. If you are using Chapter 13, you must file a repayment plan with your other bankruptcy papers.

The court will appoint an official called a "trustee" to oversee your bankruptcy case. If you file for Chapter 7 bankruptcy, the trustee is responsible for reviewing your paperwork, collecting any property that is not exempt, and selling it to pay your creditors. In a Chapter 13 case, the trustee will pay your creditors out of the monthly payments you make under your repayment plan.

If you file for Chapter 7 bankruptcy, your case will probably be over in six months. At that time, the court will "discharge" (eliminate) your debts, except for those which you will continue to owe. A Chapter 13 case lasts for three to five years, depending on the length of your repayment plan. If you complete your plan, the court will discharge your remaining debts, except for those which you will continue to owe. If you cannot complete your plan, the trustee may give you a grace period, reduce your total monthly payments, or extend your repayment period. If circumstances beyond your control prevent you from completing the plan, the court might discharge your debts.

After You File for Bankruptcy
When you file for bankruptcy, the automatic stay immediately stops most collection actions against you by a creditor, collection agency, or government entity. The automatic stay, however, will not stop the IRS from proceeding with an audit or issuing a tax assessment. Creditors may ask the court to lift the stay to allow them to collect a particular debt; if this happens, you will have an opportunity to argue against the creditor.

How Often Can You File?
You cannot file for Chapter 7 bankruptcy if you received a discharge in a previous Chapter 7 case within the last eight years, or a discharge in a previous Chapter 13 case within the last six years. Chapter 13 bankruptcy has no such restriction; you can file for it at any time. Also, you cannot file for Chapter 7 bankruptcy if a previous case was dismissed within the past 180 days because you violated a court order; the court ruled that your filing was fraudulent or an abuse of the bankruptcy system; or you requested the dismissal after a creditor asked the court to lift the automatic stay.

Property You Can Keep
When you file for Chapter 7 bankruptcy, you may claim certain assets as exempt—property that can't be taken and sold by the trustee. In California, you must choose between two different lists of exemptions. The first list (called "system 1") is typically used by filers who have some equity in homes they own; the second (called "system 2") allows filers to exempt almost $20,000 of any type of property. Here are some of the items included in each system:
System 1
  - Equity in a home up to:
    — $50,000 if you are single and not disabled

— $75,000 if you are married

— $150,000 if you are 65 or older or physically or mentally disabled, or if you are 55 or older and earn under $15,000 per year (single) or $20,000 per year (married)

- Life insurance loan value to $9,700
- Appliances, furnishings, clothing
- Social Security deposits to $2,425 ($3,650 if married)
- Health aids
- Jewelry, heirlooms, and art to $6,075
- Motor vehicles to $2,300
- Public benefits
- Tools used in your trade or profession to $6,075, and
- 75% of your wages.

System 2

- Equity in a home or burial plot to $18,675
- ERISA-qualified retirement benefits
- Animals, crops, appliances, furnishings, household goods, books, musical instruments, and clothing to $475 per item
- Health aids
- Jewelry to $1,225
- Motor vehicle to $2,975
- Public benefits
- Tools used in your trade or profession to $1,875, and
- Unused portion of the $18,675 available toward the equity in your home or burial plot, plus $925, for any property.

Debts That Survive Bankruptcy

You are not allowed to discharge these debts in bankruptcy:

- child support and alimony
- certain tax debts
- personal injury debts caused by your intoxicated driving
- student loans, unless repayment would cause undue hardship
- debts you couldn't discharge in a previous bankruptcy, and
- fines and penalties imposed for violating the law, such as traffic tickets, criminal court penalties, and criminal restitution.

In addition, the following debts are not dischargeable in Chapter 7, if a creditor objects to the debt's discharge and the court agrees:

- debts incurred by fraud, such as lying on a credit application
- credit purchases of $500 or more for luxury goods or services within 90 days of the bankruptcy filing
- most loans or cash advances of $750 or more within 90 days of the bankruptcy filing
- debts arising from willful and malicious injury to another or another's property, including assault, battery, false imprisonment, libel, and slander, and
- debts from embezzlement, larceny (theft), or breach of trust.

CHECKS

You may have more rights than you know when it comes to dealing with a financial institution about checks you write or receive.

Check Holds

Financial institutions used to make a lot of money by holding onto deposits for a few days before letting the depositor withdraw the funds. Now, state and federal laws restrict this practice. You can withdraw the money from government checks, cashier's checks, electronic deposits, and money orders the day after you deposit them. When you deposit a non–next day check, the bank must make the first $100 available for withdrawal the following business day. Local checks (for Northern Californians, checks drawn on financial institutions in Northern California and parts of Nevada; for Southern Californians, checks drawn on financial institutions in Southern California, Arizona, and the Las Vegas area) cannot be held more than two business days. Other checks cannot be held more than five business days. A financial institution can, however, hold a local check for seven business days and a nonlocal check for 11 business days if the check is for over $5,000 or is a redeposited bounced check, if the deposit account is frequently overdrawn, or if the financial institution has reason to believe the check will be uncollectible.

These check hold rules do not apply to money market funds.

Stopping Payment

You may legally stop payment on a check if you don't do it to defraud a creditor. The stop payment order may be oral but will lapse if not confirmed in writing in 14 days. (Comm. Code § 4403.)

Stale and Postdated Checks

Financial institutions are not obligated to honor a stale check—one older than six months or 180 days. (Comm. Code § 4404.) Most do, however, unless the check says "void after six months."

A postdated check is one dated later than the date it was actually written. If you receive a postdated check and present it to a financial institution for cashing before its date, a financial institution may legally cash the check, although many refuse to do so. Except in very limited circumstances, a business may not request a postdated check. (Bus. & Prof. Code § 17538.6.)

Proper Identification

A merchant cannot refuse your check solely because you won't allow the merchant to write your credit card number on your check. Merchants can ask you to show a credit card and can record the type of card, the issuer of the card, and expiration date. Merchants can also ask to see reasonable forms of identification, such as your driver's license, and may record that number on your check. (Civ. Code § 1725.)

Checks for Payment in Full

In a dispute between two parties about money owed, sometimes one party will send the other a check for part of the amount with a notation on the check stating, "Cashing this check constitutes payment in full." If a recipient cashes such a check, it amounts to accepting a settlement for that amount. The recipient of such a check cannot cross out the "full payment" language, deposit the check, and sue for the balance owed. Cashing the check will settle the matter unless the recipient cashed the check without noticing the "paid in full" notation. However, if this was the case, the recipient must offer a check or money order for repayment of the amount within 90 days after the first check is cashed. (Comm. Code § 3311.)

Bad Checks

If a check bounces, the recipient may be entitled to collect up to three times the amount of the check. The recipient must first demand, by certified mail, that the person who wrote the check pay the amount of the check, the cost of certified mail, and the bad check fee assessed against the recipient, within 30 days. The letter must also inform the person who wrote the check that the recipient may be able to collect triple the amount of the check if the person who wrote the check doesn't respond to the demand letter. If the person who bounced the check does not pay within 30 days and does not have a good faith dispute with the recipient, the recipient has two options:

- Sue for the original amount of the bounced check plus three times that amount—with a minimum of $100 and a maximum of $1,500—as a penalty. (Civ. Code § 1719.) The check writer is not liable if he or she has written confirmation that the check bounced due to bank error or a delay in posting the direct deposit of a Social Security or government assistance check.
- Turn the matter over to the county district attorney's office. If that office has a check diversion program, writers of bad checks may be able to avoid criminal prosecution if they make the check good and comply with other rules. A recipient who enlists the help of the district attorney cannot sue.

Someone who willfully writes a bad check, knowing the account has insufficient funds to pay it, with the intent of defrauding the recipient of the check, can be sentenced to up to one year in county jail or state prison. (Pen. Code § 476a.)

COSIGNERS' RIGHTS

A cosigner on a credit or loan application promises to pay if the primary borrower does not. If the primary borrower defaults, the cosigner's credit report may be affected. For this reason, the Federal Trade Commission requires that the cosigner be given a disclosure statement pointing out the obligations and risks. California requires that the notification shown below be given, in both English and Spanish, in ten-point type. If the contract is written in a language other than English or Spanish, the cosigner must be given notice in English and the language in which the contract is written. The notice does not have to be given to spouses who both sign a credit contract. (Civ. Code § 1799.91.)

NOTICE TO COSIGNER

You are being asked to guarantee this debt. Think carefully before you do so. If the borrower doesn't pay the debt, you will have to. Be sure you can afford to pay if you have to, and that you want to accept this responsibility. You may have to pay up to the full amount of the debt if the borrower does not pay. You may also have to pay late fees or collection costs, which increase this amount.

The creditor can collect this debt from you without first trying to collect from the borrower. The creditor can use the same collection methods against you that can be used against the borrower, such as suing you, garnishing your wages, etc. If this debt is ever in default, that fact may become part of *your* credit record.

This notice is not the contract that makes you liable for the debt.

CREDIT AND CHARGE CARDS

Both credit cards and charge cards allow you to buy goods on credit and pay later, but charge cards (such as American Express) don't usually allow you to carry an unpaid balance from month to month. Credit and charge cards are governed by your agreement with the bank, credit union, savings and loan association, merchant, or other creditor that issued the card, and by several laws: the California Song-Beverly Credit Card Act (Civ. Code §§ 1747 and following), the federal Fair Credit Billing Act (15 U.S.C. §§ 1666 and following), and the federal Truth in Lending Act (15 U.S.C. §§ 1601 and following).

Interest

Credit card companies are generally free to charge as much interest as they want. California laws prohibiting usury (exorbitantly high interest) don't apply. Because most credit card companies are based in states where there are very few consumer protections, these companies only have to follow the lenient laws in these business-friendly states, even though they serve California customers.

Unrequested Credit and Charge Cards

A company that issues credit or charge cards cannot legally send you one except in response to your request or application. However, there are no penalties against companies that send unrequested cards. If you "accept" the card—that is, if you use it, sign it, or notify the card issuer in writing that you plan to keep it—you become liable for all charges made after your acceptance. But if you do not accept the card and it is used—for example, by a thief—the company is responsible.

Disclosures

When a credit or charge card company sends you an application or pre-approval letter, it must fully disclose the terms of your agreement, including finance charges, interest rates, membership fees, and how interest rates and daily balances are calculated. (15 U.S.C. § 1637.) If the card issuer doesn't disclose this information or gives you the wrong information, you can sue for any loss you suffered as a result, including your actual damages, attorneys' fees, court costs, and twice the amount of finance charges you were wrongfully charged. (15 U.S.C. § 1640.)

The card issuer can get off the hook if, within 60 days, it notifies you of the error and makes the necessary corrections. As long as the company does not charge you any interest in excess of the amount it actually disclosed, it will probably not be liable for the error. In addition, if the card issuer's mistake was unintentional and resulted from a clerical, calculation, computer, printing, or similar error, the card issuer will not be liable.

Credit card companies that disclose marketing information to marketers of goods must provide a written notice to the cardholder—or to the applicant for a credit card—clearly stating the cardholder's right to prohibit the disclosure of any marketing information that reveals the cardholder's identity. The notice must include a preprinted form that the cardholder can use to exercise this right, and must identify a toll-free telephone number available for the same purpose. This rule does not prohibit credit card companies from giving information to consumer credit reporting agencies or companies affiliated with the card issuer. (Civ. Code § 1748.12.)

Lost, Stolen, and Borrowed Cards

Your liability for unauthorized charges made on your credit or charge card after it has been lost or stolen is limited by federal law. (15 U.S.C. § 1643.) If you give adequate notice to the card issuer within a reasonable time after you discover the loss or theft, you're not responsible for any charges made after the notification and are liable only for the first $50 of charges made before you notified the card issuer (although few card issuers ever try to collect this money).

If a friend or relative uses your card without your knowledge or permission, you are liable for the charges unless you report it as stolen. If you give someone permission to use your card, anything charged is your responsibility. If you tell the person to stop charging and they ignore you, you may still be liable to the card issuer for these charges—unless you report the card as stolen or cancel the card—although you can also try to get the money back from the person who misused your card by suing them in small claims court.

Disputes Over Credit or Charge Card Purchases

If you buy a defective item or service with a credit or charge card, you can often refuse to pay if the seller won't replace or repair the item or otherwise correct the problem. (15 U.S.C. § 1666i.)

There are some limits to this law. First, you have to try in good faith to resolve the dispute. Second, you are required to explain to the credit or charge card company in writing why you are withholding payment. Third, if you used a Visa, Mastercard, or other card not issued by the seller, you can refuse to pay only if the purchase was for more than $50 and was made within the state you live in or within 100 miles of your home.

If you used a card issued by the seller—such as a department store or gas company card—you can withhold payment regardless of where and for how much the purchase was made. The same is true if the seller obtained your order by mailing you an ad in which the card issuer participated and urged you to use the credit card in question. But you still have to try to resolve the problem first.

Billing Errors

If you find an error in your statement, you must send a letter to the company that issued the card, and the letter must be sent so that the company receives it within 60 days after it mailed the bill to you. Be sure to send the letter to the correct address for billing disputes, which you can find on the back of your bill, and which will be different from the address for sending payment. The company must acknowledge receipt of your letter within 30 days unless it corrects the bill within that time. The card issuer must correct the error or explain why it believes the amount to be correct within two billing cycles (but in no event more than 90 days). If the card company does not comply with this limit, you don't have to pay any portion of the disputed balance or associated finance charges. (15 U.S.C. § 1666.)

During the two-billing-cycle/90-day period, the company cannot report the amount to a credit bureau as delinquent or threaten or actually take any collection action against you. (15 U.S.C. § 1666a.) It can send you periodic statements, apply the amount in dispute to your credit limit (which lowers the amount available for you to charge), or charge you interest on the amount in dispute (to be dropped if you're later proven correct).

If the company violates these rules, you can sue to recover your actual losses, such as costs you incur in trying to remove erroneous information from a credit bureau file, twice the amount of any interest, attorneys' fees, and court costs. (15 U.S.C. § 1640.)

Credit Card Surcharges

Retailers cannot charge consumers a surcharge for using a credit card. Retailers can, however, offer a discount on the established price if you pay cash—which amounts to the same thing. (Civ. Code § 1748.1.)

Personal Information on Credit Card Slips

Merchants cannot ask customers to write their phone number on a credit card slip. The rule doesn't apply if the payment is a deposit or if you are having merchandise shipped, delivered, or installed, or for special orders. (Civ. Code § 1747.08.)

Debiting Bank Accounts to Pay Credit Card Bills (Setoffs)

A bank, credit union, or savings and loan cannot take money out of a deposit account to cover a missed credit card payment unless you have authorized such a transaction. (15 U.S.C. § 1666h; 12 C.F.R. § 226.12(d).)

CREDIT BUREAUS

Credit bureaus (officially called "consumer credit reporting agencies") are companies that make money by gathering and selling information about a person's credit history. The three major credit bureaus are Experian, TransUnion, and Equifax. Credit bureaus are regulated by the federal Fair Credit Reporting Act (15 U.S.C. §§ 1681 and following) and by the California Consumer Credit Reporting Agencies Act. (Civ. Code §§ 1785.1 and following.) Here are the major rules:

- Bureaus may gather information about your credit-worthiness, credit standing, credit capacity, character, general reputation, personal characteristics, or mode of living as it relates to your eligibility for credit or insurance, or for employment purposes.
- Bureaus cannot report an arrest unless it resulted in a conviction. (Civ. Code § 1785.13.)
- Bureaus can report bankruptcies for no more than ten years and can report other adverse information for no more than seven years.

Bureaus may provide this information to anyone who intends to use it in a credit transaction, for employment purposes, to determine your eligibility for government benefits, or for any other legitimate business need that relates to you.

Seeing Your File

Bureaus must show you your credit file if you present proper identification. You have a right to see your file as often as you want. You have the right to one free copy of your credit report each year. If you are denied credit because of adverse information in a credit file, you have the right to a free copy, but must request it within 60 days. You are also entitled to a free copy if you are unemployed and plan to apply for a job within 60 days, you receive public assistance, or you believe your file contains errors due to fraud. If you don't qualify for a free report, the bureau can charge you $8. (Civ. Code § 1785.17.)

Credit Scores

Most credit files also include a credit score. A credit score is a numerical calculation that is supposed to indicate the risk that you will default on your payments. A high credit score indicates less risk; a low score indicates potential problems. Credit scores typically range from lows of 300-400 to highs of 800-900.

Credit scores can determine whether you get a loan, yet federal law does not require credit bureaus to let you know what your score is. However, the three major credit bureaus (Experian, Equifax, and TransUnion) and the biggest credit scoring company (Fair, Isaac and Co.) will send you your credit score and report for a small fee (often $12.95). California law requires credit bureaus to provide consumers with their scores and related information on request. (Civ. Code § 1785.10). For more information, check the website of Consumers Union, www.consumersunion.org.

Mistakes in a Credit File

If you complain to a bureau about a mistake or inaccuracy in your file, the bureau must investigate within 30 days. If you are right, or if the creditor who provided the information can no longer verify the information, the bureau must remove it from your file.

A credit bureau must take the following steps when investigating your complaint:

- complete its investigation within 30 days of receiving your complaint (extended to 45 if the bureau receives information from you during the 30-day period)
- contact the creditor reporting the information you dispute within five days of receiving your complaint
- review and consider all relevant information submitted by you
- remove all inaccurate and unverified information and adopt procedures to keep the information from reappearing
- reinsert removed information only if the provider of the information certifies that the information is accurate and you are notified within five days of the reinsertion, and
- provide you with the results of its reinvestigation within five days of completion, including a new credit report.

In addition, creditors who report information to credit bureaus must:

- refrain from reporting information they know is incorrect
- refrain from ignoring information they know contradicts what they have on file
- refrain from reporting incorrect information once they learn that the information is, in fact, incorrect
- provide credit bureaus with correct information once they learn that the information they have been reporting is incorrect

- notify credit bureaus when you dispute information
- note when accounts are "closed by the consumer"
- provide credit bureaus with the month and year of the delinquency of all accounts placed for collection, charged off, or similarly treated, and
- finish their investigation of your dispute within the required 30-day or 45-day period.

If the credit bureau includes information in your file that you disagree with, you have the right to place a statement in your file describing your version of the dispute. If the reporting agency helps you write the summary, it must be limited to one hundred words. Otherwise there is no word limit, but it is best to keep the statement very brief. The credit bureau must give a summary of your statement to anyone who requests your file. If you request it, the bureau must also give the summary to anyone who received a copy of your file within the past six months—or two years, if your file was given out for employment purposes.

Suing a Credit Bureau

You can sue a credit bureau for negligent (unreasonably careless) or willful noncompliance with the law within two years after the bureau's harmful behavior first occurred. You can sue for actual financial loss, such as court costs, attorneys' fees, and lost wages and, if applicable, intentional infliction of emotional distress. For truly outrageous behavior, you can recover punitive damages—damages meant to punish for malicious or willful conduct. (15 U.S.C. § 1681n.))

CREDIT DISCRIMINATION

The federal Equal Credit Opportunity Act (ECOA) prohibits a creditor from refusing to grant credit because of race, color, religion, national origin, sex, marital status, or age, or because you receive public assistance. A creditor can ask about marital status, age, or public assistance, but only to determine your credit-worthiness, your credit history, and the likelihood of your continued income. (15 U.S.C. § 1691.)

The federal Fair Housing Act (FHA) (42 U.S.C. §§ 3601 and following) prohibits discrimination in residential real estate transactions. The FHA covers loans to purchase, improve, or maintain your home and loans for which your home is used as collateral, as well as sales and appraisals of homes.

California also has several laws prohibiting credit discrimination. It is against California law for creditors to:

- refuse to issue a credit card because of race, religious creed, color, national origin, ancestry, or sex (Civ. Code §1747.80)
- offer credit on less favorable terms because of marital status (Civ. Code §1812.30), or
- discriminate in home mortgage lending because of race, color, religion, sex, sexual orientation, marital status, national origin, ancestry, familial status, source of income, or disability (Gov't. Code § 12955).

Race Discrimination

In general, lenders are not allowed to ask your race on a credit application or to ascertain it by any other means (such as a credit file) other than by personal observation. A mortgage lender, however, must ask your race for the purpose of monitoring home mortgage applications. Lenders are accused of getting around race discrimination prohibitions by "redlining"— denying credit to residents of predominantly nonwhite neighborhoods.

These laws prohibit redlining:

- The federal Home Mortgage Disclosure Act requires that mortgage lenders maintain and disclose their lending practices for certain areas. (12 U.S.C. §§ 2801 and following.)
- The federal Community Reinvestment Act requires that bank mortgage lenders demonstrate that they serve the needs of the communities in which they are chartered to serve. If the bank fails to do so, bank regulators can deny the bank the right to establish branches or engage in other activity requiring regulatory approval. (12 U.S.C. §§ 2901 and following.)
- Redlining is also barred by the Fair Housing Act (42 U.S.C. §§ 3601 and following) and the Equal Credit Opportunity Act. (15 U.S.C. § 1691.)
- California law specifically prohibits redlining. (H & S Code §§ 35800 and following.)

Sex Discrimination

Discrimination based on sex is prohibited, but a creditor may ask you to designate a title (Mr., Ms., and so on) as long as they make clear that selecting one is optional. A creditor may also ask your sex when you apply for a real estate loan; this information is collected by the federal government for statistical purposes.

Marital Status Discrimination

Discrimination based on marital status (that is, because you are married, in a registered domestic partnership, or single) is prohibited under the ECOA and California law. (Civ. Code § 1812.30.) The FHA has a similar provision prohibiting discrimination on the basis of familial status.

These laws require creditors to allow a married person or domestic partner to apply for credit in his or her name only. A creditor cannot require an applicant's spouse to cosign an application. However, a creditor may ask certain questions that might disclose your marital status, such as:

- whether you pay alimony or child support
- what your income sources are (alimony or child support might be included in your answer), and
- whether any person, such as a spouse or registered domestic partner, is jointly liable for any debts you list on a credit application.

If an unmarried couple or a couple registered as domestic partners applies for a joint loan, the creditor must consider their combined income, just as it would for a married couple. (*Markham v. Colonial Mortgage Service Co.,* 605 F.2d 566 (D.C. Cir. 1979).)

DEBT COLLECTION

The law prohibits creditors from using abusive or deceptive tactics to collect a debt. The law, however, also grants powerful collection tools to creditors once they have won a lawsuit over the debt.

Important Terms

Judgment creditor. A person who has sued and won a judgment against someone else. This person is a creditor because the loser of the lawsuit owes him or her money.

Judgment debtor. The person who lost the lawsuit and owes money to the judgment creditor.

Prohibited Debt Collection Practices

Debt collection practices are governed by the federal Fair Debt Collection Practices Act (15 U.S.C. §§ 1692 and following) and California's Fair Debt Collection Practices Act. (Civ. Code §§ 1788 and following.) The federal law governs only collection agencies. The state law covers any bill collector, including collection agencies and creditors who collect debts on their own behalf. Under both laws, a debt collector may not:

- **communicate with a debtor** by:
  - calling, writing, or talking with the debtor directly, if the bill collector knows the debtor has an attorney
  - calling repeatedly or at an unusual or inconvenient place or time
  - reaching the debtor at work, if the collector knows that the debtor is prohibited from receiving collections calls at work, or
  - sending a document that misleadingly appears to be from a court, government agency, or attorney.
- **harass or abuse a debtor** by:
  - harming or threatening the debtor or another person, or the reputation or property of the debtor or another person
  - using obscene or profane language, or
  - publishing the debtor's name as a person who doesn't pay bills.
- **communicate with third parties about the debtor**, including:
  - giving false credit information about the debtor, or failing to disclose that the debtor disputes a debt, if true
  - contacting a third party (other than the debtor's spouse, parent if the debtor is a minor or lives in the same house, debtor's attorney, or a credit bureau) for any purpose except locating the debtor, verifying the debtor's employment, or finding out whether the debtor has medical insurance (for medical debts only), or
  - failing to reveal the debt collector's company name to any third party contacted, if asked.
- **make false or misleading statements**, including:
  - falsely claiming to be an attorney, police officer, or government agent
  - threatening to take action that isn't intended or can't be taken, such as stating that welfare benefits will be cut off, the debtor will be jailed, or the debtor's property will be taken, or

— falsely claiming that the debtor has committed a crime
- **use unfair or outrageous debt collection methods**, such as:
  — adding interest, fees, or charges not authorized in the original agreement or by state law
  — accepting a check postdated by more than five days, unless the collector notifies the debtor between three and ten days in advance of when he will deposit it
  — calling the debtor collect or otherwise causing the debtor to incur communications charges, or
  — sending the debtor a postcard or envelope with words or symbols on the outside that indicate the collector is trying to collect a debt.

Calling Off a Debt Collector

If you've been contacted by a collection agency, the federal Fair Debt Collection Practices Act gives you the right to tell the bill collector to cease all communications with you. Begin over the phone; follow up with a letter. If the collection agency contacts you again other than to say collection efforts are ending, or that it is going to take a specific action—such as suing you—it has violated the law.

How Judgment Creditors Can Collect Debts

Once the creditor has won a lawsuit affirming the debt, the creditor can use the following collection techniques.

Wage garnishment. A wage garnishment orders the debtor's employer to withhold a portion of the debtor's wages from each paycheck (net pay) and pay that money directly to the judgment creditor. For most judgments, the employer will withhold 25% of each paycheck; the creditor can ask that less be withheld. As much as 50% can be withheld if the debt is for spousal or child support. Garnishment lasts until the creditor collects the entire judgment or until a wage garnishment of higher priority (for spousal or child support or taxes) is instituted.

- To garnish a debtor's wages, the judgment creditor must prepare a few fill-in-the-blanks forms available free from the court clerk and send them to a local levying officer, usually a sheriff or marshal. The levying officer will serve these papers on the debtor's employer.
- A debtor who wants to protest a wage garnishment may file a "claim of exemption." The debtor must show that his entire paycheck is needed to support himself and his family. If the creditor opposes this claim, the court will decide whether or not garnishment is appropriate and, if so, in what amount.

Seizing the debtor's property. When a creditor gets the court's permission to have certain items of the debtor's property seized or sold, it's called "levying" on the judgment. A creditor can take a portion of the debtor's wages (wage garnishment), the debtor's deposit account or safe deposit box, money owed to the debtor by a third person, or the contents of a business debtor's cash register. In addition, a creditor can seize the debtor's real estate or personal property, have it sold, and collect the proceeds.

To use a levy, the judgment creditor must prepare a form (called a Writ of Execution) and send it, along with instructions and fees, to a local levying officer. The levying officer will serve these papers on the person or business that has the debtor's assets (such as a bank) and will seize or sell the debtor's property.

Some kinds of property are exempt from collection, which means the creditor can't take them or force the debtor to sell them. Whenever a creditor seeks to take a debtor's property, the debtor is given a form explaining how to file a claim of exemption. Using this form, the debtor can request a hearing to argue that the property is exempt or that it will be a financial hardship if the property is taken.

Between $50,000 and $150,000 of equity in the debtor's homestead and 75% of the debtor's wages are exempt from collection in California. In addition, the debtor can keep:

- insurance policies, including disability or health benefits, life insurance proceeds, and unmatured life insurance of up to $9,700 loan value
- pensions
- personal property, including appliances
- furnishings

- necessary food and clothing
- $2,425 of bank deposits from Social Security ($3,650 for a husband and wife or registered domestic partners)
- burial plots
- health aids
- motor vehicles worth up to $2,300
- jewelry, heirlooms, and art worth up to $6,075
- public benefits, such as welfare, Social Security, workers' compensation, and unemployment benefits, and
- tools of trade—such as materials, uniforms, books, equipment, and a motor vehicle—worth up to $6,075, if used for the debtor's work ($12,150 if used by a husband and wife in the same trade). (Civ. Proc. Code §§ 704.010 and following.)

Creditors can also place liens on a debtor's property. (See Liens, below.)

LIENS

A lien is a claim against a debtor's property for the amount of a debt. It gives the creditor the right to be paid from the proceeds if the property is sold or refinanced. A debtor may voluntarily take on a lien by pledging collateral as security for a loan or purchase. More often, liens are placed on property by creditors.

Some liens do not require a court judgment in the creditor's favor, such as:

- **Tax liens.** The IRS or Franchise Tax Board can record a lien against a debtor's property for delinquent income taxes.
- **Child support liens.** Liens for unpaid child support debts don't require a court order other than the order for support.
- **Mechanics' or materialmen's liens.** Someone who performs work or supplies materials for a house, vehicle, or other property can place a lien on that property if the bill is not paid.

Some liens can be used only by a creditor who has won a court judgment against the debtor. Among these "judicial liens" are:

- **Real estate liens.** A creditor who has a court judgment that is enforceable in California, or a workers' compensation judgment, may place a lien on the debtor's real estate. This lien must be recorded (put on file) at the county recorder's office. Any real estate the debtor purchases in that county after the lien is placed will also be subject to the real estate lien. The lien lasts for ten years unless the creditor re-records it. (Code of Civ. Proc. §§ 697.060, 697.340.)

- **Business property liens.** A creditor can create a lien that lasts for five years against a business's personal property (anything but real estate) by filing papers with the California secretary of state. This lien applies to tools, equipment, harvested crops, accounts receivable, and inventory items with a unit value of over $500, but not to cars, boats, or other vehicles. (Code of Civ. Proc. § 697.530.)
- **Liens on pending legal action.** If a debtor is involved in a lawsuit, divorce, or other legal action, a creditor may file a lien in the pending case. If the debtor wins the suit, he or she must pay the creditor before collecting his or her own judgment. (Code of Civ. Proc. § 708.440.)

LOANS

Under state and federal law, lenders must provide borrowers with certain information and options, and are restricted in the methods they can use to collect loans.

Disclosures

The federal Truth in Lending Act requires lenders to disclose certain information in writing when someone applies for a loan, such as the total amount of the loan, the annual percentage rate and amount, and any penalties for late payment or prepayment. (15 U.S.C. § 1631.)

Balloon Payments

If a loan for personal property (not real estate) includes a balloon payment—a large payment at the end of a loan period—you have the right to refinance that payment at the lender's prevailing rate when it comes due. (Civ. Code § 1807.3.)

Restricted Collection Practices

Lenders must follow certain procedures when trying to get borrowers to repay their loans. Several short-cuts have been restricted or banned.

- **Setoffs** happen when your lending institution removes money from your deposit account to cover a payment missed on your loan. This is legal only if the institution disclosed in writing, when you took out the loan, its right to use a setoff. Otherwise, you can sue for the amount taken out of your account plus any other fees or penalties. A bank cannot use a setoff in any circumstances if doing so will lower the aggregate balance of all your accounts with that bank to less than $1,000. These rules don't apply to automatic withdrawal payment plans or when the deposit account is collateral for the loan. (Fin. Code §§ 864, 6660.)

- **Confession of judgment** is a loan provision that lets a lender automatically take a judgment against you if you default, without having to sue you. Federal law prohibits such provisions in any non–real estate consumer contract. (16 C.F.R. §§ 444.1 and following.)

- **Security interest.** When you take out a secured loan, you give the creditor the right to take certain property, or a portion of it, if you don't pay. This is called a security interest. Federal law prohibits lenders from taking a security interest in the following, unless you are actually buying the item: clothing, furniture, appliances, linens, china, crockery, kitchenware, one radio and one television, wedding ring, and personal effects. (16 C.F.R. §§ 444.1 and following.)

- **Voluntary wage assignments.** Some lenders try to ensure your repayment by suggesting that you voluntarily agree to a wage assignment. This means that each time you are paid, a sum of money is deducted from your paycheck by your employer to pay the lender.

  With the exception of real estate loans, a voluntary wage assignment is allowed only if you have the power to revoke it. (16 C.F.R. §§ 444.1 and following.) If you're married, your spouse must consent before the lender can take a voluntary wage assignment. (Lab. Code § 300.)

- **Waivers of exemptions.** If a creditor sues you and wins a court judgment, or you file for bankruptcy, some of your property is protected from your creditors—that is, it can't be taken to pay what you owe. This property is called your exempt property. (See Debt Collection, above for more information.)

  Some creditors try to get around these laws by including a provision in a loan agreement that says you waive your right to keep your exempt property. These provisions are prohibited in any non–real estate consumer contract. (16 C.F.R. §§ 444.1 and following.)

REPOSSESSING PROPERTY

If you buy something on credit, pledge the item—for example, a new car— as security for the loan, and then don't keep up your loan payments, the item can be repossessed. In California, a creditor must sue you in court and obtain a court judgment before repossessing any property except a motor vehicle. (Com. Code § 9601.) Of course, if a creditor (or a "repo man") shows up without a court judgment and you give him permission to repossess your property—in other words, you give it back—it's perfectly legal. (Civ. Code § 1812.2.) You are under no obligation to give this permission, but if you don't and the creditor sues, attorneys' fees and court costs will probably be added to the amount you already owe.

Motor Vehicles

As mentioned, a lender doesn't need to sue and win a court judgment to repossess a motor vehicle; the lender is free to send a repossessor as soon as you default on your car loan payments. A repossessor can't use force to get to your vehicle—repossessions must occur without any "breach of the peace." (Revised Unif. Comm. Code § 9-609.) But a repossessor can grab your vehicle almost anytime you're not in it or standing guard. It's legal to hotwire a car, use a duplicate key, or remove a car from an open garage or carport. It's illegal to take a car from a garage where the door is closed but unlocked or to break into a locked garage, even by using a duplicate key.

When your car is repossessed, you often have a short time during which you can get it back by paying the amount of your delinquent payments, as well as all late fees and the costs the lender incurred in taking and storing it. This is called reinstatement. (Civ. Code § 2983.2.) The lender won't agree to this, however, if you have done any of the following:

- had the contract reinstated in the past
- lied on your credit application
- hidden the car to avoid repossession
- failed to take care of the car, causing its value to diminish substantially, or
- committed violence against the lender or repossessor.

Any time before the car is sold, you also have the right to redeem it by paying the entire balance of the contract, plus any past-due installments and repossession or collection costs. The lender must give you written notice that you have the right to get the car back within 15 days after the notice is mailed. If it doesn't, you may have the right to get the vehicle back for nothing—but you will have to resume making payments on your loan. If you don't contact the lender, the lender will send you a formal notice of its intent to sell the car. You then have an additional ten days to pay the entire balance of what you owe in exchange for getting it back.

If you don't pay what you owe within the time provided in the lender's notice, the property will be sold at an auction. The lender must give you 15 days' notice of the time and place of the sale. Usually, the lender invites used car dealers and others who regularly buy repossessed cars. They bid very low, so the sale of your car will likely bring in far less than what you owe the lender.

The sale price is subtracted from what you owed the lender before the car was repossessed. Then the cost of repossessing, storing, and selling the property is added to the difference, and the total is called a deficiency balance. You owe that amount to the lender. If you don't pay, the lender can sue you.

If the repossessor takes your car, you're entitled to get back all your belongings that were in the car when it was repossessed. You'll have to make a request within the time allowed in your loan agreement.

STUDENT LOANS

There are many different types of student loans. Some are arranged through the federal government, some through the states, and still others through private lenders. The most common student loans, discussed below, are funded through the federal government. If you have a loan through a state agency or private lender, you will need to contact the lender to find out more about your rights and responsibilities.

There are two main categories of federal student loans: Federal Family Education Loans (FFELs) and Federal Direct Loans. The main difference between the FFEL and Direct Loan program is that the Direct Loan program provides government loans directly to students through their schools. FFEL loans are usually made by private banks and guaranteed by the federal government.

FFELs include subsidized and unsubsidized Stafford Loans (formerly known as Guaranteed Student Loans) and parental PLUS loans. If your loan is subsidized, it means that the government pays the interest on your loan while you are in school or during any authorized periods of deferment. The FFEL category also includes Supplemental Loans for Students, but the government stopped offering these in the mid-1990s. There are also FFEL consolidation loans. There are four types of Federal Direct Loans: Subsidized Stafford Loans, Unsubsidized Stafford Loans, PLUS Loans, and Consolidation Loans.

Other important types of federal student loans include the following:

- **Perkins Loans (formerly called National Direct Student Loans and National Defense Student Loans).** A Perkins loan is a low-interest loan for undergraduate or graduate students with exceptional financial need. Perkins loans are made by schools with a combination of federal and school funds—your school is considered your lender.
- **Non–need-based loans for parents or independent students.** Parental Loans for Students (PLUS) loans are made to parents to help pay for their dependent children's education. The loans are available directly from the federal government or through banks.
- **Federal loans for healthcare professionals.**
    - Health Professions Student Loans (HPSL). HPSL loans are need-based loans made by schools to students pursuing degrees in medicine, osteopathy, dentistry, optometry, pharmacy, podiatry, or veterinary medicine.
    - Nursing Student Loans (NSL). NSL loans are need-based loans made by schools to students pursuing a course of study leading to a diploma, associate, baccalaureate, or graduate degree in nursing.
    - Health Education Assistance Loans (HEAL). HEAL loans to first-time borrowers were discontinued as of October 1, 1995; you can obtain a new HEAL loan only if you received at least one other HEAL loan before that date. HEAL loans are made by banks or schools to students in schools of medicine, osteopathy, dentistry, veterinary medicine, optometry, podiatry, public health, pharmacy, chiropractic, health administration, or clinical psychology.

- **Federal Consolidation Loans.** See Consolidating Your Loans, at the end of this chapter.

You can use the Department of Education's National Student Loan Data System to find out what type of student loan you have. This information is available online at www.nslds.ed.gov. You can also call the Federal Student Aid Information Center, 1-800-4-FED-AID (1-800-730-8913), to get this information.

Canceling a Student Loan

You may be able to cancel your student loan under limited circumstances, including:

- You become totally and permanently disabled or die. You (or your executor) can cancel any federal student loan in these circumstances. PLUS loans may be canceled if the child for whom you borrowed the money dies. PLUS loans may also be canceled if both parents die or become disabled.
- Your school closes before you can complete your program of study. You can cancel up to 100% of a Stafford, PLUS, Perkins, Direct Loan, or SLS loan made on or after January 1, 1986.
- Your school falsely certifies that you were eligible for a student loan. You can cancel up to 100% of a Stafford, PLUS, Direct Loan, or SLS loan made on or after January 1, 1986.
- Your school fails to pay you a refund you were owed. You can cancel all or a portion of a Stafford, PLUS, Direct Loan, or SLS loan made on or after January 1, 1986.

The following cancellation circumstances apply to Perkins loans only:

- You are in the U.S. military. The Defense Department will repay up to 50% of a Perkins loan if you're serving in an area of hostility or imminent danger. If you have a PLUS loan, you may be able to obtain repayment assistance (not cancellation) if the student for whom you borrowed serves in the military. For more information, contact the student's recruiting officer. Since September 11, 2001, the government has announced a number of new benefits for student loan borrowers serving in the military. This information is posted on the Department of Education website, www.ed.gov.

- You're a full-time teacher in a designated area serving low-income students. You can cancel up to 100% of a Perkins loan and some portion of a Stafford Loan, whether direct or FFEL.
- You're a full-time teacher of children with disabilities in a public or other nonprofit elementary or secondary school. You can cancel up to 100% of a Perkins loan.
- You're a full-time professional provider of early intervention services for the disabled. You can cancel up to 100% of a Perkins loan.
- You're a full-time teacher of math, a science, foreign languages, bilingual education, or another field designated as a teacher shortage area. You can cancel up to 100% of a Perkins loan.
- You're a full-time employee of a public or nonprofit agency providing services to low-income, high-risk children and their families. You can cancel up to 100% of a Perkins loan.
- You're a full-time nurse. You can cancel up to 100% of a Perkins loan.
- You're a full-time medical technician. You can cancel up to 100% of a Perkins loan.
- You're a full-time law enforcement or corrections officer. You can cancel up to 100% of a Perkins loan.
- You're a full-time staff member in a Head Start program. You can cancel up to 100% of a Perkins loan.
- You're a Peace Corps or VISTA volunteer. You can cancel up to 70% of a Perkins loan.

To cancel a federal student loan—or to determine whether you qualify for cancellation—call your loan servicer or the Department of Education's Debt Collection Services Office at 800-621-3115. The Department of Education also offers a free booklet entitled *The Student Guide*. It contains important information about canceling student loans and obtaining deferments. To order, call 800-433-3243 or visit the Department of Education's website at www.ed.gov.

Deferring Repayments

You may be able to defer (postpone) repayment of a federal student loan if you are not in default—that is, you have made your payments on time, are in the grace period after graduation, or have been granted other deferments or forbearances. The rules depend on the kind of loan you have and when you obtained it.

Deferments are never automatic. You must contact your loan servicer to apply.

Loans Disbursed On or After July 1, 1993

The following provisions apply to all loans except those for health care professionals. For all other loans, you may obtain a deferment if:

- You are enrolled in school at least half-time. You can defer interest and principal on a Perkins loan or Stafford loan. On a PLUS or SLS loan, you can defer principal only.
- You are enrolled in an approved graduate fellowship program or a rehabilitation program for the disabled. You can defer interest and principal on a Perkins loan or Stafford loan. On a PLUS or SLS loan, you can defer principal only.
- You are unable to find full-time employment. You can defer interest and principal on a Perkins loan or Stafford loan. On a PLUS or SLS loan, you can defer principal only. The deferment is for a maximum of three years.
- You are suffering from economic hardship. You are automatically entitled to the deferment if you receive public assistance. Otherwise, you will probably qualify if your total income minus your student loan payments is $800 or less per month. You can defer interest and principal on a Perkins loan or Stafford loan. On a PLUS or SLS loan, you can defer principal only. The deferment is for a maximum of three years.

The Perkins loan program offers a number of additional deferment options.

Different rules apply to deferment of most loans disbursed before July 1, 1993. These rules vary depending on the loan type. For more information about deferring these older loans, contact your loan servicer. In addition, you may defer interest and principal on loans for health care professionals.

Forbearance

During times of financial hardship, your lender may allow you to stop payment on your loan, reduce your payments, or extend the period of time over which you pay. An arrangement of this sort is called a forbearance. Forbearances are easier to obtain than deferments—you may be able to obtain a forbearance even if your loan is in default—but forbearance is the less attractive option, because interest will continue to accrue during the time when you are not making payments, no matter what type of loan you have.

Your loan servicer must give you a forbearance on a federal student loan if your federal student loan payments exceed 20% of your gross monthly income. These forbearances are granted one year at a time, up to three years in a row. Forbearances are also mandatory in cases of local or national emergency or disaster. In most other circumstances, your loan servicer may use its discretion when deciding whether or not to grant a forbearance. Congress has encouraged lenders to grant forbearances where poor health or other personal problems make it difficult for a borrower to meet his or her loan obligations.

If you qualify for a forbearance, you may be able to keep it for up to three years. Call your loan servicer to apply.

Consolidating Your Loans

You can consolidate your federal student loans through the government's direct lending program or through a private loan consolidation company. With loan consolidation, you can lower your monthly payments by extending your repayment period; you may also be able to lower your interest rate. Most loan consolidators offer flexible repayment options based on your income, and you may be able to consolidate even if your loans are in default. The main advantage of consolidation is that it generally allows you to lower your monthly payments, and you will make only one payment each month. It also allows you to lock in a fixed interest rate, a big advantage when interest rates are low. However, under current FFEL rules, you only get one chance to consolidate with a private lender. Whether consolidation will save you money or cost you more in the long run depends on how much you owe and the length of the consolidation loan. In some cases, consolidation can actually increase your total interest expense. Types of loans eligible for consolidation, repayment options, and interest rates vary slightly from lender to lender; contact loan consolidators for more information.

Defaulted Student Loans

If you're in default on your student loans (usually meaning that you haven't made any payments for nine months or more) and ignore the loan holder's attempts to contact you, expect more serious action. At a minimum, your balance will begin to rise quickly as collection fees are added. The government also has a number of ways it can come after you, including:

- **Tax refund intercept.** The Internal Revenue Service is authorized to deduct the amount of defaulted federal student loans from any income tax refund due you. You will be notified before the money is withheld and given at least 60 days to present written evidence to the agency collecting the loan, showing that the loan is either not past due or not legally enforceable.

- **Wage garnishment.** The Department of Education is obligated to garnish up to 10% (15% in some cases) of your wages—without first suing you and getting a judgment—if you've defaulted on your loan. At least 30 days before the garnishment is to begin, you will be notified and given the opportunity to object—on the ground that you returned to work within the previous 12 months after having been fired or laid off.

- **Federal benefits offsets.** The government can take certain types of federal benefits, including Social Security Retirement and Social Security Disability, and certain Black Lung and Railroad Retirement benefits. The government is limited in the amount of benefits it can take. The first $9,000 cannot be seized. (31 U.S.C. § 3716(c)(3)(A).) And it can never take an amount that exceeds 15% of your income.

Finally, you may be sued on a defaulted loan, no matter how old it is or how long ago you defaulted, but only if the Department of Education is unable to collect through a wage garnishment.

It's possible to avoid these aggressive collection tactics by negotiating a repayment plan with the holder of your loan or by consolidating your loan. If you make 12 consecutive payments, you will no longer be in default. And while you are making the 12 payments, collection efforts will be suspended. ■

Dogs

State law covers some important issues when it comes to animals, but local governments are in charge of most basic animal regulations. Most cities:

- Require owners to buy a license for each dog.
- Limit the number of pets per household.
- Require dogs to be on a leash and under control whenever they're off their owners' property, except in areas designated for unleashed dogs. (Most trails and campgrounds of the California State Park system are closed to dogs.)
- Require dogs to have a rabies vaccination and sometimes other shots, such as distemper.
- Require owners to immediately clean up dog droppings deposited anywhere except on their own property.

Many of these local laws, however, don't apply to assistance dogs trained to help owners with disabilities.

TOPICS

Destruction of Livestock by Dogs

Dog Bites and Other Injuries Caused by Dogs

Dog Pounds and Shelters

Dogs in Vehicles

Guide, Signal, and Service Dogs

Pet Stores

Unhealthy Dogs

RELATED TOPICS

Courts and Lawsuits

   Personal Injury Lawsuits

Landlords and Tenants

   Pets

Real Estate

   Noise

ADDITIONAL RESOURCES

Every Dog's Legal Guide: A Must-Have Book for Your Owner, by Mary Randolph (Nolo), is a guide to the laws that affect dog owners and their neighbors.

DESTRUCTION OF LIVESTOCK BY DOGS

Someone who owns, possesses, or keeps a dog that injures or harasses livestock is liable to the owner of the livestock for any losses. The farmer who loses livestock doesn't have to prove that the dog's owner knew that the dog posed a danger to livestock.

A farmer who catches a dog in the act of harassing or wounding livestock may kill the dog without being liable to the dog's owner for the value of the dog. (Civ. Code § 3341.)

DOG BITES AND OTHER INJURIES CAUSED BY DOGS

In California, the owner of a dog that injures someone is almost always liable for the injury. Three different legal rules impose liability; someone injured by a dog has a choice of suing under any one of them.

- **The dog bite statute.** If a dog bites someone who is in a public place or lawfully in a private place, the owner is liable for the injury. (Civ. Code § 3342(a).) The injured person does not have to prove that the dog owner did anything wrong. It doesn't matter, for example, that the owner didn't know the dog would hurt anyone or conscientiously tried to keep it from injuring anyone.

    The police and military cannot be sued if their trained dogs bite someone while they're working, as long as the government agency in charge of the dog has a written policy on proper use of its dogs. (Civ. Code § 3342(b).)

- **The common law rule.** The dog bite statute applies only to dog bites; to sue for other injuries, an injured person must prove that the dog's owner or keeper knew, or had reason to know:

    — the dog was vicious or dangerous to people, and

    — the specific tendency (for example, a tendency to knock people down) of the dog that caused the injury.

- **Negligence.** A dog owner may also be sued for negligence (unreasonable carelessness) if the owner's actions resulted in an injury. For example, a California man let his dog roam, in violation of a local leash law. The dog ran into the road, and a pickup truck crashed trying to avoid it. Two men riding in the back of the truck suffered serious permanent injuries. A judge ruled that the dog owner's violation of the leash law was negligence, and awarded the injured men $2.6 million.

A dog owner may be able to escape liability by proving that the injured person provoked the injury, or voluntarily and knowingly risked the injury.

What the Owner Is Liable For

A dog owner who is legally responsible for an injury to a person or property may be responsible for reimbursing the injured person for:

- medical bills (emergency room, office visits, hospital stays, surgery, medication, physical therapy)
- time off work
- pain and suffering, and
- property damage.

Who Is Responsible

Usually, a dog's owner is legally responsible for damage or injury the dog causes. But an injured person may also sue:

- the dog owner's parent, if the owner is less than 18 years old
- the dog owner's landlord, if the landlord knew the dog was dangerous but didn't do anything about it, or
- someone who was taking care of the dog for the owner.

Dangerous Dogs

If a dog bites someone on at least two separate occasions, or if a dog trained to fight bites someone once and causes substantial injury, any person (including the district or city attorney) can sue the dog's owner. The court will determine whether the dog is still a danger to people. The court may order the owner to take any action it decides is necessary to prevent future injury, including removing the dog from the area or destroying it. (Civ. Code § 3342.5.)

California law also sets out a procedure for having a court declare a dog "potentially dangerous" or "vicious." The owner of a dog that a judge finds to be potentially dangerous must keep the dog fenced or leashed at all times. If a court rules that a dog is vicious, it may prohibit the owner from owning a dog for up to three years. (Food and Agric. Code §§ 31601 and following.)

DOG POUNDS AND SHELTERS

A dog running loose in violation of local law can be picked up and held by city or county animal control officers. The owner will be fined and charged for the cost of impounding the dog. If the dog is unlicensed, there will be an additional fine.

Unless a dog is running at large, or an emergency requires immediate action, most courts would agree that an owner who has possession of a dog is entitled to:

- be notified before the dog is seized
- be notified before the dog is destroyed, and
- be given a chance to argue, in court, that the dog shouldn't be destroyed.

If a dog isn't claimed or adopted within a certain time, a shelter may destroy it humanely, or sell it to a research lab unless local law prohibits this. Any animal shelter, public or private, that turns dogs (alive or dead) over to a research facility must prominently post a large sign, stating that "Animals Turned In to This Shelter May Be Used for Research Purposes or to Supply Blood, Tissue, or Other Biological Products." (Civ. Code § 1834.7.)

DOGS IN VEHICLES

Dogs in the open back of a pickup must be either in a cage or cross-tied to the truck unless the sides of the truck are at least 46 inches high. The law doesn't apply to cattle or sheep dogs used by farmers and ranchers. Violators can be fined $50 to $100 for a first offense and up to $250 for a third offense. (Veh. Code §§ 23117, 42001.4.)

Kinds of Assistance Dogs

- **Guide dogs** help visually impaired owners navigate through public places.
- **Hearing or signal dogs** alert hearing-impaired people to important sounds: intruders, phones, crying babies, doorbells, and smoke alarms. In cars, they alert owners to sirens and honking drivers.
- **Service dogs** are the arms and legs of many people with a physical disability. They pull wheelchairs, carry baskets and briefcases, open doors, and turn on lights.

GUIDE, SIGNAL, AND SERVICE DOGS

Access to Public Places

Both California and federal laws guarantee disabled people with assistance dogs access to public places. (Civ. Code § 54.2.) The federal Americans With Disabilities Act (ADA) allows access to places of "public accommodation," which means anywhere the public is invited or permitted. Public accommodations include, among other places:

- restaurants and stores
- theaters
- hotels and motels
- schools
- parks, golf courses, and bowling alleys
- museums and libraries
- shopping centers and grocery stores
- convention centers and concert halls, and
- doctors' offices and hospitals. (28 C.F.R. Part 36, § 36.104.)

The federal law also requires places of public accommodation to modify their "policies, practices, or procedures to permit the use of a service animal" by a disabled person. (42 U.S.C. § 12181; 28 C.F.R. Part 36, § 36.302.)

It is illegal to impose any extra charge for admitting an assistance dog to any place the dog is allowed by law. (Civ. Code § 54.2.) Zoos are allowed to keep these dogs out of areas where zoo animals aren't separated from the public by a physical barrier, but the zoo must maintain free kennel facilities for the dogs. (Civ. Code § 54.7.)

Avoiding Problems If You Have an Assistance Dog

If you have an assistance dog, it's a good idea to carry copies of the state laws that allow you access to public places. Although the ADA, in theory, eliminates the need for such documentation, it can come in handy. If you are refused admittance to a public place, you can show the management that the law forbids such discrimination.

The Workplace

The federal Americans With Disabilities Act forbids any kind of employment discrimination against disabled persons. Employers with 15 or more employees must make "reasonable accommodations" for disabled workers. (42 U.S.C. § 12111.) The regulations interpreting the ADA say that letting a blind employee bring a guide dog to work is an example of a reasonable accommodation. If an employer refuses to allow an assistance dog and the employee sues, a court will have to decide what's reasonable under the circumstances.

Rental Housing

Generally, California landlords may refuse to rent to tenants with dogs. There are, however, a few exceptions.

Residents of public housing developments (those owned and operated by a state, county, city, or district agency) who are over the age of 60 or disabled may keep up to two small pets per apartment. (H & S Code § 19901.)

Tenants in "federally assisted" housing for the elderly or handicapped are allowed by law to own pets. (Housing and Urban-Rural Recovery Act of 1983, 12 U.S.C. § 1701r-1.) This rule applies even if the federal government does not own the rental housing—it's enough that a federal agency (the U.S. Department of Housing and Urban Development, for example) subsidizes it.

It is illegal to refuse to rent housing to someone because that person uses a guide, signal, or service dog. (Civ. Code § 54.1(5).) These dogs are normally so well trained and well behaved that a landlord has little reason to object to them anyway. The law allows landlords to include reasonable regulations in the lease or rental agreement. The owners, like all dog owners, are liable for any damage the dogs cause.

Government Assistance for Low-Income Owners

The Internal Revenue Service recognizes guide dogs as a legitimate medical expense, which can be deducted for federal income tax purposes. (Treas. Reg. § 1.213-1(e)(1)(iii).)

To help with the expenses of keeping a guide, service, or signal dog, California gives a small monthly payment for dog food and other costs to low-income disabled owners. (Welf. & Inst. Code § 12553.)

The federal government may also pay for a guide dog for a veteran who is entitled to federal disability compensation. (38 U.S.C. § 1714.) The costs paid for may include travel expenses incurred when the veteran goes to pick up the dog from a training center.

PET STORES

To prevent California consumers from buying an unhealthy puppy imported into the state from a midwestern "puppy mill," California retail pet dealers must post, on the dog's cage, a sign giving the state where the dog was bred. They must also post, close to the cages, a notice stating that information about the source and health of the dogs is available to prospective buyers.

Every retail seller of a dog must also fill out and give the buyer a written form, which is provided by the state Department of Consumer Affairs. The form lists:

- where the dog came from, if it came from a licensed dealer
- its birth date
- its immunization record
- a record of any known sickness the dog has, and
- a record of any veterinary treatment or medication received by the dog while with a retail pet dealer.

The dealer must also give the buyer one of the following:
- a signed statement that the dog has no known disease or illness and no known hereditary condition that adversely affects the dog's health or is likely to affect it in the future, or
- a record of any known disease or condition that affects the dog's health at the time of sale or is likely to affect it in the future, along with a statement signed by a licensed veterinarian that authorizes the sale; recommends necessary treatment, if any; and verifies that the disease or condition does not require hospitalization or surgical procedures.

Dealers are also required to give prospective buyers additional information on the breeder and broker, purebred registration, past disease, and the dog's parents' registration number, if any, from the Orthopedic Foundation for Animals.

Dealers who knowingly sell sick animals are subject to a penalty of up to $1,000. (H & S Code §§ 122125 and following.)

UNHEALTHY DOGS

California's Pet Protection Act protects consumers who buy sick dogs from pet stores. The law protects owners who discover that their pet is sick within 15 days after taking the dog home or, in the case of hereditary problems, within one year.

Notifying the Pet Dealer

The owner must get a written statement from a California veterinarian stating that the dog is sick or that the dog has a hereditary disease that adversely affects the dog's health or is likely to require hospitalization or surgery. (H & S Code § 122160.)

The owner must deliver the statement and the veterinarian's name and telephone number to the pet dealer no later than five days after the diagnosis is made. (H & S Code § 122170.)

The Owner's Options

The dog owner then has three choices:

- **Return the dog** for a refund of the purchase price and reimbursement for reasonable veterinary fees up to the cost of the dog.
- **Exchange the dog** for another of equal value and get reimbursement for reasonable veterinary fees up to the cost of the dog.
- **Keep the dog** and receive reimbursement for reasonable veterinary fees up to 150% of the purchase price of the pet. (H & S Code § 122160.)

The Pet Dealer's Response

If the pet dealer doesn't dispute the diagnosis, the refund and reimbursement must be paid within ten days after the dealer receives the veterinarian's statement. (H & S Code § 122180.) If the pet dealer wants to dispute the diagnosis, the dealer can require the owner to have the dog examined by another veterinarian of the pet dealer's choosing. The pet dealer must pay for the exam. (H & S Code § 122185.)

If the Dog Dies

If the dog dies, the owner can choose to receive a refund or a replacement dog plus reimbursement for reasonable veterinary fees for the diagnosis and treatment of the dog. The owner must give the pet dealer a written statement from a California veterinarian, stating that the dog died from either:

- an illness that existed within 15 days after the buyer took the dog home, or
- a congenital or hereditary condition that was diagnosed by the veterinarian within one year after the buyer took the dog home. (H & S Code § 122160.)

To make sure consumers know their rights, the statute requires pet stores to give buyers a written notice explaining them. ■

Employees' Rights

Both California and federal law protect the rights of workers. Employees have the right to work free of discrimination, harassment, environmental hazards, violations of their privacy, and other legal transgressions. Employees also have the right to certain workplace benefits, including time off in certain circumstances. This chapter explains the rules.

TOPICS

Acquired Immune Deficiency Syndrome (AIDS)
Child Labor
Discrimination
Domestic Violence
Drug Testing
English-Only Rules
Equal Pay
Family and Medical Leave
Firing
Health and Safety Regulations
Health Insurance
Immigrant Workers
Independent Contractors
Lie Detector Tests
Personnel Files
Pregnancy
Psychological Testing
Sexual Harassment
Smoking Policies
Unemployment Insurance
Unions
Vacations
Wage and Hour Restrictions
Workers' Compensation

RELATED TOPICS

Consumers' Rights

Health Insurance

Courts and Lawsuits

Jury Duty

Government Benefits

Disability Insurance

Small Businesses

Responsibility to Employees

ADDITIONAL RESOURCES

The California Department of Fair Employment and Housing, 800-884-1684, www.dfeh.ca.gov, takes complaints about discrimination and harassment and provides legal information on state employment law.

The California Department of Industrial Relations, 415-703-5070, www.dir. ca.gov, takes complaints and provides information about wage and hour issues, workplace health and safety, and workers' compensation.

California Workers' Comp: How to Take Charge When You're Injured on the Job, by Christopher A. Ball (Nolo), includes all the forms and information necessary to file and handle a workers' comp claim.

Employment Law Center of the Legal Aid Society of San Francisco, 600 Harrison Street, Suite 120, San Francisco, CA 94107, 415-864-8848, www. las-elc.org, offers information and assistance to low-income workers with legal problems. The Center also operates the Bay Area Workers' Rights Clinics, which provide direct help to employees in a variety of legal situations.

The Equal Employment Opportunity Commission, 800-669-4000, www. eeoc.gov, takes complaints about discrimination and harassment and offers legal information about federal employment law.

Equal Rights Advocates, 1663 Mission Street, Suite 250, San Francisco, CA 94103, provides general information, 415-621-0672, and advice and counseling, 800-839-4372. You can find ERA online at www.equalrights. org. Information is available on legal issues affecting women and girls, including sex discrimination, sexual harassment, and work and family concerns.

Job Accommodation Network, P.O. Box 6080, Morgantown, WV 26506, 800-526-7234, www.jan.wvu.edu, provides information and free consulting services about workplace accommodations for people with disabilities.

9to5, National Association of Working Women, 207 East Buffalo Street #211, Milwaukee, WI 53202, 800-522-0925, www.9to5.org, maintains a hotline and provides information and referrals to local groups.

National Employment Lawyers Association, 44 Montgomery Street, Suite 2080, San Francisco, CA 94104, 415-296-7629, www.nela.org, provides a directory of attorneys specializing in employment law.

Pension Rights Center, 1350 Connecticut Ave NW, Suite 206, Washington, DC 20036, www.pensionrights.org, offers free publications on pensions and retirement programs.

Positive Resource Center, 785 Market Street, 10th Floor, San Francisco, CA 94103, 415-777-0333, http://positiveresource.org, provides assistance for people with HIV who are returning to work: job referrals, computer training, resume assistance, and information about interacting with employers. The organization also provides benefits counseling to help those with HIV access public and private insurance, disability, and health care benefits.

Working for Yourself: Law & Taxes for Independent Contractors, Freelancers & Consultants, by Stephen Fishman (Nolo), provides legal information and written agreements for those who are self-employed.

Workplace Fairness, 44 Montgomery Street, Suite 2080, San Francisco, CA 94104, 415-362-7373, www.workplacefairness.org, provides comprehensive free information about workers' rights.

Your Rights in the Workplace, by Barbara Kate Repa (Nolo), is a comprehensive guide to employee rights. It includes information on state laws, resources for workers, and much more.

ACQUIRED IMMUNE DEFICIENCY SYNDROME (AIDS)

Many American workers are infected with HIV, the virus that can cause
Acquired Immune Deficiency Syndrome (AIDS). Although the virus is not
spread through the kind of casual contact that typically takes place at work,
some employers and employees have reacted to the spread of AIDS with
panic—and a strong prejudice against working with people with HIV.

California and federal courts have ruled that AIDS and HIV infection are
disabilities, so infected workers are protected by federal, state, and local
laws prohibiting discrimination against the disabled, including the federal
Americans With Disabilities Act (ADA) and California's Fair Employment
and Housing Act (FEHA). Under the ADA, it is illegal for any company
employing 15 or more people to discriminate against workers because they
are HIV-infected or have AIDS. The FEHA prohibits discrimination by any
company with five or more employees.

Employers covered by these laws must make reasonable
accommodations to allow employees with AIDS or HIV to continue
working. Such accommodations may include extended leave, reassignment
to less strenuous positions within the company, and flexible work
schedules.

Most California courts have ruled that HIV- or AIDS-infected workers
must be allowed to keep working if they can do their jobs once the
employer makes some reasonable accommodation.

In addition, a number of California municipalities, including Berkeley,
Los Angeles, and San Francisco, have enacted laws explicitly prohibiting
discrimination in employment based on AIDS.

HIV Testing

An employer cannot use the results of an HIV test as a basis for deciding
whether to hire a worker. (H & S Code § 120980.)

The laws on job discrimination based on AIDS are evolving rapidly. For
more information, contact the AIDS Legal Referral Panel, 415-701-1100,
www.alrp.org; or the California AIDS Information hotline, 800-367-2437.

CHILD LABOR

Federal law generally prohibits employing children under the age of 14. (29 U.S.C. §§ 203, 212, and 213.) A person who is at least 16 years old may be employed in nonhazardous jobs (most jobs except for mining, manufacturing, meatpacking, roofing, and excavation), as long as the job doesn't have a negative effect on the young employee's schooling or health. To work in occupations that the Department of Labor deems hazardous, the employee must be at least 18 years old. To determine what types of jobs are currently considered hazardous for the purposes of the federal Fair Labor Standards Act, call your local office of the Labor Department's Wage and Hour Division or go to the Department's website for teenage workers, www.youthrules.dol.gov.

The law restricts when and for how many hours workers ages 14 and 15 may be employed. Here are the rules:

- They may work no more than three hours on a school day and no more than 18 hours in a school week.
- They may work no more than eight hours on a nonschool day and no more than 40 hours in a nonschool week.
- During the period that starts with the day after Labor Day and ends at midnight on May 31, their workday may not begin earlier than 7 a.m. or end later than 7 p.m.
- From June 1 through Labor Day, their workday may not begin earlier than 7 a.m., but it can end as late as 9 p.m.

California law also restricts the hours of workers aged 16 and 17, as follows:

- They may work no more than four hours on a school day.
- They may not be required to work before 5 a.m. or after 10 p.m. on any day preceding a school day.
- They may not be required to work past 12:30 a.m. on any day preceding a nonschool day.
- They may work no more than eight hours a day and 48 hours per week. (Lab. Code § 1391.)

Jobs Without Restrictions

Some industries have obtained special exemptions from the legal restrictions on child labor. Children of any age may perform in television, movie, or theatrical productions, for example.

Farm Labor

Less stringent restrictions apply to children who work on farms. For example, children of any age may do nonhazardous work on a farm outside of school hours if the farm is owned or operated by their parents.

DISCRIMINATION

Many kinds of discrimination in the workplace are prohibited by local, state, and federal law.

Title VII

Title VII of the Civil Rights Act of 1964 is the primary federal law outlawing discrimination on the basis of race, skin color, gender, religion, or national origin. The Equal Employment Opportunity Commission (EEOC) is the federal agency that administers and enforces Title VII.

Title VII applies to all companies and labor unions with 15 or more employees. It also governs employment agencies, state and local governments, and apprenticeship programs. Title VII covers discrimination in every aspect of the employment relationship, from help wanted ads to workplace conditions, performance reviews, and post-employment references.

A number of other federal laws in addition to Title VII fight unfair workplace discrimination:

- The Equal Pay Act requires employers to pay equal wages to men and women performing the same jobs, with a few limited exceptions.
- The Age Discrimination in Employment Act (ADEA) prohibits workplace discrimination against employees who are at least 40 years old. The Older Workers Benefit Protection Act (OWBPA) is an amendment to the ADEA that specifically outlaws discrimination in employment benefit programs on the basis of age; it too applies only to employees age 40 and older. The OWBPA requires employers to

follow strict rules when asking older workers to give up their right to sue for age discrimination.

- The Pregnancy Discrimination Act (PDA) makes it illegal for an employer to discriminate against pregnant women in hiring, pay, benefits, or firing.
- The Americans With Disabilities Act (ADA) makes it illegal to discriminate against people because of their physical or mental disabilities.

California Fair Employment and Housing Act

Most California workers also are covered by the Fair Employment and Housing Act (FEHA), which prohibits discrimination based on race, religion, color, national origin, ancestry, physical handicap, medical condition, marital status, gender, age, pregnancy, childbirth or related medical conditions, political activity, or arrests or detentions that did not result in a criminal conviction. California law covers all workplaces with five or more employees and covers the entire employment relationship, from hiring through firing. (Gov't. Code §§ 12900-12996.) In 2003, California amended the FEHA to prohibit discrimination on the basis of gender identity, becoming the first state in the nation to protect transgendered persons from discrimination in employment and housing. (Gov't. Code §§ 12926, 12949.)

An additional state law makes it illegal to discriminate against gays and lesbians in the workplace or to coerce or influence workers' political activities. (Lab. Code §§ 1101 and 1102.)

DOMESTIC VIOLENCE

California employers must give employees who have been victims of domestic violence time off to deal with certain related issues. A worker can take time off to seek medical care for injuries; obtain services from a shelter, domestic violence program, or rape crisis center; get psychological counseling; or take steps to plan for future safety, such as relocating. California law also requires all employers—regardless of size—to allow domestic violence victims to take leave to seek legal protection (such as a restraining order) for themselves or their children, or to testify at a court hearing. Employers cannot fire or discriminate or retaliate against an employee for exercising these rights. Most of these rules apply only to companies that employ 25 or more workers. (Lab. Code §§ 230 and 230.1.)

Leave taken under this law may count against the employee's 12-week annual allotment of family and medical leave, if the employee is eligible for such leave. (See Family and Medical Leave, below.)

DRUG TESTING

Any company that intends to conduct drug testing on job candidates usually includes in its job application an agreement to submit to such testing. The applicant agrees by signing the application. If, in the process of applying for a job, you are asked to agree to drug testing, you have little choice but to agree to the tests or drop out as an applicant.

The rules are somewhat different when it comes to people who have already been hired. Many employers connected with the federal government are specifically authorized to periodically test some employees for drug use. For example, the Department of Transportation requires drug testing for some critical positions, such as airline pilots.

Private employers can usually test employees for drug and alcohol use only if it relates to performance and behavior on the job. Unless a problem surfaces that indicates an employee may be working below par or endangering the safety of others because of substance abuse, there is generally no legal right to perform a drug test. Also, employers must make reasonable efforts to safeguard the privacy of any employee who is actually enrolled in a drug treatment program. (Lab. Code §§ 1025 and 1026.)

Companies that conduct blanket drug tests of all employees or randomly test employees without justification can be sued for invasion of privacy and infliction of emotional harm. And California courts have repeatedly held that drug tests given without notice violate public policy.

ENGLISH-ONLY RULES

California law generally prohibits employers from adopting English-only policies, which require employees to speak only English on the job. Exceptions are allowed where there is a clear business necessity for the rule, such as for air traffic controllers or for those who must deal with customers who speak only English, and where there is no alternative that would achieve these goals as effectively. Employers who have a workplace rule requiring employees to speak English must first notify all employees of the rule, inform them when English must be spoken, and explain the consequences of breaking the rule.

If you believe your employer has imposed an illegal or unfair language requirement, contact the Language Rights Project of the Employment Law Center of the Legal Aid Society of San Francisco, 800-864-1664.

EQUAL PAY

The Equal Pay Act (29 U.S.C. § 206) is a federal antidiscrimination law, enforced by the Equal Employment Opportunity Commission, that requires employers to pay male and female employees equally for equal work. It also provides that fringe benefits, including pension retirement plans, must not discriminate between men and women performing equal work. Although the Act protects both men and women, it has almost always been applied to situations where women are paid less than men for doing similar jobs.

Pay systems that result in employees of one sex being paid less than the other for equal work are allowed under the Equal Pay Act only if the pay system is actually based on a factor other than gender—such as seniority, merit, or quantity or quality of production.

Jobs don't have to be identical for the courts to consider them equal, but they have to be quite similar. In general, courts have ruled that two jobs are equal when both require the same levels of skill, effort, and responsibility and are performed under similar conditions.

FAMILY AND MEDICAL LEAVE

Both the federal Family and Medical Leave Act or FMLA (29 U.S.C. §§ 2601 and following) and the California Family Rights Act (Gov. Code §12945.2) require employers to allow their employees up to twelve weeks of unpaid leave each year to care for a newborn or newly adopted child; to care for a spouse, parent, or child with a serious medical condition (California law also covers domestic partners); or to recuperate from their own serious medical condition. However, these laws apply only to companies that employ 50 or more workers within a 75-mile radius of the employee's workplace. Workers are entitled to leave only if they have been employed for at least a year, and for at least 1,250 hours in the year prior to the leave request.

Although this leave is generally unpaid, employees can receive wage replacement for some of their time off, in certain circumstances. Employees who take family medical leave to care for an ill spouse, domestic partner, parent, or child, or who take leave after the birth or placement of an adoptive child, can receive up to six weeks of partial wage replacement. Employees will be paid approximately 55% of their regular weekly pay, up to a limit of $804 per week in 2006. This money comes from employee contributions to the State Disability Insurance (SDI) fund. Those contributions increased in 2004 to fund the new leave entitlement. For more information on this program, visit the website of California's Employment Development Department, www.edd.ca.gov.

In California, workers may take up to four months of unpaid leave for pregnancy, childbirth, and related medical conditions. This leave is in addition to the time off provided by the Family Rights Act—for example, an employee could take up to four months of unpaid pregnancy and childbirth leave, then take an additional 12 weeks of family leave to care for and bond with her child. Federal and state law require employers to grant men the same options for taking leave from their jobs to care for a child as it grants to women. To do otherwise is illegal discrimination based on gender. California law also prohibits workplace discrimination based on marital status. For example, it's illegal for an employer to offer parental leave only to married employees.

Additional California laws give employees in private industry the right to take time off from work to deal with specific parental responsibilities. State law provides that:

- An employer may not discriminate against an employee who takes time off to attend a child's school conference, provided that the employee gives the employer reasonable notice of the need to attend the conference. (Lab. Code § 230.7.)
- Companies with 25 or more employees may not fire or discriminate against an employee who is a parent or guardian of any child in daycare at a licensed facility or in kindergarten through 12th grade for taking up to 40 hours leave from work each school year, per child, to visit the child's school. The time off may not exceed eight hours per calendar month. The employee must give the employer reasonable notice of the need for the leave. (Lab. Code § 230.8.)

Also see Domestic Violence, above.

FIRING

Under California law, the private employment relationship is presumed to be "at will." This means that workers may quit at any time, for any reason, and employers may fire workers at any time, for any reason, unless (1) the reason for firing is discriminatory or violates public policy or (2) the worker has an employment contract limiting the employer's right to fire at will.

Most employees who are fired have no legal right to notice, no right to contest their dismissals, and no right to severance pay. The only thing they're entitled to is a final paycheck, including all vacation pay already earned. State law gives employees the right to get their final paychecks immediately, with some exceptions for employees of the movie, petroleum, and farming industries.

Illegal Reasons for Firing

Even though employers have fairly wide latitude in deciding whether to fire workers, there are some legal limits. An employer can't fire you for a reason that's illegal. If you believe you have been fired illegally, you should seek some legal advice to find out whether you might have grounds for a lawsuit or at least some good leverage to negotiate a reinstatement or a severance package.

In California, the following are some illegal reasons for firing:

- **Discrimination.** An employer may not fire you because of your race, color, national origin, gender, gender identity, religion, disability, age (if you are at least 40 years old), marital status, sexual orientation, or medical condition. If you believe that you were fired for a discriminatory reason, you should contact the Department of Fair Employment and Housing at 800-884-1684, www.dfeh.ca.gov.
- **Retaliation.** You cannot be fired for complaining about harassment or discrimination, for filing a workers' compensation claim, for union activities or other collective actions to improve the terms and conditions of employment, for complaining about a health and safety violation, or for complaining about a wage and hour issue (for example, the employer's failure to pay overtime).

- **Violation of public policy.** If you are fired for exercising a legal right (such as the right to vote or the right to take family medical leave), refusing to break the law (for example, by refusing to submit false business tax returns), or reporting illegal conduct (whistleblowing), your employer may have violated public policy. In these situations, courts have recognized that society's interest in protecting these rights is so strong that employers may not punish employees who exercise them.

- **Breach of contract.** If you have a written employment contract, your employer must honor its terms—including any terms on when and why you can be fired—or face liability for breach of contract. Even if you don't have a written contract, you may be able to show that you were promised, implicitly or explicitly, that you wouldn't be fired without good cause. For example, if your boss repeatedly told you that your job was secure, and led you to believe, through statements in the employee handbook or other policies, that employees wouldn't be fired without a good reason, you might have a claim for breach of an implied contract.

- **Fraud.** If your employer made false promises to get you to take a job, then fired you, you may have a legal claim for fraud.

HEALTH AND SAFETY REGULATIONS

California has its own occupational safety and health program—Cal/OSHA—that protects workers' rights to safe and healthy work conditions. The law covers all workers in the state, including those employed by state and local government, but does not cover federal employees. (Lab. Code §§ 6304 and 6400.)

Cal/OSHA Requirements

Employers must have an Injury and Illness Prevention Program, which must be in writing and tailored to the needs of the individual workplace. (Lab. Code §§ 6401.7) At a minimum, each program must:

- identify who at the company is responsible for enforcing health and safety measures

- set out the employer's system for guaranteeing safe work practices, which may include training and discipline
- spell out how employees can complain about unsafe conditions and hazards in the workplace, and
- schedule periodic inspections to identify unsafe conditions and work practices.

Employers who employ fewer than 10 workers are subject to less stringent requirements. (See 8 Cal. Code. Regs § 3203 for more information on Injury and Illness Prevention Program rules.)

Depending on the types of hazards and workplaces involved, the employer's responsibility for creating and maintaining a safe workplace can include such diverse things as labeling potentially hazardous substances, upgrading or removing machinery that poses a danger, providing employees with special breathing equipment to protect workers' lungs from dust created by a manufacturing process, improving lighting above work areas, vaccinating against diseases that can be contracted at work, or even tracking the effects of workplace conditions on employees' health through periodic medical examinations.

Posting Requirements

The law also requires employers to give employees access to laws and information on workplace health and safety. Employers must display the poster "Safety and Health Protection on the Job" where it can easily be read by all employees. Employers must also post any citations issued against them by Cal/OSHA for health and safety violations.

Retaliation Is Prohibited

It is illegal for an employer to fire or punish an employee for filing a safety complaint, refusing to perform any work that would violate a safety standard or order, or participating in an investigation of a safety violation. Cal/OSHA can order an employer who violates this rule to return the employee to the job and to reimburse him or her for damages such as lost wages, the value of lost benefits, and the cost of searching for a new job.

Walking Off the Job

OSHA gives you the right to refuse to continue doing your job in extreme circumstances that represent an immediate and substantial danger to your personal safety. If you walk off a job because of a safety hazard, be sure to contact the nearest OSHA office as soon as you're out of danger.

Enforcing Your OSHA Rights

If you believe there are serious health and safety problems at your workplace, you can file a complaint by contacting the nearest OSHA office. Look in the phone book under California, State of–Department of Industrial Relations, Division of Occupational Safety and Health or Division of Labor Standards Enforcement. Or you can fill out a complaint online by visiting Cal/OSHA's website at www.dir.ca.gov/DOSH.

HEALTH INSURANCE

Workers who have been covered by health insurance on the job and who have not been fired for gross misconduct may have the right to continue health insurance coverage when employment ends. Under the federal Consolidated Omnibus Budget Reconciliation Act, or COBRA (29 U.S.C. § 1162), employers must offer a former employee the option of continuing to be covered by the company's group health insurance plan at the worker's own expense for at least 18 months after employment ends. Coverage for family members is also included. In some other circumstances, such as the death of the employee, that employee's dependents can continue coverage for up to 36 months.

COBRA also requires that the cost of continuing group health coverage must be similar to the cost of covering people who are still working for the employer.

IMMIGRANT WORKERS

The Immigration Reform and Control Act, or IRCA (8 U.S.C. §§ 1101 and following), is a federal law that restricts the flow of foreign workers into American workplaces. IRCA covers all employees hired since November 6, 1986, except those who work occasionally in private homes as domestic workers. Independent contractors aren't covered.

Under IRCA, it is illegal for an employer to:

- hire a worker who the employer knows has not been granted permission by the U.S. Citizenship and Immigration Service (USCIS) to be employed in the United States (through a green card, visa, or USCIS work permit)
- hire any worker who has not completed USCIS Form I-9, the Employment Eligibility Verification Form
- continue to employ an unauthorized worker—often called an illegal alien or undocumented alien—hired after November 6, 1986, or
- discriminate against workers based on their citizenship status (as long as they are legally authorized to work in this country).

Filing USCIS Form I-9

Employees must fill out their section of Form I-9 by the end of the first day on a new job. They then have three business days to present the new employer with documents that prove their identity and eligibility to work in the United States.

Native-born adults can typically prove employment eligibility by producing a Social Security card, a birth certificate issued by the state of birth, or a current U.S. passport. If you don't have a passport, a current California driver's license or photo identification card will typically prove your legal identity.

Non-native-born adults can prove identity using a passport of their home country. To prove eligibility to work, however, they will also have to show a green card, visa of a type that allows work, or work permit ("Employment Authorization Document").

INDEPENDENT CONTRACTORS

Independent contractors are not protected by most of the workplace rights guaranteed by law to employees. The relationship between independent contractors and the company or person paying for their work is covered not by the law of the workplace, but by contract law.

An independent contractor is a businessperson—someone who does contract, consulting, or freelance work for a company, often on a project basis. For example, a computer consultant might receive a flat fee to install a software system and train a company's employees on how to use it. To be considered an independent contractor, a person must control both the outcome of the project and how it is accomplished. Also, an independent contractor must offer services to the public at large, not just to one company.

Employee or Independent Contractor?

Common examples of those who typically work as independent contractors are lawyers, accountants, decorators, and computer consultants. But to avoid paying benefits (and employment taxes), some employers try to classify people who should be considered employees as independent contractors. The factors the IRS uses to determine whether a worker is an employee or a contractor are summarized in the chart below. The IRS is primarily concerned with:

- your behavior on the job
- your finances, and
- your relationship to the hiring firm.

Factors the IRS Considers

CONTROL OVER YOUR WORK

You will more likely be considered an independent contractor (IC) if you:
- are not given instructions on how to work by the hiring firm, and/or
- provide your own training.

You will more likely be considered an employee if you:
- receive instructions that you must follow about how to do your work from the hiring firm, and/or
- receive detailed training from the hiring firm.

CONTROL OVER YOUR FINANCES

You will more likely be considered an IC if you:
- have a significant investment in your own equipment and facilities
- pay business or travel expenses yourself
- make your services available to the public
- are paid by the job, and/or
- have opportunity for profit or loss.

You will more likely be considered an employee if you:
- have equipment and facilities provided by the hiring firm free of charge
- get reimbursed for your business or traveling expenses
- make no effort to market your services to the public
- are paid by the hour or other unit of time, or
- have no opportunity for profit or loss—for example, because you're paid by the hour and have all expenses reimbursed.

RELATIONSHIP OF THE WORKER AND HIRING FIRM

You will more likely be considered an IC if you:
- don't receive employee benefits such as health insurance
- sign an IC agreement with the hiring firm
- can't quit or be fired at will, or
- are performing services that are not a part of the hiring firm's regular business activities.

You will more likely be considered an employee if you:
- receive employee benefits from the hiring firm
- have no written IC agreement
- can quit at any time without incurring any liability to the hiring firm
- can be fired at any time by the hiring firm, and/or
- are performing services that are part of the hiring firm's core business.

LIE DETECTOR TESTS

The federal Employee Polygraph Protection Act (29 U.S.C. § 2001) and a similar state law (Lab. Code § 432.2) virtually outlaw the use of lie detectors in connection with employment. That law covers all private employers in interstate commerce, which includes just about every private company that uses the U.S. mail or the telephone system.

Under the federal Act, it is illegal for all private companies to:

- require, request, suggest, or cause any employee or job applicant to submit to a lie detector test
- use, accept, refer to, or inquire about the results of any lie detector test conducted on an employee or job applicant
- dismiss, discipline, discriminate against, or threaten to take action against any employee or job applicant who refuses to take a lie detector test, or
- discriminate against or fire those who use its protections.

Under California law, employers may ask employees or applicants to take a lie detector test, but only if the employer first advises them, in writing, of their legal right to refuse.

When Lie Detector Tests Can Be Used

The Employee Polygraph Protection Act allows lie detector tests to be used in connection with jobs in security and handling drugs, or in investigating a specific theft or other suspected crime. However, employees who will be required to take a test as part of an investigation of an employment-related crime must be given written notice of their rights, as well as a copy of all questions that will be asked during the test.

The Act does not apply to—and lie detector tests are allowed for— employees of federal, state, or local government. The Act also doesn't apply to certain jobs that involve sensitive work relating to national defense.

Enforcing the Law

The Employee Polygraph Protection Act is enforced by the U.S. Department of Labor. If you have questions about whether the Act applies to your job, or if you suspect that you have been illegally subjected to polygraph testing, call the Labor Department's Wage and Hour Division or visit the Department's website at www.dol.gov/esa/whd.

PERSONNEL FILES

The best way to find out what a company knows about you, or what it is saying about you to businesses and people outside the company who inquire, is to obtain a copy of your employment file. California law gives employees broad access to their employment records. Employees have the right to demand a copy of any document they have signed concerning their employment. Employees also have the right to inspect the employer's records relating to the employee's performance or to any grievance concerning the employee.

Each employer must make these records available to employees in one of the following ways:

- The employer must keep a copy of the records at the place where the employee works.
- The employer must make the records available to the employee at the place where the employee works within a reasonable time after the employee asks to see the records.
- The employer must permit the employee to inspect the records at the place where the records are kept.

Employees do not have the right to see every document in their personnel files: Records relating to a criminal investigation and letters of reference do not have to be disclosed. (Lab. Code §§ 432, 1198.5.)

PREGNANCY

The federal Pregnancy Discrimination Act outlaws discrimination against women on the basis of pregnancy, childbirth, or any related medical condition. The Act is part of Title VII of the Civil Rights Act of 1964, 42 U.S.C. §§ 2000e and following. It only applies to employers with 15 or more employees.

The Act provides that if an employee is temporarily unable to perform her job because of a pregnancy-related condition, an employer must treat her as it does any other "temporarily disabled employee." It may arrange for a pregnant woman to do modified tasks, give alternate work assignments, give disability leave, or provide for leave without pay—and it must make such arrangements if it does so for other disabled employees.

The law also specifies that:

- An employer cannot refuse to hire or promote a woman solely because she is pregnant, as long as she is able to perform the key functions of the job.
- Pregnant employees who need time off from work must receive the same treatment as employees who take time off because of other medical conditions. This protection includes women who must take time off from work to recover from an abortion.
- An employer cannot refuse to provide health insurance benefits that cover pregnancy if it provides such benefits to cover other medical conditions.
- A woman cannot be required to take a leave from work during her pregnancy if she remains able to do her job.
- A woman cannot be forced to take a minimum amount of time off from work after giving birth.
- An employer cannot limit pregnancy benefits to married employees.

California law, which applies to all employers regardless of size, requires employers to give female employees up to four months of unpaid leave for pregnancy or childbirth. (Gov't. Code § 12945.) Their jobs must be held open for them on return just as jobs are held open for employees on family or medical leave. See Family and Medical Leave, above.

PSYCHOLOGICAL TESTING

Some employers use written questionnaires to help them try to predict whether or not a person would lie, steal, or be unreliable if hired for a particular job.

The legality of these tests is very questionable, particularly in California, where courts have held that psychological tests may violate the right to privacy guaranteed by the state constitution. Employees have filed—and won—lawsuits challenging psychological testing on a variety of legal grounds, including:

- violation of their right to privacy (where the test asks questions on personal topics, such as religious beliefs, sexual practices, or sexual orientation), and
- discrimination (where the test has the effect of screening out applicants in a protected group, such as women or African Americans).

Psychological tests may also qualify as "medical tests" when they elicit answers that suggest a mental disorder or impairment. Such tests could be illegal under the Americans With Disabilities Act and California's Fair Employment and Housing Act, which prohibit employers from asking about an applicant's medical history or conducting a medical exam before making a job offer.

SEXUAL HARASSMENT

Sexual harassment is any unwelcome sexual advance or conduct that creates an intimidating, hostile, or offensive work environment. Both federal and state laws prohibit such behavior. In the workplace, sexual harassment ranges from sexist jokes and innuendos to outright sexual assault. Although the laws protect men as well as women from being harassed at work and protect employees from same-sex harassment, most cases and complaints involve men harassing women.

What Employees Can Do

If you feel you are being harassed at work, you have several options. You should start by taking action within your workplace, such as confronting the harasser and demanding a stop to the harassment. If the company has an internal policy or procedure that explains how to complain about harassment internally, you should follow it—not only to stop the harassment, but also to protect your legal rights if you later decide to sue. Under federal law, an employee who wants to hold an employer liable for certain kinds of harassment must make an internal complaint if the company has an established, effective complaint procedure. California has not adopted this requirement, but it does allow employers to limit their liability in a lawsuit, if the employee could have prevented some or all of the harm she suffered had she made an internal complaint.

If you don't get satisfaction from following internal complaint procedures, you can take legal action:

- **File a complaint with a government agency.** Filing a complaint under federal or state law sets in motion an investigation that may resolve the complaint. It is also a necessary first step if you later want to file a harassment lawsuit. Because sexual harassment is prohibited under both state law (the Fair Employment and Housing Act or FEHA,

Gov't. Code §§ 12900 to 12996) and federal law (the Civil Rights Act of 1964), you may file your complaint with either a state or federal agency. If your employer has fewer than 15 employees (the minimum for federal discrimination claims), you should file with the state, because California's antiharassment laws apply to all employers, regardless of size. Because a claim filed in the FEHA office is automatically filed with the EEOC as well, you need not agonize over which to choose. But you should file your complaint as soon as possible. You must file a federal claim within 300 days (and a state claim within one year) after the harassment occurred. The advantage of filing and pursuing a state claim is that you are allowed to collect as high an amount in damages as you are able to prove. In federal claims, the amount you can collect will be limited, depending on how many employees there are in your workplace.

- **File a lawsuit.** You can also file a private lawsuit for sexual harassment or under some other legal theory, such as intentional infliction of emotional distress or assault. You will probably need to hire a lawyer to help you.

Filing a Harassment Claim

To file a harassment claim with the state agency, contact the California Department of Fair Employment and Housing, 800-884-1684. To file a complaint with the EEOC, call 800-669-4000—you will be automatically connected to your nearest office. (You can also find a list of EEOC offices on the EEOC website at www.eeoc.gov.)

SMOKING POLICIES

California law prohibits anyone from smoking in an enclosed place of employment. In addition, California employers may not knowingly or intentionally permit smoking in an enclosed place of employment. There are several exceptions: Smoking may be permitted in 65% of the rooms in a hotel or motel, designated lobby areas, meeting and banquet rooms (except when food is being served), tobacco shops, and warehouses.

Employers must also take reasonable steps to prevent nonemployees from smoking in nonsmoking areas, and may not require employees to enter a smoking-designated area as part of their work duties. Local ordinances may be more restrictive, but not less so. (Lab. Code § 6404.5.)

UNEMPLOYMENT INSURANCE

Unemployment insurance, also called UI or unemployment compensation, provides you with some income replacement if you lose your job. The UI program is run jointly by the federal government and the states, and is paid for primarily by a tax on employers. Eligible employees can receive between 12 and 26 weeks of full benefits during the year after they file a claim, depending on their prior earnings.

Unemployment insurance covers most employees at all levels, including part-time and temporary workers. Those not covered include people employed by small farms; casual domestic workers and babysitters; newspaper carriers under age 18; children employed by their parents, spouses, or children; employees of religious organizations; and elected officials.

Eligibility for Benefits

To qualify for benefits, you must have left your job for "good cause," which includes leaving because you were laid off, the job was eliminated, or your employer went bankrupt. Good cause also includes leaving because of excessive cost or time to travel to work, because a doctor advised you to change jobs for health reasons, or to accompany your spouse to a new locality. In addition, you must:

- be available to be recalled to your old job or to work in a similar one
- be physically able to perform your old job or a similar one, and
- be actively seeking work in a reasonable and customary way.

Even if you're covered by unemployment insurance and otherwise eligible to receive it, you may be disqualified from receiving benefits if you:

- refused to accept a similar job without good reason
- quit your job without good reason
- lied or failed to disclose a material fact in applying for benefits, or
- were fired from your job for misconduct—such as stealing, drinking, or sleeping on the job.

However, mere inefficiency, poor job performance because of inability or incapacity, or inadvertent mistakes will not be considered job misconduct that will disqualify you from receiving benefits.

Calculating Benefits

To calculate your benefits, the unemployment insurance office uses a rather complicated formula premised on the base period of your wages. The weekly amount you may receive ranges from $40 to $450, depending on the amount of your previous earnings.

To file a claim, go to the nearest unemployment insurance office or check the Employment Development Department (EDD) website at www.edd. ca.gov. After you file, you will have to follow up periodically to state that you are still unemployed, and to show that you are actively seeking work.

If your claim is denied, you'll be notified in writing of that decision, the reason for it, and the number of days you have to appeal the decision. (Unemp. Ins. Code §§ 1251 and following.)

You can find a list of offices and an online claim form, as well as lots of helpful information on unemployment insurance, at the EDD website.

UNIONS

The National Labor Relations Act, or NLRA (29 U.S.C. §§ 151 and following), requires most employers and unions to negotiate fairly with each other until they agree to a contract that spells out the terms and conditions of employment for the unionized workers—including pay rates, hours, and work conditions.

Generally, the courts have ruled that employees have rights to:

- discuss union membership and read and distribute union-related literature during nonwork time in nonwork areas (such as an employee lounge)
- sign a card asking an employer to recognize a union and bargain with it, sign petitions and grievances concerning employment terms and conditions, and ask coworkers to sign petitions and grievances, and
- display pro-union sentiments by wearing message-bearing items such as hats, pins, and T-shirts on the job.

An employer may not:
- grant or promise employees promotions, pay raises, desirable work assignments, or other special favors if they oppose unionizing efforts
- dismiss, harass, reassign, or otherwise punish or discipline employees (or threaten to do so) if they support unionization
- close down a worksite or transfer work or reduce benefits to pressure employees not to support unionization, or
- use state funds to assist, promote, or deter union organizing, if the employer is a state contractor, conducts business on state property pursuant to a contract or concession agreement, or receives more than $10,000 from the state in any year for participating in a state program.

The NLRA also prohibits unions from interfering with employees' rights to reject or change union membership. Unions may not:
- restrain or coerce employees to keep them from exercising their rights under the NLRA; this includes violence and threats of violence against people who reject union membership
- cause or encourage an employer to discriminate against an employee or group of employees because of their de-unionization activities
- interfere in any way with an employee's right to freely express opinions on union membership
- fail or refuse to bargain in good faith with an employer, or
- prevent employees from going to work by using such tactics as mass picketing.

In general, the courts have recognized an employee's right to refuse to join a union on religious grounds. However, the employee may still be required to pay union dues and fees. Employees who object to this requirement on religious grounds or because they don't support the union's political activities can arrange to pay the dues amount to a nonlabor, nonreligious charitable organization.

Additional Information

Contact the local office of the NLRB, listed in the federal government section of the telephone directory. You can also visit the Board's website at www.nlrb.gov. If you are having specific problems with a union at work, contact the California AFL-CIO headquarters at the California Labor Federation, 600 Grand Avenue, Suite 410, Oakland, CA, 94610, 510-663-4000, www.calaborfed.org.

VACATIONS

No state or federal law requires an employer to offer paid vacation. However, California employers are subject to some strict legal controls regarding how and when employees must be paid for vacation time, if the employer does choose to offer it. (See Wage and Hour Restrictions.)

WAGE AND HOUR RESTRICTIONS

The federal Fair Labor Standards Act, or FLSA (29 U.S.C. §§ 201 and following), establishes minimum pay and hour rules. The FLSA applies to employers with annual sales of $500,000 or more and employers that are engaged in interstate commerce, which includes nearly all workplaces.

Some employees are exempt from the FLSA, including:

- executive, administrative, and professional workers
- employees in training
- transportation industry workers
- employees who work outside the country
- people with severe physical handicaps employed in special workshops
- volunteers in nonprofit organizations
- mental patients or patient-workers at rehabilitation facilities, and
- prison laborers.

Minimum Wage

The FLSA and California law require that you be paid at least the minimum wage—currently $6.75 per hour under California law. Employers may pay on the basis of time at work, piece rates, or some other measurement, but in all cases, an employee's pay divided by the hours worked during the pay period must equal or exceed the minimum wage. Some additional rules on pay rates:

- **Tips.** California employers may not take their employees' tips or credit those tips against the minimum wage. The employer must pay at least the minimum hourly wage; tips earned are in addition to this compensation. Employees may be required to pool tips or "tip out" with other employees who also provided services to the customer. For example, in a restaurant, wait staff might be required to pool their tips with bussers and food preparers.

- **Commissions.** Commissions paid for sales may take the place of wages for purposes of the FLSA. However, if the commissions do not equal the minimum wage, the employer must make up the difference.

Overtime

Under California law, eligible employees who work more than eight hours in a day or more than 40 hours in one week must be paid at least one and one-half times their regular rate of pay for all hours worked in excess of eight or 40. However, many employees are not eligible for overtime pay, including managers, supervisors, high-level decision makers, administrators, professionals, and others.

Final Paychecks

State law controls how soon your final paycheck must be given to you if you are fired or quit work. If you're fired, you have the right to get your final paycheck immediately—with some special exceptions for employees of the movie, petroleum, and farming industries. If you quit, you are entitled to your paycheck within 72 hours, or immediately if you've given 72 hours' notice. (Lab. Code §§ 201 and 202.) Employers may pay you through direct deposit, if you received your wages that way while employed.

Some counties, cities, and towns have passed their own wage laws. Check with the legal department of the county or municipality in which you work.

Wage and Hour Information

For more information about the FLSA or to file a complaint, contact your local office of the Wage and Hour Division of the U.S. Department of Labor. You can find a list of offices—and information on federal wage and hour laws—at the Division's website at www.dol.gov/esa/whd.

For information about California wage and hour laws, contact the California Department of Industrial Relations at 888-275-9243, or refer to the Department's website at www.dir.ca.gov.

WORKERS' COMPENSATION

The workers' compensation system provides benefits and income to employees who are injured or become ill because of their jobs. The insured worker pays no premiums and no deductible; the system is funded primarily by insurance premiums paid by employers. If an injured employee is killed on the job, benefits may also extend to the worker's dependents. In most circumstances, workers' compensation protects employers from being sued for work-related injuries or deaths—workers whose injuries are covered by workers' compensation cannot file a lawsuit against their employer for the same injuries.

To be covered by workers' compensation, the injury needn't be caused by a sudden accident, such as a fall. With a few exceptions, any injury that occurs in connection with work is covered.

A common illness becomes an occupational illness for purposes of workers' compensation when the nature of a job increases the worker's chances of suffering from that disease. Illnesses that are the gradual result of work conditions—for example, emotional illness, repetitive motion injuries, and stress-related digestive problems—increasingly are being recognized by the courts as covered by workers' compensation insurance. Particularly for psychiatric and other stress-related injuries, however, the injured worker must prove that the job itself mostly contributed to the injury.

The California workers' compensation system entitles workers to receive:

- **Medical treatment** necessary to cure or relieve the effects of an accident or injury caused at work. This includes doctors' bills, hospitalization, physical restoration, surgical and chiropractic care, nursing services, dental care, prescriptions, X-rays, laboratory studies, and other necessary and reasonable care ordered by a physician.
- **Temporary disability payments.** The employee is entitled to a portion of his or her wages while off work and recovering from the illness or injury. This amount is not subject to income tax.
- **Permanent disability payments.** A worker whose ability to participate in the open job market is impaired will receive monetary compensation. An employee's benefit may be increased if the injury was due to the employer's willful misconduct.

- **Vocational rehabilitation.** Workers who can't return to their jobs due to the injury may be entitled to participate in a back-to-work program, which may include job modification or retraining.

Filing a workers' compensation claim. The first step in every workers' compensation claim is to inform your employer of your injury as soon as possible and get any medical care required. Under new rules adopted in 2004, you may be required to see a doctor selected and approved by your employer, rather than your own doctor, if you want to be reimbursed.

Typically, your employer will have a claim form for you to fill out or will obtain a form quickly. Your employer then submits the paperwork to the proper insurance carrier. You must also file a separate claim with the Workers' Compensation Appeals Board, the agency that oversees workers' compensation in California.

For more information or to file a claim, contact the local office of the Division of Worker's Compensation, listed in the state government section of your telephone directory. You can also refer to the Division's website at www.dir.ca.gov/DWC. For fact sheets and other information on workers' compensation, including details on the 2004 changes to the workers' compensation system, check out the website of the Employment Law Center of the Legal Aid Society of San Francisco, www.las-elc.org. ■

Government Benefits

Many government programs provide food, housing, income, and medical benefits to needy Californians. Here we cover some programs that are run by the state or are jointly administered by federal and state agencies.

California or U.S. residency or citizenship is required for nearly all government benefit programs.

TOPICS

Disability Insurance

Medi-Cal

Medicare

Social Security

Supplemental Security Income

Veterans' Benefits

RELATED TOPICS

Citizens' Rights

California Citizenship and Residency

United States Citizenship

Landlords and Tenants

Evictions

ADDITIONAL RESOURCES

Social Security, Medicare & Government Pensions, by Joseph Matthews with Dorothy Matthews Berman (Nolo), explains the rules of these federal programs and discusses how to deal with the government bureaucracies.

Long-Term Care: How to Plan & Pay for It, by Joseph Matthews (Nolo), explains the Medi-Cal benefits available for long-term home health care and nursing facility care.

The Clearinghouse Review, a periodical published primarily for Legal Aid and Legal Services lawyers, contains articles on all federal government benefits programs.

Nolo's Guide to Social Security Disability: Getting & Keeping Your Benefits, by David Morton, III, M.D. (Nolo), explains eligibility, medical determinations of disability, and how to apply for federal benefits.

U.S. Immigration Made Easy, by Ilona Bray (Nolo), explains many ways to get permanent resident status.

Fiancé & Marriage Visas: A Couple's Guide to U.S. Immigration, by Ilona Bray (Nolo), explains the law and procedures for getting permanent resident status through marriage.

Becoming a U.S. Citizen: A Guide to the Law, Exam & Interview, by Ilona Bray (Nolo), explains how green card holders can apply to naturalize.

DISABILITY INSURANCE

State and federal disability insurance programs are designed to help disabled workers who can't work. However, these programs differ regarding who is eligible, how much they'll receive in benefits , and for how long. You may also be eligible for private disability benefits from your employer.

Federal Benefits

If you have a permanent or long-term disability, you can apply for federal disability benefits distributed through the Social Security program. To qualify, you must not only be disabled, but also be eligible for Social Security based on your work history. Your dependents can also receive benefits under this program.

To be eligible, you must meet both of the following criteria:

- **Be disabled.** This means that you have a physical or mental impairment that prevents you from doing any substantial gainful work—that is, work for which you can expect to receive more than $860 per month. The impairment must be expected to last at least 12 months or to result in your death. Your disability must be verified by a doctor.

- **Have the required number of work credits.** These credits are calculated by Social Security based on the number of calendar quarters you've worked in covered employment. Most people who have worked at least a few years and paid into the Social Security fund are covered.

You can apply for Social Security benefits at any Social Security Administration office. Benefits don't begin until six months after the onset of the disability. You may be eligible for back payments if you wait to apply, but back payments are limited to the 12 months before you filed your application.

The amount of your payments is based on your salary or wage history. The amount won't be as much as you made before your injury.

For more information, see the Social Security website at www .socialsecurity.gov.

State Disability Insurance (SDI)

SDI is a California program for workers who are temporarily or permanently disabled. It is much more inclusive than the federal program. (Unemp. Ins. Code §§ 2601 and following.)

You are eligible to receive SDI if your doctor certifies that you have any non-work-related physical or mental illness or injury that prevents you from doing your regular or customary work. Elective surgery, pregnancy, childbirth, adoption, and related conditions are all included as disabilities, as is being quarantined by a health officer or being treated in a residential facility for acute alcoholism or drug-induced illness.

You cannot receive SDI if any of the following are true:

- You left your job and were not actively looking for work when you became disabled.
- You are already collecting workers' compensation in an amount greater than or equal to what your SDI benefit would be (you can collect the difference if your workers' compensation payments are less than your SDI benefits).
- You are receiving unemployment insurance benefits.
- You are incarcerated or become disabled while committing a felony.
- You are receiving full wages from your employer.

To apply, you and your doctor must fill out a form. You can get the form from your local SDI office (a division of the Employment Development Department), from the Employment Development Department in Sacramento, or online at www.edd.ca.gov (under "How to File a Claim," click "Disability Insurance," then "Forms and Publications"). You must file for benefits no earlier than nine days but no later than 49 days after your disability starts.

For the first week after you file your application, you are not eligible for any benefits. After that week, if you meet the other requirements, you will begin receiving checks. It may take up to two weeks for your first check to arrive.

How much you'll receive is based on your earnings during a 12-month period ending about six months before your disability. When you get an application form, you will also receive instructions for figuring out your precise benefit amount.

MEDI-CAL

Medi-Cal (called Medicaid outside of California) is a program established by the federal government and administered by the state that helps pay medical costs for qualified needy people. (42 U.S.C. § 1396(a)-(q).) It is available only to individuals who have limited incomes and assets. If you meet the eligibility requirement for both programs, you may be able to receive both Medicare (a federal program, discussed below) and Medi-Cal benefits.

Eligibility

If you are receiving Supplemental Security Income (SSI), CalWORKS refugee assistance, or foster care or adoption assistance benefits, you are automatically eligible for Medi-Cal. Otherwise, to apply for Medi-Cal you must be one of the following:

- the parent or caretaker relative of children under 21 years old living in your home, where the other parent is deceased, incapacitated, unemployed, or absent from the home
- under 21 yourself
- age 65 or over
- disabled or blind
- diagnosed with cervical or breast cancer
- pregnant
- a refugee who has been living in the U.S. less than eight months, or
- living in a skilled nursing or intermediate care facility.

Only those who have limited resources qualify for Medi-Cal—usually you must have no more than $6,000 in assets (adjusted annually). Not counted in your available assets are your home and your car. Your income must also be limited—but state authorities subtract your actual medical bills when evaluating your income and assets for Medi-Cal eligibility.

Generally, Medi-Cal won't consider the income or assets of your children or any other relatives in deciding your eligibility, unless you receive regular financial support from a relative. If you live with your spouse, his or her income will be counted as your income. Different rules apply if your husband or wife is in a nursing facility.

To apply for Medi-Cal, you or your representative may file a written application in person at the local county social services office, or you can download an application and mail it in according to the instructions at www.dhs.ca.gov/mcs/medi-calhome/MC210.htm.

Coverage

Medi-Cal covers a wide range of treatment and services. The care or service must be prescribed by a doctor and provided by a doctor or facility that "participates" in Medi-Cal. Also, inpatient services must be approved as "medically necessary" by the facility. And Medi-Cal coverage for certain medical services must be approved by a Medi-Cal consultant before you receive them.

Hospitals, doctors, and other providers of medical care that accept Medi-Cal patients must accept Medi-Cal's payment as payment in full. If you're eligible for both Medicare and Medi-Cal, and you're treated by a medical facility or doctor that accepts Medi-Cal patients, the treating physician must accept from Medicare and Medi-Cal the total fee that Medicare determines is reasonable. You cannot be billed for any extra amounts for the covered services.

MEDICARE

Medicare is a federal program designed to help seniors and some disabled Americans pay for medical costs. The program is divided into three parts: Part A is hospital insurance, Part B is medical insurance, and Part D is prescription drug coverage.

Part A: Hospital Insurance

These people are automatically eligible to receive Part A coverage:

- those 65 or older and eligible for Social Security retirement benefits or for civil service retirement benefits
- those under 65 who have been entitled to Social Security disability benefits for 24 months, or
- anyone who has permanent kidney failure requiring dialysis or a kidney transplant.

If you have any trouble qualifying for Medicare based on kidney failure, contact the National Kidney Foundation, 30 East 33rd Street, New York, NY 10016, 800-622-9010, www.kidney.org.

If you're 65 or over but not automatically eligible for Part A insurance, you can still enroll in the Medicare hospital insurance program. You must pay a monthly premium of up to $393, depending on the number of work credits you have (2006 rules). The premium increases by 10% for each year after your 65th birthday during which you're not enrolled.

You will also have to pay an initial "hospital insurance deductible," $952 in 2006, which increases every year. Part A hospital insurance pays a portion of hospital and inpatient treatment costs. However, only treatment that is medically reasonable and necessary is covered. The hospital or skilled nursing facility must be approved by Medicare and accept Medicare payment, and the specific care and treatment you receive must be prescribed by a doctor.

Among the specific things Part A insurance pays while you're in the hospital are:

- a semi-private room (two to four beds per room) and all your meals, including any special medically required diets
- regular nursing services
- special care units, such as intensive care, coronary care, or a private hospital room if medically necessary
- drugs, medical supplies, and appliances furnished by the facility (casts, splints, wheelchair)
- hospital lab tests, X-rays, and radiation treatment billed by the hospital
- operating and recovery room costs
- blood transfusions over three pints
- rehabilitation services while you're in the hospital or nursing facility, and
- part-time skilled nursing care and physical therapy and speech therapy provided in the hospital or nursing facility.

Part A insurance does not pay for:

- television, radio, or telephone in your hospital room
- private-duty nurses
- a private room, unless medically necessary, or
- the first three pints of blood you receive, unless you make arrangements for their replacement.

Part B: Medical Insurance

Part B medical insurance pays some of the costs of treatment by your doctor either in or out of the hospital, and some medical expenses incurred outside the hospital.

Anyone who is age 65 or older and a U.S. citizen or lawful permanent resident who has lived in the U.S. with a green card for five years is eligible. If you want Part B medical insurance, you must enroll in the program and pay a monthly premium ($88.50 in 2006). In most years, this premium is raised slightly on January 1.

Part B insurance pays only a fraction of most people's medical bills. First, you must pay an annual deductible ($124 in 2006). Also, many major medical expenses are not covered. For treatment that is covered, Medicare pays only 80% of what it considers to be a reasonable charge for the doctor's services—which may be much less than the doctor charged you.

Part B insurance pays for:

- doctors' services, including a one-time physical within the first six months of your Part B coverage, and surgery, provided at a hospital, at the doctor's office, or at home
- mammograms, bone density tests, and Pap smears for women patients
- colorectal cancer screening, if a doctor deems it necessary
- prostate cancer screening for men over 55
- cholesterol tests
- medical services provided by nurses, surgical assistants, or laboratory or X-ray technicians
- services provided by pathologists or radiologists while you're an inpatient at a hospital
- outpatient hospital treatment, such as emergency room or clinic charges,
  X-rays, and injections
- an annual flu shot
- diabetes screening, supplies, and self-management training
- an ambulance, if required for a trip to or from a hospital or skilled nursing facility
- drugs or other medicine administered to you at the hospital or doctor's office
- medical equipment and supplies, such as splints, casts, prosthetic devices, body braces, heart pacemakers, corrective lenses after a cataract operation, oxygen equipment, glucose monitoring equipment for diabetes patients, wheelchairs, and hospital beds

- some kinds of oral surgery
- some of the cost of outpatient physical and speech therapy
- day treatment for mental health
- manual manipulation of out-of-place vertebrae by a chiropractor, and
- part-time skilled nursing care and physical therapy and speech therapy provided in your home.

Medicare Part B medical insurance does not pay for:

- routine physical examinations
- treatment that isn't "medically necessary," including some elective and most cosmetic surgery and virtually all forms of alternative medical care such as acupuncture, acupressure, and homeopathy
- vaccinations and immunizations
- drugs—prescription or not—that you can administer or take yourself at home
- routine eye or hearing examinations, eye glasses, contact lenses (except after a cataract operation), or hearing aids
- general dental or periodontal work, and
- routine foot care.

Part D: Prescription Drug Coverage

As of January 1, 2006, Medicare began covering some of the costs of prescription medications you take at home. This Medicare Part D benefit is administered through private insurance companies that offer Medicare-approved prescription drug plans, and through Medicare Advantage managed care plans that include a Part D drug benefit. The Part D program replaces drug coverage through medigap plans, many managed care plans, Medicare drug discount cards, and most Medicaid coverage. It does not replace employer-sponsored prescription drug coverage for Medicare beneficiaries if that coverage is at least equal to the coverage offered by a basic Medicare Part D plan. For many people, Medicare Part D reduces their out-of-pocket costs for prescription drugs.

Anyone who is entitled to Medicare Part A coverage (whether actually enrolled in it or not) or who is currently enrolled in Medicare Part B, may join a Medicare Part D plan. This is true regardless of whether a persons' Medicare eligibility is based on age or disability. Except for people who also receive benefits from Medicaid (Medi-Cal in California), enrollment in Part D is voluntary.

The cost structure of Medicare Part D is complicated. If you qualify for a low-income subsidy, the cost for prescription drugs is minimal. Most people, however, will pay a monthly premium, an annual deductible, and a co-payment for each prescription they fill. In 2006, the average premium for Part D coverage is about $32 per month, the average annual deductible is $250, and the average copayment is 25% of the cost of covered drugs. It is important to understand that each Part D prescription drug plan will cover only those drugs specifically included on its "formulary" (a list of the drugs the plan covers). Before selecting a plan, be sure to find out whether the medications you regularly take are covered.

Medicare Part D is mandatory for people who are also enrolled in Medicaid. For everyone else, enrollment is optional. But, Medicare has created a financial penalty for those who delay enrolling. For every month you delay enrolling after you first become eligible, your premium will be 1% higher. And that increase is permanent. For example, if you wait to join a Part D plan for two years after you are first eligible for Part D coverage, you will always pay 24% (1% per month for 24 months) more in premiums for any plan you join. Because of this penalty, it makes sense for most people to join a Part D plan as soon as possible.

To figure out which Part D plan is best for you, there are several agencies that will help:

- The Centers for Medicare and Medicaid Services (CMS), the federal agency that administers the Medicare program, provides personalized help in locating Part D plans. Contact CMS at 1-800-MEDICARE (1-800-633-4227) or www.medicare.gov.
- Every state has a certified program that provides free advice to consumers about Medicare, Medicaid, and other health insurance matters. Contact the State Health Insurance Assistance Program (SHIP) or Health Insurance Counseling and Advocacy Program (HICAP) office near you.
- Your state's Department of Insurance.

SOCIAL SECURITY

Social Security is a combination of federal programs designed to pay benefits to workers and their dependents. (42 U.S.C. §§ 301 and following.) Benefits are paid based on the worker's average wage in jobs covered by Social Security over his or her working life. The three basic categories of benefits under Social Security are:

- **Retirement benefits.** You may choose to begin receiving your retirement benefits any time after you reach age 62, but the amount of benefits goes up for each year you wait to retire until you reach age 70.
- **Dependents' and survivors' benefits.** If you're a spouse, age 62 or older, of a retired or disabled worker, or a surviving spouse, age 60 or older, of a deceased worker who would have qualified for retirement or disability benefits, you and your children may be entitled to benefits based on the worker's earning record. You may also be eligible for these benefits if you're 62 or older and divorced, if your marriage to the worker lasted at least ten years, you've been divorced at least two years, and you have not remarried.
- **Disability benefits.** See Disability Insurance.

Qualifying for Benefits

The specific requirements within each program vary. However, to qualify for all benefits, the worker must have worked in "covered employment" for a sufficient number of years, which differs depending on when he or she reaches age 62, becomes disabled, or dies. Any job or self-employment from which Social Security taxes are reported is covered employment.

The worker must have accumulated enough "work credits" from covered employment to be covered by Social Security. Work credits are measured in quarter-years (January through March is the first quarter of each year, April through June is the second, and so on). The worker receives credit for every quarter in which he or she earned more than the required minimum amount of money. The number of work credits the worker needs depends on the benefits for which the worker applies and the age at which he or she applies.

If the worker is eligible for benefits, the amount he or she will receive is determined by the worker's history of all reported earnings in covered employment since beginning to work.

SUPPLEMENTAL SECURITY INCOME

Supplemental Security Income (SSI) is a joint federal-state program intended to guarantee a minimum income to elderly, blind, and disabled people. (42 U.S.C. §§ 1381 to 1385.) To be eligible for SSI, you must meet four requirements:

1. You must be 65 or over, blind, or disabled. You're considered legally blind if your vision is no better than 20/200 or your field of vision is limited to 20 degrees or less, even with corrective lenses. You're considered disabled if you have a physical or mental impairment that prevents you from doing any substantial work and that is expected to last at least 12 months or to result in your death.

2. Your monthly income must fall under certain limits. Any income you earn in wages or self-employment, and any money you receive from investments, Social Security benefits, pensions, annuities, royalties, gifts, rents, or interest on savings, as well as regular food and housing provided by others, is counted as income for determining SSI eligibility.

Some things don't count as income, including:

- the first $20 per month you receive from any source (except other public assistance based on need)
- the first $65 per month of your earned income (wages or self-employment), plus one-half of all your earned income over $65 a month
- irregular or infrequent earned income (such as from a one-time-only job) if such income isn't more than $10 a month
- irregular or infrequent unearned income (such as a gift or dividend on an investment) up to $20 per month
- food and shelter from nonprofit agencies
- if you're a student under age 22, earnings up to $1,410 per month to a maximum of $5,670 per year
- food stamps, energy assistance, or housing assistance from a federal program run by a state or local government agency, and
- some work-related expenses for blind or disabled people paid by public assistance.

3. Your assets, not counting your home and car, must not be worth more than $2,000 ($3,000 for a married couple). Some items aren't counted, including:

- your automobile, if you or a member of your household use it for transportation
- your personal property and household goods
- wedding and engagement rings
- property essential to self-support, such as tools or machines used in your trade
- grants, scholarships, fellowships, or gifts used for tuition and educational expenses (for nine months after you receive them)
- life insurance policies with a total face value of $1,500 or less per person and term life insurance policies with no cash surrender value, and
- funds—up to $1,500—specifically earmarked for burial expenses and a burial plot for each spouse.

4. As of February 1, 1997, a new applicant for SSI benefits must be one of the following:

- a citizen of the United States or a legal resident who has worked in the U.S. and paid Social Security taxes for at least ten years
- a legal resident who is, or is the spouse of, a veteran of the U.S. military, or
- a person granted political asylum or refugee status.

If you are not a citizen but were a legal resident of the U.S. who was receiving SSI benefits as of August 22, 1996, you may continue receiving those benefits. Also, if you were a permanent legal resident of the U.S. as of August 22, 1996 and you are blind or disabled, you may be eligible to receive SSI benefits.

Amount of Benefits

The maximum SSI payment is the same as the monthly income limits for eligibility, which depend on your type of disability and your projected ability to return to work in the future. These maximum benefit amounts, though, are reduced by any income you make.

If you qualify for SSI payments, you may also qualify for additional benefits offered by state and county programs. These benefits may include allowances for guide dogs if you are blind, and stipends for in-home support services and protective services. For more information, contact your local welfare office.

A few additional rules apply:
- Your benefit check will be reduced by one dollar for every two dollars you earn in current wages or self-employment over $65 a month.
- Your payment will be reduced dollar for dollar by the amount of unearned income you receive over $20 a month; such income includes your Social Security benefits, pensions, annuities, interest on savings, dividends, or any money from investments or property you own.
- Your SSI payment will be reduced by up to one-third if you live in a friend or relative's home and don't pay for your food or shelter there.

How to Apply for SSI Benefits

Apply for SSI benefits at your local Social Security office. After you complete the necessary paperwork, it will take from four to eight weeks to receive your first regular monthly SSI check. To find the address and working hours of the office nearest to you, call 800-772-1213, or check the Social Security Administration's website at www.socialsecurity.gov.

VETERANS' BENEFITS

Federal Benefits

Veterans may be entitled to numerous benefits from the federal government, depending on their service history. Although the eligibility requirements for each benefit are different, almost all benefits require that you have an honorable or general discharge. In addition, you must have been in active service to be eligible for most benefits. (38 U.S.C. §§ 101 and following.)

Federal benefits are managed by the Department of Veterans Affairs (VA) and include:
- health care benefits (VA hospitals, outpatient treatment, and nursing home facilities)
- disability compensation for service-related injuries
- housing for older veterans and homeless veterans
- overseas benefits
- death and burial benefits

- education and training (including low-cost student loans, grants, and vocational rehabilitation training)
- employment preferences for civil service and other government jobs
- benefits for owners of small or disadvantaged businesses
- home loan guaranties
- life insurance, and
- pensions.

For information on additional VA benefits and claims procedures, contact a VA regional office or visit the VA website at www.va.gov. To speak with someone at the office nearest you, call 800-827-1000 for most benefits, or 877-222-8387 for health care benefits.

For information and advocacy, you can also contact Swords to Plowshares, a veterans' rights organization, at 415-252-4788 or www.swords-to-plowshares.org.

State Benefits
State law provides California veterans with additional benefits. State benefits are administered by the California Department of Veterans Affairs (CDVA) and include:

- **Home loan benefits.** The Cal-Vet home loan program provides low-cost, low-interest financing to eligible veterans for the purchase of primary residences in California. (Mil. & Vet. Code §§ 985 and following.) For more information, call the CDVA, 800-952-5626, or visit its website at www.cdva.ca.gov.
- **Education and training benefits for children and dependents.** The CDVA administers a program that waives college fees for dependant children and spouses of service-related disabled or service-related deceased veterans. (Mil. & Vet. Code §§ 891 and following.) Information about the state waiver of fees can be obtained by contacting your local County Veterans Service Office, listed in the government pages of your telephone book and at www.cacvso.org.
- **Elderly and homeless housing benefits.** Veterans' Homes provide long-term residential care, assisted living, and skilled nursing for California veterans. (Mil. & Vet. Code §§ 1010 and following.) California has three such facilities, one at Yountville in Northern California and two in Southern California; one in Chula Vista and

one in Barstow. Additional facilities are being planned. To be eligible for admission, a veteran must be at least 62 years old or disabled and must be a California resident who served honorably. For information on income limitations and fees, call the home in which you're interested. For Yountville, call 800-404-8387. For the Barstow home, call 800-746-0606. For information on the Chula Vista home, call 888-857-2164.

For information on additional state benefits, call the CDVA, or visit its website at www.cdva.ca.gov. ■

Inheritance and Wills

There are many ways to pass your property to those you want to have it after you die. Each has advantages: Some avoid probate court proceedings, while others save on taxes or give more flexibility to those who inherit your property. If you don't leave clear instructions, state law determines who inherits your property.

TOPICS

Executors and Administrators

Gift and Estate Tax

Inheritance by a Spouse

Inheritance by Children

Inheritance When There's No Will

Joint Tenancy

Payable-on-Death Bank Accounts

Probate

Transfer-on-Death Registration for Securities

Trusts

Wills

RELATED TOPICS

Children

Guardianships

Relationships

Community and Separate Property

Gay and Lesbian Couples

Serious Illness

Durable Power of Attorney for Finances

Durable Power of Attorney for Health Care

Medical Directives (Living Wills and Powers of Attorney)

ADDITIONAL RESOURCES

Quicken WillMaker Plus (Nolo) software lets you create a valid will, durable power of attorney for finances, health care directive, and final arrangements document.

Nolo's Simple Will Book, by Denis Clifford (Nolo), contains a detailed discussion and forms (tear-out and on CD-ROM) for creating a will.

Plan Your Estate, by Denis Clifford and Cora Jordan (Nolo), is a detailed guide to estate planning, including trusts, estate taxes, charitable gifts, and other topics.

8 Ways to Avoid Probate, by Mary Randolph (Nolo), explains easy and inexpensive ways to spare your family the cost and delay of probate proceedings after your death.

Estate Planning Basics, by Denis Clifford (Nolo), is a concise introduction to all major estate planning issues.

Make Your Own Living Trust, by Denis Clifford (Nolo), explains how a living trust can help you avoid probate fees and lower estate taxes. It contains forms with which you can prepare your own living trust.

Special Needs Trusts: Protect Your Child's Financial Future, by Stephen Elias (Nolo) explains what a special needs trust is and how to create one if circumstances require it.

How to Probate an Estate in California, by Julia Nissley (Nolo), contains all the forms and instructions for probating an estate in California.

The IRS website, www.irs.gov, offers some useful documents, including IRS Instructions for Form 706, Federal Estate Tax Return, and IRS Publication 448, *Federal Estate and Gift Taxes*.

EXECUTORS AND ADMINISTRATORS

The executor is the person named in a will to wind up a deceased person's affairs. In many cases, this means handling the probate proceedings. (See Probate.)

If probate is required, the first thing an executor does is file the will and a document called "Petition for Probate" with the local probate (superior) court. Unless the executor named in the will is clearly not fit to serve, the court will issue a document called "Letters Testamentary," which gives the executor legal authority to act on behalf of the estate.

If there is no will, or the person appointed in the will cannot serve, the court appoints an "administrator," who has the same duties as an executor. State law determines who is appointed. The surviving spouse or registered domestic partner is the first choice. If there is none, the deceased person's children are appointed, and so on down a list of relatives allowed to serve. (Prob. Code § 8461.)

The executor or administrator must:

- get certified copies of the death certificate
- handle probate, if required
- locate will beneficiaries
- inventory the deceased person's assets and safe deposit box, and manage the property during the probate process
- collect the deceased person's mail
- cancel credit cards and subscriptions
- notify Social Security and Medi-Cal, if necessary
- collect death benefits and insurance proceeds
- file the deceased person's final state and federal income tax returns
- file federal and California estate tax returns, if required
- pay debts, and
- transfer property that doesn't go through probate, including community property left to the surviving spouse and joint tenancy property.

The executor may hire a lawyer or other professional to handle any or all of these duties, and pay the lawyer's fee from estate assets.

GIFT AND ESTATE TAX

Federal gift and estate tax is assessed when someone gives away a large amount of property, either during life or at death. The giver, not the recipient, is taxed. The tax rate is the same whether the property is given before or after death.

Most people pay no federal gift or estate tax, because anyone may give away (during life or at death) a substantial amount of property. For deaths through 2008, every person can leave $2 million worth of property free of federal estate tax. That amount will increase to $3.5 million in 2009. The estate tax is scheduled to expire altogether in 2010, but will come back again for deaths in 2011 unless Congress acts.

Gifts of any amount to a spouse who is a U.S. citizen, to a tax-exempt organization, or for medical expenses or school tuition are always exempt from gift/estate tax.

Gift Tax

By taxing property regardless of when it's given, the gift tax is intended to thwart people who try to avoid estate tax by giving property away before they die. Any gift worth more than $12,000 given to one person in one year is subject to the federal gift tax. Each member of a married couple gets this annual exclusion, so together they can give up to $24,000 per recipient per year, without reducing either's exempt amount. So, in practice, people can give away substantial amounts of property and avoid the estate tax assessed at death.

EXAMPLE: *Robin gives her son $7,000 in cash and $10,000 in real estate in one calendar year. She must file a gift tax return for the amount over $12,000. She will not have to pay tax now but will use $5,000 of her exempt amount, leaving that amount $5,000 smaller when she dies (assuming she makes no more nonexempt gifts). If Robin waited until next year to give the real estate, both gifts would be entirely exempt.*

You must file a gift tax return if you give away more than the annual exclusion amount to one person (not including a tax-exempt organization), even if you do not have to pay any tax now. Gift tax returns must be filed with a regular annual income tax return. They can be tricky; you'll need help from a tax preparer or tax attorney.

Estate Tax

A federal estate tax return (IRS Form 706) must be filed within nine months after death for someone whose gross estate (everything owned at the date of death) exceeds the exempt amount for the year of death.

The return must be filed even if no tax is due. For example, if someone leaves $2.5 million to his wife, no tax will be due (because property left to a U.S. citizen spouse is tax-exempt), but an estate tax return must be filed.

California has no state gift or estate tax.

INHERITANCE BY A SPOUSE

Each member of a married couple owns half of the couple's community property, and is free to leave it to whomever he or she pleases. The other spouse has no claim to it. Separate property may also be left to a beneficiary of the owner's choosing.

If a married person dies without a will, however, all community property goes to the surviving spouse. The survivor also inherits some or all of the separately owned property, depending on whether or not the deceased spouse left surviving children or other close relatives.

A Spouse's Right to Inherit

The law tries to make sure that no one is unintentionally omitted from his or her spouse's will. If someone marries after making a will and then dies without changing that will to provide for the new spouse (or indicating in the will an intent to disinherit the new spouse), the surviving spouse may have a claim to some of the deceased spouse's property. Specifically, the spouse is entitled to:

- the deceased spouse's half of the couple's community property and quasi-community property
- up to one-half of the deceased spouse's separate property.

This property is called the spouse's "share" of the deceased spouse's estate. (Prob. Code §§ 6560-6562.)

Inheritance Without Probate

If a couple (spouses or registered domestic partners) holds title to property as "survivorship community property," the survivor automatically inherits sole ownership of the property when the first one dies. No probate is required; the procedure is the same as that for joint tenancy property. (Civ. Code § 682.1.)

Even if property isn't held this way, however, formal probate isn't required for any property left without restriction to a surviving spouse or registered domestic partner, regardless of the size of the estate. (Prob. Code § 13500.) Two simple documents may be used to transfer ownership to the survivor, depending on the type of property involved.

Spousal Property Order. A court order, called a Spousal Property Order, is required to transfer ownership of certain types of property, including real estate owned in the name of the deceased person alone, or stocks and bonds. The survivor must submit a Spousal Property Petition to the local superior court. The petition is a fill-in-the-blanks form provided by the court. The survivor must also mail notice of the petition to people who might be interested: close relatives and the beneficiaries of the deceased person's will. If no one objects, the court will issue a Spousal Property Order, officially transferring ownership to the survivor. The entire procedure takes about a month.

Affidavit for community property real estate. The survivor may take over all community property without probate, unless the deceased person willed his or her one-half interest or a portion of it to someone else. The only restriction is a 40-day waiting period before the survivor may sell or otherwise dispose of any community real estate—a provision that allows others to assert any claims they may have on the property. (Prob. Code § 13540.)

For community real estate, most title insurance companies will accept a simple form affidavit to establish ownership in the name of the survivor alone. The affidavit is a document that describes the property and contains other recording information, which can be taken from the original deed. The survivor must sign the affidavit in the presence of a notary public and then record it, along with a certified copy of the deceased person's death certificate, in the county recorder's office in the county where the property is located. No court need be involved, but it's a good idea to check with the title company before using the affidavit, because that company may have specific requirements.

INHERITANCE BY CHILDREN

A Child's Right to Inherit

If you have or adopt a child after you make a will, and don't provide for the child in the will, he or she is still entitled to a share of your estate. The share is what the child would have been entitled to if you had died without a valid will. (See Inheritance When There's No Will.)

There are several important exceptions to this general rule. The child is not entitled to inherit anything if any of the following is true:

- The will makes it clear that you intentionally disinherited the child.
- You left everything, or almost everything, to the child's other parent.
- You provided for the child outside the will. (Prob. Code §§ 6570, 6571.)

Inheritance by Minor Children

If a minor (a child under 18) inherits up to $5,000 worth of property, it can simply be given to the minor's parents. (Prob. Code § 3401.) But if a minor inherits property worth more than $5,000, a more formal arrangement is required. If the giver did not make other arrangements, the executor can name a "custodian" for up to $10,000 (larger amounts need court approval), or a court will appoint a property guardian (one of the child's parents, if possible) to manage the property.

Avoiding Property Guardianship Proceedings

There are several ways to leave money or valuable property to a minor without creating a guardianship:

- **Leave the property to an adult.** Many people don't leave property directly to a child. Instead, they leave it to the child's parent or to the person they expect to have care and custody of the child if neither parent is available. There's no formal legal arrangement, but they trust the adult to use the property for the child's benefit.
- **Name a custodian** under the California Uniform Transfers to Minors Act. You can name a "custodian" to manage property you leave a child until the child reaches an age you choose, from 18 to 25. (Prob. Code §§ 3900-3925.) The custodian is responsible for collecting and investing the property and using it for the child's needs. No court supervises the custodian.

- **Create a child's trust.** You can establish a trust for a minor in your will or living trust. You must choose an adult who will manage the property and dole it out for the child's education, health, and other needs. The trust ends at whatever age you designate, and any remaining property is turned over to the child outright.

Children With Special Needs

These property management options are not designed to provide long-term property management for a child with serious disabilities. You may want to create what's called a special needs trust to leave the child property while preserving the child's eligibility for government benefits (especially Medi-Cal). See *Special Needs Trusts: Protect Your Child's Financial Future*, by Stephen Elias (Nolo).

INHERITANCE WHEN THERE'S NO WILL

When someone dies without a will ("intestate"), that person's property goes to the closest relatives, under California's "intestate succession" law. (Prob. Code §§ 6400-6414.) Here are the basic rules:

- The surviving spouse or domestic partner inherits all community property. The survivor also inherits one-third, one-half, or all of the separate property, depending on whether or not there are surviving children or other close relatives. The rest of the separate property is divided into shares and distributed to the children, parents, grandparents, and/or siblings of the deceased person.
- If the deceased person was single, his or her children inherit all the property. If there are no surviving children, more distant relatives inherit it.
- If someone dies without a will and leaves only more distant relatives (no spouse, children, grandchildren, great-grandchildren, parents or their issue, or grandparents or their issue), then the property goes to the "next of kin," as defined by Probate Code § 6402.

To inherit property from someone who dies without a will, a person must survive the deceased person for at least 120 hours. (Prob. Code § 6403.)

These rules apply only to personal property and real estate in California; real estate in another state is passed according to the intestate succession law of the state in which it is located.

Adopted Children

Under the intestate succession law, a child who has been adopted may inherit from a birth parent only if both of the following are true:

- The deceased parent and the adopted child lived together at any time as parent and child, or the natural parent was married to or living with the other natural parent at the time of the child's conception and died before the child was born.
- The adoption was by the spouse of either of the natural parents or took place after the death of either natural parent. (Prob. Code § 6451.)

JOINT TENANCY

Joint tenancy is a way two or more people can hold title to property they own together. The most important feature of joint tenancy is that when one joint owner (called a joint tenant) dies, the surviving owner(s) automatically get complete ownership of the property, without probate. This is called the "right of survivorship." The surviving owners need only fill out some simple paperwork to transfer the property into their names alone.

A joint tenant cannot leave his or her share of the property to anyone other than the surviving joint tenants. So, for example, if a joint tenant leaves a will giving her share of the property to her son instead of the other joint tenant, the will would have no effect. However, a joint tenant can, while still alive, transfer the interest in the property or change the way title is held to get around this rule. (Civ. Code § 683.2.)

Joint tenancy often works well for unmarried owners who acquire real estate or other valuable property together. If they take title in joint tenancy, probate is avoided when the first owner dies. Married couples are usually better off (because of tax advantages) taking title as community property or community property with right of survivorship.

Creating a Joint Tenancy

To create a joint tenancy, all the co-owners need to do is call themselves joint tenants on the document that shows ownership of property, such as a deed to real estate, a car's title slip, or a card establishing a bank account.

Drawbacks of Joint Tenancy

Joint tenancy has some disadvantages that may make it a poor estate planning choice, depending on the circumstances. For example, an older person who, seeking only to avoid probate, puts solely owned property into joint tenancy with someone else may be surprised to learn that he or she has given up half ownership of the property. The new owner can sell or mortgage his or her share, or it could be taken by creditors.

Other potential drawbacks of joint tenancy:

- If one joint tenant becomes incapacitated and cannot make decisions, and has not created a durable power of attorney to authorize someone else to act for her, the other owners must get legal authority to sell or mortgage the property. That may mean going to court to get someone (called a conservator) appointed to manage the incapacitated person's affairs.

- If you create a joint tenancy by making another person a co-owner, federal gift tax may be assessed on the transfer. However, if two or more people open a bank account in joint tenancy, but one person puts all or most of the money in, no gift tax is assessed against that person. But tax may be assessed when a joint tenant who has contributed little or nothing to the account withdraws money from it. Also, the recipient loses a future income tax benefit by receiving the property while the giver is alive, rather than at his or her death. Because of IRS "tax basis" rules, if the value of the real estate goes up, the taxable profit will be greater when the property is eventually sold.

- If spouses own property as joint tenants, the surviving spouse could miss out on a big income tax break later, when the property is sold. If the value of property owned in joint tenancy has gone up since the spouses acquired the property, the surviving spouse gets a stepped-up tax basis only for that half of the property owned by the deceased spouse. (The tax basis is the amount from which taxable profit is figured when property is sold; the basis is "stepped up" to the value at the time of death.) To get a stepped-up basis on the whole thing, the surviving spouse must prove that the property was actually community property; the IRS presumes that property held in joint tenancy is not community property.

PAYABLE-ON-DEATH BANK ACCOUNTS

Setting up a payable-on-death account, also called an informal bank account trust or revocable trust account, is an easy way to transfer cash at your death, quickly and without probate. All you do is designate one or more persons you want to receive the money in the account when you die.

You can do this with any kind of bank account, including savings, checking, or certificate of deposit accounts, by filling out a simple form at your bank. You can also name a beneficiary to receive certain kinds of government securities, including bonds, Treasury Bills, and Treasury Notes, at your death.

During your life, the beneficiary has no right to the money in the account. You can withdraw some or all of the money, close the account, or change the beneficiary at any time. When you die, the beneficiary can claim the money by showing the bank the death certificate.

PROBATE

Probate generally refers to the process by which a deceased person's will is proved valid in court, the person's debts and taxes are paid, and the remaining property is distributed to inheritors. If there is no will, property must still go through probate unless the deceased person made other arrangements.

The executor named in the will (or, if there is no will, an administrator appointed by the court) is in charge of handling probate paperwork and managing the deceased person's property until it's distributed. In many cases, probate can be handled entirely by mail, without any court appearances.

Cost and Delay

Usually, California probate takes seven months to a year, but it can take longer if the estate is complicated. During that time, the beneficiaries get nothing unless the judge allows the immediate family an allowance.

If an attorney is hired, lawyer, court, and other fees can eat up 5% or more of a deceased person's estate (the property left at death). State statutes contain a formula for setting lawyer fees, although clients are free to negotiate a different amount. Because the statutory fees are based on the gross (not net) value of the deceased person's property, they often bear no relation to the actual work done. Under the statute, a lawyer may collect:

- 4% of the first $100,000 of the gross value of the probate estate (the property that goes through probate)
- 3% of the next $100,000
- 2% of the next $800,000
- 1% of the next $9 million
- 1/2% of the next $15 million, and
- a "reasonable amount" (determined by the court) of everything above $25 million. (Prob. Code § 10810.)

That means that if an estate has a gross value of $600,000—even if the deceased person's equity were only $200,000—an attorney could collect $15,000. That figure doesn't include court fees or accountants' and appraisers' bills.

What Property Goes Through Probate

Property left by a will must go through probate before it can be transferred to the beneficiaries. If you don't make a will or some other arrangement (living trust or joint tenancy, for example) to designate who gets your property, the property also goes through probate. It is distributed to your surviving spouse or registered domestic partner or to your closest relatives, according to California's "intestate succession" law.

Several kinds of property can be transferred to beneficiaries without formal probate, including:

- property held as community property with the right of survivorship
- property left through a living trust
- property held in joint tenancy
- funds in a payable-on-death bank account
- life insurance proceeds, and
- funds for which a beneficiary was designated (for example, funds in an Individual Retirement Account).

A streamlined probate court procedure is available for other kinds of property, including:

- property left to a surviving spouse, and
- property in small estates (less than $100,000, not counting property left to a surviving spouse, property in a living trust, and joint tenancy property).

Avoiding Probate

In most instances, if there are no fears of huge creditors' claims and no fights among relatives, formal probate court proceedings are a waste of time and money. Many people avoid probate by using a living trust or other method that allows property to pass directly to inheritors without probate.

TRANSFER-ON-DEATH REGISTRATION FOR SECURITIES

You may name a beneficiary to inherit your stocks or mutual fund accounts without probate. To do this, you must contact your broker or mutual fund company and register the securities in what is called "transfer-on-death" or "beneficiary" form. All you do is fill out a form provided by the broker naming the beneficiary (and alternate beneficiary, if the broker allows this and you want to do it). The law that allows this registration is called the Uniform Transfer-on-Death Securities Registration Act.

During your life, the beneficiaries you name have no right to the stocks, and you are free to change your mind at any time. After your death, the beneficiary must provide proof of identity and proof of the death to the stock transfer agent or mutual fund company, which will handle the transfer without involvement of the probate court.

TRUSTS

A trust is an arrangement under which one person, called the trustee, holds legal title to property on behalf of another, called the beneficiary. You can create a trust by preparing and signing a document called a Declaration of Trust.

Once the trust has been created, you can transfer property to it by registering title in the trustee's name as trustee of the trust.

Trusts can serve many different purposes. Some help people save on estate taxes or probate court costs, and some are designed to manage property over many years. Here, briefly, are the most common and useful kinds of trusts.

Children's Trusts

If you want to leave a substantial amount of property to a child under 18, it is fairly common to arrange for a child's trust to be set up at your death if the child is still a minor. (See Inheritance by Minor Children, above.)

Flexible Trusts

If you don't want to decide how your property will be spent after your death, you can create a "sprinkling trust." It authorizes the trustee to decide how to spend trust money for the different beneficiaries you name.

Generation-Skipping Trusts

A "generation-skipping" trust is sometimes used by people concerned about federal estate taxes. (For information about the federal estate tax threshold, see Gift and Estate Tax, above.) This trust won't reduce your own estate tax liability; it can, however, exempt up to $2 million from tax in the next generation.

With this kind of trust, your children are entitled to income from trust property you leave them, but they can't touch the principal. The principal goes to your grandchildren at the death of your children. The property you leave in such a trust is included in your taxable estate when you die. But it's not included in your children's taxable estate when they die (assuming there is an estate tax at that time).

Simple Living Trusts

A basic revocable living trust lets your property pass to those you want to inherit it without the supervision of the probate court, saving a significant amount of time and money. A living trust performs the same function as a will, but wills are generally subject to probate.

A basic revocable living trust is a simple kind of trust. You transfer ownership of some or all of your property to yourself as trustee, so you keep full power over trust property. (If you make a shared trust with your spouse, you become cotrustees.) This means that you keep absolute control over the property in your living trust. You can revoke (terminate) the trust at any time.

After you die, the person you named in your trust document to be the "successor trustee" takes over. When the first grantor dies, the trust becomes irrevocable, and the successor trustee must notify all the trust beneficiaries and heirs of that fact. The successor trustee is in charge of transferring the trust property to the family, friends, or charities you named as the trust beneficiaries. No probate is necessary for property that was transferred to the living trust. In most cases, all your property can be distributed within a few weeks—compared to many months or even years for probate. When all the property has been transferred to the beneficiaries, the living trust ceases to exist.

Having your property in a basic probate-avoidance living trust does not affect your taxes. You report any income from trust property on your own income tax return. And after your death, property in trust is treated the same as other property you own when it comes to federal estate tax.

Special Needs Trusts

A person with a physical or mental disability may not be able to handle property, at any age. Often, the solution is to establish a trust with a competent adult as trustee to manage the trust property. These trusts must be drafted carefully so that they don't jeopardize the beneficiary's eligibility for government benefits. See *Special Needs Trusts: Protect Your Child's Financial Future*, by Stephen Elias (Nolo).

Spendthrift Trusts

If you want to leave property to an adult who just can't handle money, a "spendthrift trust" is a good idea. The trustee controls the purse strings, which keeps the money from being squandered by the beneficiary. And special language in the trust document prevents trust property from being seized by the beneficiary's creditors (as far as is legally possible).

Tax-Saving AB Trusts

Older couples who have amassed a significant amount of property are often concerned about the bite that federal estate taxes will take out of that wealth when they die. At first glance, there doesn't seem to be a problem, because no federal estate tax is assessed on property left to a surviving spouse who is a U.S. citizen. This is called the marital deduction. But, in fact, this just postpones estate tax until the second spouse dies and no marital deduction is available. Most elderly couples who have a combined estate large enough to be subject to estate tax should avoid leaving large sums to each other.

One way around this trap is for each spouse to put his or her property into an AB trust, sometimes called a "bypass trust" or "spousal trust." When one spouse dies, his or her half of the property goes to the children—with the crucial condition that the surviving spouse gets the right to use the property for life and is entitled to any income it generates. The surviving spouse is usually also given limited power to use up some or all of the trust principal if it's necessary for medical expenses or other basic needs. When the second spouse dies, the trust property goes to the children outright. Using this kind of trust keeps the second spouse's taxable estate half as large as it would be if the property were left to the spouse.

An AB trust can restrict the use of property for years after the first spouse's death. A couple who makes one must be sure that the surviving spouse will be financially and emotionally comfortable receiving only the income from the property placed in trust, with the children (or others) as the trust's final beneficiaries. Many younger and middle-aged couples find it best to simply leave all the property to the surviving spouse, who will have plenty of time and opportunity to enjoy it.

WILLS

A will is a document in which you specify what is to be done with your property when you die. In it, you can also name an executor, who will wind up your affairs after your death, and a guardian to care for your minor children and their property.

Writing a Will

Anyone 18 or older who is of sound mind can make a valid will.

The best way to make a will is to produce it with a typewriter or computer, then sign and date it in front of at least two witnesses who don't stand to inherit anything under the terms of the will. The witnesses sign a statement under oath that they saw you sign the will; this allows a probate court, after your death, to accept the will as valid. An entirely handwritten will is valid in California, but it's not recommended; after your death such a will is easier to challenge in court because no witnesses will be available to testify that they saw you sign it.

Updating a Will

There are two ways to change a will. You can add a supplement, called a codicil, or just revoke the old one and start fresh. To avoid the possibility of conflicts between the original will and a codicil, it's usually preferable to revoke the old one and prepare a whole new will. It's not much more work, because a codicil must be signed and witnessed just like the original will.

Probate Avoidance

Property left through a will often cannot be transferred to the beneficiaries without the approval of the probate court. To avoid probate's expense and delay, many people use probate-avoidance devices, such as living trusts, to leave property. Even if you do this, you should have a will; it's an essential back-up device for property that you don't get around to transferring to your living trust. ■

Landlords and Tenants

State law defines many of the rights and responsibilities of California landlords and tenants. We cover these legal rules here, as well as some practical issues, such as roommates' obligations to each other and rental listing services.

In some cities, rent control or other ordinances provide greater protections for tenants than the state requires, and often substantially limit the landlord's ability to evict tenants and raise rents. If you are a landlord or tenant in a mobile home park or marina, special state laws (and some local ordinances) apply. This chapter does not cover these situations, nor does it apply to commercial tenants. Tenants who are residents of condominiums, townhouses, or planned developments are subject to the homeowners' associations' covenants, codes and restrictions ("CC&Rs"), but these rules themselves must be consistent with state and local laws.

TOPICS

Bankruptcy of Landlord or Tenant
Condition of Rented Premises
Condominium Conversion
Cosigning Leases and Rental Agreements
Deposits, Fees, and Last Month's Rents
Discrimination
Evictions
Leases and Rental Agreements
Managers
Pets
Privacy and the Landlord's Right to Enter
Rent
Rent Control
Rental Listing Services
Renter's Tax Credit

Retaliatory Evictions and Rent Increases
Roommates
Sale of Rented Property
Tenancies in Common

RELATED TOPICS
Courts and Lawsuits
Personal Injury Lawsuits
Real Estate
Noise
Nuisance

ADDITIONAL RESOURCES

California Tenants' Rights, by Janet Portman and David Brown (Nolo), is a detailed discussion of California landlord-tenant law, including how to handle an eviction lawsuit.

The California Landlord's Law Book: Rights and Responsibilities, by David Brown, Janet Portman and Ralph Warner (Nolo), explains the law (including local rent control rules) California landlords need to know.

The California Landlord's Law Book: Evictions, by David Brown (Nolo), contains all the forms and instructions for handling an eviction lawsuit without a lawyer.

Renters' Rights: The Basics, by Janet Portman and Marcia Stewart (Nolo), explains tenants' rights and responsibilities and provides practical, understandable solutions.

BANKRUPTCY OF LANDLORD OR TENANT

The bankruptcy of the landlord or tenant has a substantial impact on the tenancy.

If the Tenant Files for Bankruptcy

A tenant's bankruptcy does not terminate his or her lease, even if the lease has a clause in it that authorizes immediate termination in the event that the tenant becomes insolvent or bankrupt. These clauses are unenforceable. (11 USC § 365(e).) When a tenant has filed for bankruptcy and fails to pay rent or violates another term of the tenancy (such as keeping a pet in violation of a no-pets clause), the landlord can't deliver a termination notice or proceed with an eviction. This prohibition is known as the "automatic stay," and it means that landlords must go to the federal bankruptcy court and ask the judge to "lift," or remove the stay. (U.S. Code § 365(e).) In most cases, judges lift the stay within a matter of days and landlords proceed with the termination and eviction.

The automatic stay does not apply, however if the landlord completed the eviction proceeding and got a judgment for possession *before* the tenant filed for bankruptcy. Under the Bankruptcy Abuse Prevention and Consumer Protection Act of 2005, landlords can proceed with the eviction without having to go to court and ask for the stay to be lifted.

In very narrow circumstances, and only for evictions based on rent nonpayment, a tenant can stop the eviction even if the landlord got a judgment before the tenant filed for bankruptcy. (11 USC §§ 362(a)(1), (2), and (3); *In Re Butler*, 271 B.R. 867 (2002).) Nor may a landlord enforce a judgment for back rent without applying for "relief from stay" from the bankruptcy court.

The landlord may not use the security deposit to offset past due rent. If the landlord violates this or any aspect of the automatic stay (such as filing or proceeding with an eviction), the landlord will be liable to the tenant for any actual damages the tenant incurs and possibly for punitive damages (meant to punish the landlord) as well.

The automatic stay does not affect lawsuits initiated by the tenant before the filing date of the bankruptcy petition—these may continue, and landlords are free to continue to defend themselves.

After a tenant files a petition for bankruptcy, the tenant or possibly the bankruptcy trustee (appointed by the bankruptcy court to oversee the bankruptcy case) must decide whether to "assume" (carry on with) or "reject" (terminate) the lease. In a Chapter 7 bankruptcy, the decision must be made within 60 days; in a Chapter 11, 12, or 13 case, the decision can be made any time before the tenant's reorganization plan is confirmed by the bankruptcy court. Whether the lease is assumed or rejected is a matter of business judgment, and will depend on whether the trustee thinks that continuation of the lease will benefit the bankrupt tenant's creditors, who are hoping to get something out of the tenant's assets. If the lease is assumed, the trustee has the power to assign the lease to a third party, even if a clause in the lease prohibits assignment. (11 USC §§ 365(f)(1),(3).) But in order for the lease to be assumed or assigned, the tenant must promptly pay (or provide adequate assurances that he will pay) any unpaid back rent and any damages caused by his default. The tenant must also give the landlord adequate assurances that he will be able to pay future rent. (11 USC §§ 365(b)(1)(A), (B), and (C).) Residential leases are rarely, if ever, rejected by the trustee or assigned to a third party.

If the Landlord Files for Bankruptcy

If the landlord files for bankruptcy, the trustee for the landlord's bankrupt estate will have the same choice as that faced by a bankrupt tenant: whether to assume or reject the leases held by his tenants. If the landlord or trustee decides to reject them, the tenants can either:

- treat the lease as terminated, vacate the premises, and, if desired, sue for damages (such as moving expenses or the cost of finding a new home), or
- stay until the lease expires. If the landlord does not deliver services because of his weakened financial condition (for example, he drains the pool because he cannot afford the upkeep), the tenant can deduct an appropriate amount from the rent. (11 USC §§ 365(h)(1)(A)(i), (ii).)

CONDITION OF RENTED PREMISES

Several state laws set housing standards for the physical condition of residential rental property, both when the tenant moves in and during the tenancy.

Habitability Requirements

All rental units in California must:

- be weatherproof, waterproof, and rodent-proof (Civ. Code § 1941.1)
- have plumbing in good condition (every unit must have a toilet, wash basin, and bathtub or shower) (Civ. Code § 1941.1)
- have a kitchen with a sink (H & S § 17920.3)
- provide hot water (at least 110 degrees F.) (Civ. Code § 1941.1; H & S Code § 17920.3)
- have adequate heat (Civ. Code § 1941.1; H & S Code § 17920.3)
- have natural light through windows or skylights (H & S Code § 17920.3)
- provide electric power if it is available in the area, complete with safe and proper wiring (Civ. Code § 1941.1)
- have a smoke detector (for multiple-unit buildings) (H & S Code § 13113.7)
- have specified door and window locks (Civ. Code § 1941.3)
- have adequate garbage storage and removal facilities. (Civ. Code § 1941; H & S Code § 17920.3), and
- have a telephone jack and inside phone wiring (Civ. Code § 1941.4; Public Utilities Code § 788).

Your city or county may have other requirements. Check with your local building inspector or health department.

When Premises Are Uninhabitable

If the landlord doesn't meet these minimum requirements, the tenant has several options:

- **Move out.** Even in the middle of a lease (or without the 30 days' notice required under a rental agreement), a tenant can simply move out when landlords know about but fail to make needed repairs of furnish services. (Civ. Code § 1942.) Landlords may be required to pay "relocation benefits" to tenants who must move to allow repairs to be made. (H & S Code § 17980.7.)

- **Withhold rent.** All leases and rental agreements include an implied promise that the landlord will keep the premises in a habitable condition. (*Green v. Superior Court*, 10 Cal. 3d 616 (1974).) If the landlord is in serious violation of this standard, the tenant may withhold rent until the problem is fixed. The tenant cannot, however, withhold rent or sue the landlord if the violations are minor or the tenant has contributed to the poor condition of the premises. (Civ. Code §§ 1929, 1942(c).) The tenant must notify the landlord and wait a reasonable amount of time (up to 35 days) to fix the problem before withholding rent. In Los Angeles County, and the city of Sacramento, tenants must pay their rent withheld into an escrow account administered by the county if their landlord fails to make repairs ordered by the building or health department.
- **Call the building inspector.** This local agency—usually part of the Department of Public Works—can order the landlord to make repairs. If the landlord fails to make repairs within 60 days of being ordered to do so, tenants may sue the landlord and recover any expenses the landlord's actions have cost them, plus an additional $100 to $1,000, plus attorney fees. The court can also order the landlord to repair substandard conditions that significantly affect the occupants' health and safety and can continue to oversee the matter until the repairs are made. (Civ. Code § 1942.4.) The city or county may also bring a lawsuit, or even criminal charges, against a landlord who fails to make repairs demanded by local officials. (H & S Code §§ 17995-17995.5.)
- **Sue the landlord.** A tenant may sue the landlord and receive compensation for discomfort, annoyance, and emotional distress; and for the difference between the rent paid and the (lower) value of the substandard rental. Tenants can even ask the court to appoint a receiver, who would be authorized to collect rents, manage the property, and supervise the necessary repairs. After the repairs are made and the court discharges the receiver, the court may keep the case open for up to 18 months to monitor the situation. (H & S Code § 17980.7.)

Tenant's Right to Repair and Deduct

If a landlord fails to make a repair that is directly related to the habitability of the premises, the tenant can make necessary repairs or hire someone to make them, and deduct the cost from the next month's rent. Before having the repairs done, the tenant must give the landlord or manager written or oral notice of the problem and a reasonable amount of time in which to make the repairs. The repairs cannot cost more than one month's rent, and the problem must not have been caused by a careless or intentional act of the tenant or a guest. This "repair and deduct" remedy can be used only twice in a 12-month period. (Civ. Code § 1942.) Two or more tenants may pool their maximum repair and deduct amounts to accomplish more expensive repairs.

Landlord's Liability for Injuries

A landlord may be liable to the tenant—or others—for injuries caused by dangerous or defective conditions that the landlord knew about but failed to repair. For example, if the tenant is hurt falling on a broken stair, the landlord may be responsible.

A landlord may also be liable for tenant injuries and property damage resulting from the criminal acts of others, but only if the crime was facilitated by the landlord's unreasonable act—for example, failing to fix a defective lock or install adequate lighting. A landlord can also be liable for damage or injury caused by problem tenants or their guests. For example, tenants and others who become victims of the crime that surrounds a drug dealer's home may sue a landlord who does nothing to stop drug dealing on his property.

Disclosure of Utility Arrangements

If the landlord does not provide separate gas and electric meters for each tenant's unit, the landlord must disclose the nature of the sharing situation to all tenants before they sign any rental agreement or lease. The landlord must make a written agreement with the tenant as to how utility charges will be divided. If the landlord pays utility costs and passes them on to the tenant in the form of rent, the amount may be limited by rent control ordinances. (Civ. Code § 1940.9.)

Disclosure of Lead Paint Hazards

Landlords must tell tenants about any lead paint they know of in the rented premises or in the common areas. They must also give tenants the federally approved pamphlet, "Disclosure of Information on Lead-Based Paint or Lead-Based Paint Hazards." Landlords are not required to remove or seal lead-based paint, but may be held liable if a tenant is poisoned from a lead paint problem the landlord knew about but did not remedy. Post-1978 housing is exempt from disclosure requirements, as are studios, short-term vacation rentals, single rooms rented in residential homes, housing certified as lead-free by a state-accredited lead inspector, and housing for seniors or persons with disabilities (unless a child under six years of age is present or expected to live there). If a landlord undertakes significant renovations that will disturb lead-painted surfaces, the contractor (or landlord) must notify tenants. (42 U.S. Code § 4852d ("Title Ten"); 24 Code of Federal Regulations Part 35 and 40; Code of Federal Regulations Part 745.)

Disclosure of Sex Offender Database

For some years, the law has provided that every lease or rental agreement must include a paragraph informing tenants about the California Department of Justice database that includes the names of sex offenders and the communities (by zip code) where they live (Civ. Code § 2079.10.). In addition, courts have held that a landlord who knows that someone who poses a risk to tenants lives nearby must warn tenants about the individual.

CONDOMINIUM CONVERSION

Where there's a shortage of new homes, many landlords find it profitable to convert their buildings from rental units to owner-occupied condominiums. Instead of paying monthly rent, residents own their apartments and a share of the common space, such as halls and grounds. In many cities, landlords must pay a fee or tax per unit converted. A state law known as the Ellis Act controls condominium conversions in properties where there are four or more rental units. (Gov't. Code §§ 7060 and following.)

Before a rental unit is converted to a condominium, the landlord must obtain an approved subdivision map from the local governing agency. Existing tenants are entitled to:

- At least 60 days' written notice of the landlord's intention to file an application for an approved map. Tenants who are at least 62 years old or disabled, and have lived in the unit for at least one year, are entitled to one year's notice. However, these tenants must tell the landlord that they are eligible for this extended period within 60 days after the landlord files his notice of intent to convert.

- If the map has been approved, at least 180 days' written notice of intent to convert before their tenancy is terminated. If a tenant's lease has more than 180 days left to run, the tenant can stay as long as the lease specifies.

- The first right to buy the apartment on at least the same terms that the apartment will be offered to the public, with 90 days to decide. (Gov't. Code § 66427.1.)

Tenants who begin their tenancy *after* the map approval are entitled to:

- written notice, before the lease is signed, that the rental unit has been approved for sale as a condominium project, and that if it is sold, the lease may be terminated, and

- at least 90 days' written notice prior to the offer to sell, during which time the tenant has the right of first refusal.

Many cities and a few counties have stricter rules governing condominium conversions. Check with your local planning commission.

COSIGNING LEASES AND RENTAL AGREEMENTS

Some landlords require that certain tenants (for example, students or persons without steady income) get a parent or friend who is financially secure to cosign the lease or rental agreements. Typically, these contracts require the cosigner to pay for rent or damage to the rental unit if the tenant can't or won't pay.

If a landlord and tenant change the terms of the rental agreement or lease without the approval of the cosigner, the cosigner is no longer liable for unpaid rent or damages. The changed agreement is considered a new contract—one the cosigner didn't agree to. (Civ. Code § 2819; *Wexler v. McLucas,* 48 Cal. App. 3d Supp. 9 (1975).)

DEPOSITS, FEES, AND LAST MONTH'S RENT

All deposits and fees required by a landlord that are intended to cover unpaid rent, cleaning, or damage beyond normal wear and tear are refundable. (Civ. Code § 1950.5.) For example, a so-called nonrefundable move-in, transfer, cleaning, or pet fee must be refunded if the tenant moves out leaving the premises clean and undamaged. Expenses incurred when the tenant moves in, such as the value of the landlord's time spent familiarizing the tenant with the property, cannot be billed separately and can only be charged as part of the deposit deductions.

Limits on Credit-Check and Screening Fees

Landlords may charge up to $33 for a credit or background check, including the "actual out-of-pocket costs" of obtaining a credit report, plus "the reasonable value" of the time spent checking background information on a potential tenant. (Civ. Code § 1950.6.) The limit may be increased based on the Consumer Price Index for the nearest metropolitan area.

Limits on Deposits

The amount a landlord can collect as a deposit is limited by state law:
- **Unfurnished units.** The total of all deposits and fees, including last month's rent, may not exceed the amount of two months' rent (two-and-one-half times rent if the tenant has a waterbed).
- **Furnished units.** The total of all deposits and fees, including last month's rent, may not exceed three months' rent (three-and-one-half times rent if the tenant has a waterbed). (Civ. Code § 1950.5.)
- **Pet deposits.** A landlord may not charge an extra pet deposit for trained guide dogs, signal dogs, or service dogs. (Civ. Code § 54.2.)

Increases in Deposits

If the tenant and landlord have signed a written lease, the deposit may not be increased during the terms of a lease unless the lease allows it (and in no event may it be increased beyond the legal limit). If the premises are rented under a month-to-month rental agreement, the landlord may increase the deposit after giving the tenant 30 days' written notice, unless a city rent control ordinance prohibits it. If the rent is increased and the security deposit is described as a multiple of the rent (for example, "one month's rent"), the security deposit may increase as well.

Inspection Before Move-Out

Landlords must give tenants an opportunity to be present at an initial move-out inspection, at which the landlord and tenant inspect the rental and the landlord identifies probable security deposit deductions for damage or uncleanliness. (Civ. Code § 1950.5(f).) Written notice of the right to the inspection must be sent to the tenant before the tenant's planned departure; if the tenant requests the inspection, the landlord must schedule the inspection no sooner than two weeks before the planned departure, and give 48 hours' written notice of the day and time. At the inspection, the landlord should identify probable deductions and give tenants a written, verbatim statement of their rights by quoting from the Civil Code section noted above. If the tenant does not remedy the problems, or problems could not be detected due to the presence of the tenant's belongings, the landlord may deduct as needed. The landlord may also deduct for damage or uncleanliness that appeared after the inspection.

Interest

California law does not require a landlord to pay interest on deposits. However, ordinances in the cities of Berkeley, East Palo Alto, Hayward, Los Angeles, San Francisco, Santa Cruz, Santa Monica, Watsonville, and West Hollywood do require it. Check with your city clerk for information about local laws.

Return of Deposits

The landlord has three weeks after the tenant has vacated the premises to return the tenant's entire deposit or provide an itemized written statement, documented by receipts and invoices, listing the amount of and reason for any portion of the deposit not returned, together with a check for the balance. (Civ. Code § 1950.5 (f).)

A landlord can withhold only the amount necessary to:

- pay overdue rent
- repair damage caused by the tenant—exclusive of ordinary wear and tear
- clean the premises to the level of cleanliness present when the rental began
- replace personal property of the landlord—such as furnishings—if the rental agreement or lease includes these items.

If a landlord, without a good reason and in "bad faith," doesn't refund the tenant's deposit within three weeks, a court may order the landlord to pay the tenant up to twice the monthly rent in damages, in addition to returning the amount improperly withheld. (Civ. Code § 1950.5 (l).)

If there is a written lease or rental agreement, the tenant has up to four years to sue, measured from the date the tenancy expired or the landlord's failure to properly refund the deposit, whichever occurred later. If there is no written lease or rental agreement, the tenant has two years to sue. (Code of Civ. Proc. §§ 337 (1), 337.2, 343; *Trypucko v. Clark*, 142 Cal. App. 3d Supp. 1 (1983).)

DISCRIMINATION

Discrimination in renting housing is illegal if it is based on a group characteristic such as race, religion, ethnic background or national origin, sex, marital status (including unmarried couples), age, families with children (except in certain designated senior housing), disability, sexual orientation, HIV status, personal characteristic or trait, or receipt of public assistance. And a landlord may not discriminate against a person who associates with anyone in these protected groups. However, advertisements for a roomer in a single family residence may specify that the rental is available only to persons of one sex. (Gov't. Code § 12927 (c)(2)(B).)

A landlord may adopt income criteria and apply them equally to all tenants, but if the tenant's rent is paid in part by a government assistance program (such as "Section 8"), the landlord may not require a rent-to-income ratio that fails to include the portion paid by the government as part of the tenant's "income."

Courts and government housing agencies can levy substantial fines against landlords who unlawfully discriminate, and can order a landlord to rent to any person discriminated against. (Civ. Code § 51; *Marina Point v. Wolfson*, 30 Cal. 3d 721 (1982); *Harris v. Capitol Growth Investors XIV*, 52 Cal. 3d 1142 (1991); *Smith v. Fair Employment and Housing Commission*, 12 Cal. 4th 1143 (1996).)

EVICTIONS

A landlord must file a lawsuit to evict a tenant. The case is called an unlawful detainer action.

Giving the Tenant Notice

A landlord may not file for eviction until the tenant gets proper written notice of the landlord's intent to end the tenancy. If the tenant has a month-to-month rental agreement, a landlord must provide 30 days' written notice to end the tenancy if the landlord is terminating for reasons other than lease violations. Unless local law requires it, the landlord does not have to give a reason for ending the tenancy. However, in many rent control cities, this notice must state a "just cause" (a legitimate reason, from a list in the ordinance) for ending a tenancy, except when the tenant is guilty of serious misconduct. A 30-day notice can be given any time during the month; it need not coincide with the date rent is due. If the tenant doesn't move out after the 30 days, the landlord can file an eviction lawsuit.

When the tenant fails to pay rent, violates a lease or rental agreement clause, seriously damages the premises, or uses the property for an illegal purpose, only three days' notice is required to terminate the tenancy. If the violation can be corrected (the tenant could pay overdue rent or get rid of a pet whose presence violates the lease, for example), the notice must give the tenant a choice: Remedy the problem in three days, or move. For very serious problems, such as drug dealing, the termination notice can simply require the tenant to leave within three days.

The Eviction Process

If an appropriate three-day or 30-day notice to terminate the tenancy has been properly served on (delivered to) the tenant and that time has passed without the tenant moving out or correcting the violation, the landlord can file an eviction (unlawful detainer) lawsuit. After a summons and complaint are served on the tenant, the tenant has five days to file a written response (15 days if the tenant wasn't personally served). A court hearing is then held, usually within 20 days of the landlord's request.

If the court finds in favor of the landlord, it will award the landlord a judgment for possession of the property. A sheriff will then give the tenant a "writ of execution," ordering him or her to leave within five days or be physically removed.

To appeal an eviction order, a tenant must file a notice of appeal within 30 days of receiving notice of the court judgment. To stay in a rental unit pending the outcome of an appeal, the tenant must also be granted a stay of eviction by the trial court. To get a stay of eviction, the tenant must show that both of the following are true:

- The tenant will suffer extreme hardship if he or she is evicted.
- The landlord will not be hurt by the stay. This usually means that the tenant must pay rent and agree to any other conditions imposed by the judge.

Defenses to an Eviction

These are the most common grounds on which tenants fight eviction:

- The landlord's claim that the tenant violated a lease or rental agreement provision is false.
- Rent was withheld because the premises were uninhabitable.
- The landlord is attempting to evict the tenant for exercising a tenancy-related legal right, such as complaining to a city official about substandard conditions.
- The landlord failed to give the tenant proper legal notices either to end the tenancy or to initiate the eviction lawsuit.
- The landlord does not have just cause to evict, in rent control cities where it is required.

Illegal Evictions

It is illegal for a landlord to evict a tenant by force or threat. (Code of Civ. Proc. §§ 1159-1179.) It is also illegal for a landlord to:

- lock the tenant out or change locks
- remove doors or windows
- remove the tenant's furniture or property, or
- shut off any utilities or cause them to be shut off. (Civ. Code § 789.3.)

Any provision in a lease or rental agreement that purports to allow any of these actions is void. In the case of an unlawful lock-out, property removal, or utility shutoff, the landlord can be penalized up to $100 per day, with a $250 minimum, and must also reimburse the tenant for actual losses.

Landlords cannot legally terminate a tenancy because of race, religion, or other arbitrary reasons or as a means of retaliating against a tenant for exercising a tenant right, such as using the "repair and deduct" statute, complaining to a housing authority, or organizing a tenants' group.

LEASES AND RENTAL AGREEMENTS

Leases and rental agreements are contracts to rent property. They usually contain provisions regulating the rent, number of occupants, types and number of pets, amount of deposits, noise, who pays for utilities, and the tenant's and landlord's duties to maintain and repair the premises. They can be written or oral, but an oral agreement will be enforced by a court for only one year from the date the agreement was made.

Leases

A lease gives a tenant the right to occupy a rental unit at a fixed rent for a certain number of months or years, as long as the tenant pays the rent and complies with other lease provisions. If a tenant moves out before the lease expires, the landlord is owed the remaining rent due under the lease, less the amount the landlord could recover by using reasonable efforts to find a new tenant.

At the end of the lease term, the landlord can ask the tenant to leave without stating a reason, unless a local rent control ordinance requires "just cause" for nonrenewals. If the tenant stays on, some leases provide for an automatic renewal for the same time period as the original lease. To be legal, this provision must be printed in at least eight-point boldface type, immediately above the tenant's signature. (Civ. Code § 1945.5.) In the absence of such a renewal provision, the tenant becomes a month-to-month tenant under the terms of the original lease when the original lease expires. (Civ. Code § 1945.)

Rental Agreements

Usually, a rental agreement is from month-to-month, but periods as short as seven days are legal. For monthly rentals, the tenant can move or the landlord can raise the rent, change other terms of the rental agreement, or order the tenant to move on 30 days' written notice. The notice period can be extended beyond 30 days, but only if the landlord and tenant have agreed. (Civ. Code § 1946.)

In some cities with rent control ordinances, a landlord must show "just cause" to end the tenancy, such as the landlord's need to move in.

MANAGERS

A landlord must give tenants the name and address of someone authorized to accept legal documents on the landlord's behalf. (Civ. Code § 1962.7.) This can be either the landlord or the manager. This notification must be in writing if the tenant has a written lease or rental agreement, and available on demand if the rental agreement is oral. If the landlord fails to provide this information, and if an agent of the landlord (such as a manager) handled the rental negotiations, the tenant is entitled to serve legal papers on the agent. If there is no agent, the tenant can send legal papers by certified mail to the same address where rent is paid. (Civ. Code § 1962.7.)

Any apartment complex with 16 or more rental units must employ a resident manager. (Cal. Code of Regulations, Title 25, § 42.)

A landlord is legally responsible for the acts of a manager or management company acting within the scope of their duties. For example, if a manager illegally refuses to rent to a couple with children, the landlord (along with the manager or management company) will be liable.

> ## Tips for Landlords
>
> Landlords can avoid being held liable for a manager's acts by:
> - thoroughly checking the manager's employment history and checking for prior criminal convictions that would affect the manager's ability to do the job well
> - limiting, in writing, the authority delegated to a manager
> - making sure the manager understands and applies basic landlord/tenant law, especially the duty not to discriminate against applicants or tenants or retaliate against tenants who exercise their lawful rights
> - buying insurance that covers the illegal acts of managers, and
> - setting up an easy way for tenants to communicate directly with the landlord if they believe the manager is doing a poor job or violating their rights.

PETS

A landlord can prohibit a tenant from keeping any pet except service or companion animals for physically or mentally disabled persons. (Civ. Code § 54.1.) If a pet deposit is charged, it must be refundable and, when added to the rest of the security deposit, it cannot make the sum higher than that allowed by the security deposit statute. (Civ. Code § 1950.5.) A landlord may not charge an extra pet deposit for service or companion animals. (Civ. Code § 54.2.) If a tenant's pet injures someone, and the landlord knew (or had reason to know) that the pet was dangerous, the landlord can be held liable, even if the injury occurs off the premises. (*Uccello v. Laudenslayer*, 44 Cal. App. 3d 504 (1975).)

See Dogs: Guide, Signal, and Service Dogs.

PRIVACY AND THE LANDLORD'S RIGHT TO ENTER

Tenants are guaranteed reasonable privacy. (Civ. Code § 1953(a)(1).) This right can't be waived or modified by any lease or rental agreement provision. A landlord, manager, or employee may enter the tenant's premises while the tenant is living there only:

- in case of emergency
- to make necessary or agreed-on repairs (or to assess the need for them)
- when the tenant gives permission
- to conduct a requested move-out inspection, or
- to show the property to a prospective tenant or purchaser. (Civ. Code § 1954.)

Except for emergencies and when the tenant gives permission, the landlord, manager, employee, or contractor can enter only during "normal business hours," which aren't defined in the statute. The tenant must also receive reasonable notice. 24-hour notice is presumed to be reasonable, except in the case of a pre-move-out inspection, where 48 hours are required.

RENT

The landlord and tenant may agree on any dollar amount for rent, except in certain cities covered by rent control. (See "Rent Control," below.)

When Rent Is Due

By custom, almost all leases and rental agreements require rent to be paid monthly, in advance. Most often, rent is due on the first day of the month. However, it is legal for a landlord to require rent to be paid at different intervals or on a different day of the month.

Rent Increases

If the tenant and landlord have signed a fixed-term lease, the rent can't be raised unless the lease allows it. At the end of a lease, rent may be raised to any amount, except in cities covered by rent control. The landlord is not required to give the tenant a formal written notice of such an increase but can inform the tenant at any time before the lease expires.

If the tenant is renting under an oral or written month-to-month tenancy, the landlord can usually increase the rent by any amount if the landlord gives the tenant 30 days' written notice. However, if the rent increase, plus any other increases imposed during the 12 prior months, adds up to more than 10% of the lowest rent charged during those 12 months, the landlord must give 60 days' notice of the increase. (Civ. Code § 827(b).) Ninety days' notice is required to terminate a government-subsidized tenancy. (Civ. Code § 1954.535.) Local rent control ordinances may further limit the increase allowed.

Late Fees

A late fee is legal only if it closely approximates the actual damages to the landlord from a late payment. A court will not enforce late fees unless the lease or rental agreement includes a late fees clause with wording substantially like this: "Because Landlord and Tenant agree that actual damages for late rent payments are very difficult or impossible to determine, Landlord and Tenant agree to the following stated late charge as liquidated damages." *Orozco v. Casimiro,* 212 Cal. App. 4th Supp. 7 (2004).) In general, a late fee must have a cap and should not exceed 3% – 5% of the rent.

RENT CONTROL

Although there is no statewide law that *imposes* rent control, there is a state law that regulates the extent to which individual cities may control rents (the Costa-Hawkins Rental Housing Act, Civ. Code §§ 1954.50 and following). The law provides as follows:

- **Vacancy decontrol.** Landlords may raise rents to any level after a tenant leaves, assigns, or subleases the premises. However, when the property is rerented, a city's rent control ordinance will once again apply and will limit rent increases for the new tenants in that residence. The only exception is where the city rent control ordinance provides that, upon vacancy, the property is no longer subject to rent control (as is the case in Hayward, Palm Springs, and Thousand Oaks).
- **Single family homes and condominiums.** These are not subject to any rent control once a rental is vacated.
- **New construction.** Dwellings certified for occupancy on or after February 1, 1995 will not be subject to rent control.

Rent Control Cities

Berkeley	Hayward	San Francisco
Beverly Hills	Los Angeles	San Jose
Campbell	Los Gatos	Santa Monica
East Palo Alto	Oakland	Thousand Oaks
Fremont	Palm Springs	West Hollywood

Rent control ordinances generally control more than how much rent a landlord may charge; they often govern how and under what circumstances a landlord may terminate a tenancy as well. Rent control laws fall into two broad categories.

Weak Rent Control

California cities with weak rent control are Campbell, Fremont, Hayward, Los Gatos, Oakland, and San Jose.

In these cities, landlords can raise rent by a generous (to the landlord) annual percentage. Additional rent increases are possible if the tenant doesn't object. Landlords need not register units with any government agency. Just cause for eviction is not required except in Hayward and Oakland.

Moderate to Strict Rent Control

The rent control laws of Beverly Hills, Los Angeles, Palm Springs, San Francisco, and Thousand Oaks have traditionally been considered moderate, while the rent control laws of Berkeley, East Palo Alto, Santa Monica, and West Hollywood are considered strict.

These cities keep a fairly tight limit on annual rent increases. To raise rent above the limit, a landlord must get permission from the local rent board. The landlord must justify the need for the increase, based on certain cost factors listed in the city rent control ordinance, such as increased taxes or property improvements. Moderate and strict rent control cities also require the landlord to show just cause for eviction.

Until 1996, the main difference between moderate and strict rent control was that cities following the moderate approach allowed some form of vacancy decontrol, while strict rent control cities did not. But state law now requires all cities to allow vacancy decontrol. This means there is now little difference between rent control in moderate cities and rent control in strict cities. (One of the remaining differences is that landlords in strict rent control cities must register their properties with the rent control board. Berkeley and Santa Monica also allow tenants to petition for lower rents based on a landlord's failure to maintain or repair rental property.)

No matter what type of rent control a city has—weak, moderate, or strict—landlords may not raise rents (even after a voluntary vacancy, sublease, assignment, or eviction for cause) if the landlord has been cited for serious health, safety, or fire or building code violations that the landlord has failed to remedy for six months preceding the vacancy.

RENTAL LISTING SERVICES

Rental listing services charge a fee in exchange for allowing people who are looking for apartments to use their listings. These businesses must be licensed with the California Department of Real Estate, and must offer prospective customers a written contract that spells out all terms of the agreement, including the costs of the service and the customer's rental specifications (number of bedrooms, locale or neighborhood, maximum rent, and so on). The length of the contract may not exceed 90 days.

The listing service must offer three available rental units that match the specifications of the contract within five days after a customer enters into the contract, or give a full refund. The customer must demand the refund in writing within ten days of the expiration of the five-day period.

If the customer finds a rental through another source, or fails to find a rental while using the listing service, the agency must refund all but $25 of the fee—if the customer requests this refund in writing within ten days of the expiration of the contract. The refund must be made within ten days of receipt of the customer's written demand.

Every contract must advise the customer in capitalized, bold, or italicized print of his right to a refund as described above. The notice must also tell the customer that if the service fails to abide by the refund procedure, and if the failure is willful and in bad faith, the customer may sue the service for actual damages plus punitive damages of up to $500. (Bus. & Prof. Code §§ 10167 and following.)

RENTER'S TAX CREDIT

After being suspended by the governor for many years, the renter's tax credit is back. For tax year 2005, married couples filing joint returns, heads of households, and surviving spouses may claim a $120 tax credit if their adjusted gross income is $61,588 or less. Individuals may claim a $60 credit if their income is $30,794 or less. To qualify, you must live in a California rental unit for at least half of the taxable year. And you can't take the credit if someone else (such as your parents) claims you as a dependent on their tax return. Credit amounts will be adjusted yearly. (Rev. and Tax Code § 17053.5.) (Ca. 540 and 540A, 2005 Personal Income Tax Instructions.)

RETALIATORY EVICTIONS AND RENT INCREASES

It is illegal for a landlord to evict a tenant, raise the rent, or decrease services because a tenant takes advantage of any legal right, such as the right to withhold rent because the premises are uninhabitable, the right to repair a serious defect and deduct the cost from rent payments, or the right to organize or join a tenants' organization. (Civ. Code § 1942.5.)

If a tenant (whose rent is paid up) complains to a government agency about defects in the premises or claims that the rental unit is uninhabitable in a lawsuit or arbitration proceeding, and the landlord subsequently raises the rent, decreases services, or evicts the tenant within 180 days, the law presumes that the landlord's action was retaliatory. (Civ. Code § 1942.5(a).)

A tenant who claims retaliation took place more than 180 days after complaining to a government agency must prove that the rent increase, tenancy termination, or decrease in service was retaliatory.

ROOMMATES

People who share rental premises—and have each signed the lease—have legal rights and obligations to each other and to the landlord.

Legal Obligations of Roommates

Tenants who enter into a lease or rental agreement (written or oral) are each obligated to the landlord for all rent and the cost of repairing all damage to the unit. Tenants may agree among themselves—orally or in writing—to split deposits, rent, and chores necessary to maintain the premises in any way they wish. Should one tenant fail to pay his or her fair share, the others are still obligated to pay the landlord, but also have the right to sue the other tenant for the agreed-upon amount.

New Roommates, Assignments, and Sublets

Many written lease and rental agreements limit the number of people who can live in the unit and state that all tenants must be named on the lease or rental agreement, or specifically prohibit letting others live there without the landlord's consent. A tenant may violate this provision by:

- leaving without the landlord's permission in the middle of a month or lease term and letting someone take over the remainder of the lease or rental agreement (this is called assignment of the lease) without the landlord's permission
- renting the rental property to someone else temporarily without the landlord's permission (subletting)—for example, during a vacation, or
- allowing a new person to become a permanent occupant, without the consent of the landlord.

The landlord may evict a tenant who violates the lease or rental agreement in any of these ways. However, if a person moves into a rental unit without permission from the landlord, but the landlord accepts rent from that person and otherwise treats the new occupant as a tenant, the landlord may lose the right to evict. In addition, rent control ordinances in some cities (notably, San Francisco) may limit the landlord's opportunity to disapprove of a new roommate who replaces an existing one.

SALE OF RENTED PROPERTY

When a landlord sells a rental house or apartment building, and the new owner steps in as the landlord, the new owner is subject to the terms of the lease or rental agreement that the previous owner made with the tenants.

The former landlord must transfer all security deposits, less any legal deduction for damage to the unit, to either the tenants or the new owner. If the seller transfers deposits to the new owner, the seller must give tenants a written notice of the change of ownership, itemizing all deductions (such as back rent) and giving the new owner's name, address, and phone number. (Civ. Code § 1950.4(8)(1).) If the former landlord does not transfer the entire deposit, the new owners can require that tenants make up the difference only if they were notified of the deduction and the deposit was legally withheld. (Civ. Code § 1950.5.) If the old owner doesn't give the required notice, the new owner will be responsible for returning the entire original security deposit (less legitimate deductions) when the tenant moves out.

Foreclosure Sales

When property is sold through a nonjudicial foreclosure (a foreclosure with no court involvement), the new owner must honor the leases of the existing tenants whose tenancies were created before the deed of trust or mortgage was recorded in the County Recorder's Office. If a tenant began his tenancy after the recording of the mortgage or deed of trust, or if there is a clause in the rental agreement or lease that specifies that the lease will be "junior" or "subordinate" to any deeds of trust or mortgages placed on the property, the lease is automatically terminated by the sale, and the new owner can begin eviction proceedings with a three-day notice. (Code of Civil Procedure §§ 1161a and following; *R-Ranch Markets No. 2, Inc. v. Old Stone Bank*, 16 Cal. App. 4th 1323 (1993).)

TENANCIES IN COMMON

Owners who wish to withdraw from the rental business often sell small rental properties to two, three, or four owners, each of whom intends to occupy a unit. This type of ownership is known as a "tenancy in common." It differs from condominium ownership in that the individual owners of a tenancy in common decide among themselves who will live where (by contrast, condominium owners own specific parts of the building).

New owners who intend to convert a rental building into a tenancy in common must comply with the notice requirements of the Ellis Act, as explained in Condominium Conversion, above. ■

Real Estate

You can buy or sell property on your own, without a real estate agent or lawyer. As a seller, you are bound only by a legal duty to disclose certain problems with the property and not to discriminate against prospective buyers for arbitrary reasons. If a real estate agent is involved in the transaction, his or her role is also restricted by law.

Here we cover the practical, financial aspects of property ownership, including taxes, taking title, and neighborhood disputes.

TOPICS

Adverse Possession
Buying and Selling a House
Deeds
Earthquake Insurance
Easements
Fences
Homestead
Mortgages
Noise
Nuisance
Property Taxes
Solar Energy
Taxes From the Sale of a House
Title Searches and Insurance
Title to Real Estate
Trees
Views
Zoning

RELATED TOPICS

Consumers' Rights

Contractors

Debts, Loans, and Credit

Liens

Inheritance and Wills

Joint Tenancy

Landlords and Tenants

Relationships

Community and Separate Property

ADDITIONAL RESOURCES

How to Buy a House in California, by Ralph Warner, Ira Serkes, and George Devine (Nolo), explains all the details of the house-buying process and contains tear-out contracts and disclosure forms.

Neighbor Law: Fences, Trees, Boundaries & Noise, by Cora Jordan (Nolo), explains the laws that affect neighbors and shows how to resolve common disputes without lawsuits.

For Sale by Owner in California, by George Devine (Nolo), takes homeowners through the process of selling a house in California, with or without a real estate agent.

Deeds for California Real Estate, by Mary Randolph (Nolo), contains tear-out deed forms and instructions for transferring California real estate.

The California Association of Realtors (CAR) provides a variety of consumer information online, including updates on state and federal legislation and links to sites for California home buyers and sellers. Includes real estate listing information and a directory of California Realtors. Visit CAR's website at www.car.org.

The Internal Revenue Service (IRS) offers a wealth of information on current tax laws involving real estate transactions. If you're selling your house, for example, see IRS Publication 523, *Selling Your Home*. Contact the IRS by phone at 800-829-1040, or online at www.irs.gov.

The California Franchise Tax Board provides information on California tax rules and procedures. Contact the Board at 800-338-0505 or check their website at www.ftb.ca.gov.

The California Seismic Safety Commission provides seismic hazard disclosure forms and booklets for a small charge. Call or write to the Commission at 1755 Creekside Oaks Drive, Suite 100, Sacramento, CA 95833, 916-263-5506. For more information and a list of publications, visit the Commission's website at www.seismic.ca.gov.

The California Department of Health Services provides information on environmental lead hazards, including a list of state-certified lead inspectors and testing laboratories. For details, contact the Department's Childhood Lead Poisoning Prevention Branch at 510-622-5000 or check their website at www.dhs.ca.gov/childlead.

The National Lead Information Center provides information on lead hazards and federal disclosure requirements. The Center can be reached by phone at 800-424-LEAD or online at www.epa.gov/lead.

The California Department of Real Estate (DRE) licenses real estate agents and brokers. To file a complaint about an agent's fraudulent or dishonest acts, or to find out whether an agent's license has been suspended or revoked, contact the nearest DRE office. See the DRE website (www.dre.ca.gov) for updated information on real estate laws and regulations.

The California Home Page (www.state.ca.us) provides extensive information for home buyers in the "Golden State"—from schools and jobs to business and environmental programs.

ADVERSE POSSESSION

You can gain ownership of someone else's property by "adverse possession" when you use the property for five years openly, continuously, and exclusively, without the owner's permission and while paying the annual real estate taxes. (Code of Civ. Proc. § 325.) Property owners may prevent this by giving the trespasser permission to use the land (put it in writing).

Trespassers can also gain the right to use a portion of someone else's property for a particular purpose. This is called a "prescriptive easement." (See Easements.)

BUYING AND SELLING A HOUSE

You can legally buy or sell your own California house without a real estate broker or attorney—as long as you (and all other owners) are sane and at least 18 years old.

Real Estate Brokers

With a few exceptions, anyone who represents you in selling a house must have an active real estate broker's license or be a licensed agent supervised by an active licensed broker. If you pay someone who is not known to have a real estate license, you can be fined up to $100. A nonlicensed agent can be fined up to $10,000 and sentenced to six months in county jail. (Bus. & Prof. Code §§ 10138-39.)

A broker can legally represent the buyer, the seller, or both. Traditionally, all brokers and agents (even those who primarily help the buyer) legally represent and are paid by the seller. However, it is increasingly common for buyers to insist on dual agency, which means the broker legally represents both buyer and seller even though the seller pays the commission. And some buyers hire and pay their own agent.

Payment and commissions. It is illegal for brokers to get together and establish a statewide or regionwide commission rate. By common practice, however, most real estate brokers set their individual commissions at 5–7% of the sale price of a house. Some discount rates are available. Brokers must tell prospective clients that commissions are negotiable.

Usually, brokers are paid when a house closes escrow. However, if a seller lists a house with a broker under an Exclusive Authorization or

Exclusive Agency contract, and the broker brings an offer that meets or exceeds the listing price and terms, the seller owes a commission— whether or not the seller goes through with the sale.

Disclosure

Real Estate Transfer Disclosure Statement. Sellers must give buyers a disclosure form, called a Real Estate Transfer Disclosure Statement. (Civ. Code §§ 1102-1102.6.) Sellers are expected to know about and disclose pretty much anything that might affect the house's value, such as:

- neighborhood nuisances, including noise problems
- environmental hazards such as asbestos or lead-based paint
- whether work done on the house was according to local building codes and done with permits
- any restrictions on the use of the property, such as zoning ordinances, planning restrictions, and "covenants, conditions, and restrictions" (CC&Rs) and homeowners' association dues
- whether the various features and appliances, such as a water heater or dishwasher, are in operating condition
- existence of any window security bars, including any safety-release mechanisms, and
- defective conditions such as a leaky roof or problems with electrical or plumbing systems.

Sellers are responsible for disclosing only information within their personal knowledge. However, they must fill out the form honestly and must take "ordinary care" in obtaining information about the property that, as a reasonable homeowner, they should know. If a seller carelessly or intentionally makes an error or omission in the disclosure statement, the sale is still valid, but the seller will be liable for any actual losses the buyer suffers as a result.

Real estate agents (brokers and salespeople) must conduct a "reasonably competent and diligent" visual inspection of property and disclose to buyers anything that would affect the value or desirability of the property. (Civ. Code §§ 2079, 2079.3.) Agents do not have to inspect inaccessible areas or review public documents affecting title to or use of the property.

A prospective purchaser who doesn't receive a copy of the disclosure statement until after making an offer to buy the house has three days from the date of the disclosure statement (five days if the statement was mailed, rather than personally delivered) to withdraw the offer. (Civ. Code § 1102.3.)

Natural Hazard Disclosure Statement. Sellers must also give prospective buyers a Natural Hazard Disclosure Statement (Civ. Code § 1103.2.)—or use a Local Option Real Estate Disclosure Statement (Civ. Code § 1102.6.a)—if the property is in one of several specific types of hazard areas:

- a flood hazard zone designated by the Federal Emergency Management Area (FEMA) (42 U.S.C. §§ 4001 and following)
- an area of potential flooding (due to dam failure) as identified by the Office of Emergency Services (Gov't. Code § 8589.5)
- a very high fire hazard severity zone (Gov't. Code §§ 51178, 51179) or a wildland area containing substantial forest fire risks and hazards (Pub. Res. Code § 4125)
- a delineated earthquake fault zone as identified by the California State Geologist (Pub. Res. Code § 2622), or
- a seismic hazards zone (Pub. Res. Code § 2696).

Sellers must also provide a disclosure statement if the house has any known seismic deficiencies, such as a lack of bolts or other anchors between the house and its foundation. (Gov't. Code § 8897.)

Lead-based paint disclosures. Under California law, sellers must disclose lead-based paint hazards to prospective buyers on a Real Estate Transfer Disclosure Statement. (Civil Code § 1102.6.) Furthermore, sellers of houses built before 1978 must comply with the Residential Lead-Based Paint Hazard Reduction Act of 1992, also known as Title X. (42 U.S. Code § 4852d.) Sellers must:

- disclose all known lead-based paint and hazards in the house
- give buyers a pamphlet prepared by the U.S. Environmental Protection Agency (EPA) called *Protect Your Family From Lead in Your Home,* or the California Enviromental Protection Agency's booklet *Residential Environmental Hazards: A Guide for Homeowners, Landlords and Tenants, and Buyers* (for information about how to obtain these pamphlets, see the Additional Resources section at the beginning of this chapter)

- include certain warning language in the contract as well as signed statements from all parties verifying that all requirements were completed
- keep signed acknowledgments for three years as proof of compliance, and
- give buyers a ten-day opportunity to test the housing for lead.

Registered sex offenders. All contracts for the sale of a house or other residential real estate must include a notice, in not less than eight-point type, regarding the availability of a database maintained by law enforcement authorities on the location of registered sex offenders. (Civ. Code § 2079.10a.)

Discrimination

It's illegal to discriminate in the sale of real property on the basis of race, sex, marital status, or other group characteristics.

The House Sales Contract

A contract to sell real estate must be in writing to be valid. An oral offer to purchase real estate is legally worthless—meaning a seller is out of luck if the buyer wants out of the deal. (Civ. Code § 1624.)

The asking price listed in a newspaper ad or flyer is just a starting point for negotiations over price and other terms of sale. A seller is not obligated to sell at the advertised price even if someone offers that amount. The seller may be holding out for a higher bid.

Deposits and contingencies. Most sellers require the buyer to put down a deposit when the buyer makes an offer. Most buyers make their offers contingent upon several factors, such as the house passing a physical inspection or the buyer being able to arrange financing. If the deal doesn't go through because a contingency can't be fulfilled, the seller must return the deposit.

If the buyer backs out simply because she changes her mind, or doesn't try in good faith to fulfill a contingency (for instance, the buyer doesn't apply for a loan), the seller need not return the entire deposit. Most house purchase contracts put a ceiling on the amount the seller can keep in this situation. California law generally prohibits sellers from keeping more than 3% of the agreed-upon sale price. (Civ. Code § 1675.)

Breach of contract. If the seller backs out of the deal, the prospective buyer can mediate, arbitrate, or sue. If it comes to a lawsuit, the buyer will probably ask the court to order the seller to go through with the sale and pay the buyer's out-of-pocket losses.

A real estate purchase contract is enforceable even if the buyer or the seller dies, because a deceased person's estate is responsible for fulfilling that person's lawful obligations. If the executors of the deceased person's estate want to get out of the deal, however, they may negotiate a release.

New construction defect legislation in California sets up a procedure that requires consumers who purchase new homes and discover construction defects to bring their complaints directly to builders, who then have a specified amount of time to correct the defect or make a cash settlement. If they do neither, and no agreement is reached, the homeowner can then file a lawsuit. (Civ. Code §§ 911, 912, 938, 942, 943.)

DEEDS

A deed is a document that transfers ownership of real estate.

Kinds of Deeds

In California, the most common kinds of deeds are grant, quitclaim, and trust deeds.

- **Grant deed.** The most commonly used type of deed. It guarantees that the land being transferred hasn't already been transferred to someone else or been encumbered, except as specified in the deed. (Civ. Code § 1113.)
- **Quitclaim deed.** A deed that is used to give up one's claims to land. It makes no promises about the title being transferred; the maker of a quitclaim deed simply transfers whatever interest in the land he or she may have. Quitclaims are often used when couples divorce; one spouse signs a quitclaim deed, giving up any potential claims to the other's property. The other spouse doesn't have to worry about a claim being made later.
- **Trust deed (deed of trust).** A trust deed is not like other deeds—it's more like a mortgage. It is used when someone pledges real estate as security for a loan, in conjunction with a promissory note (a written promise to pay back the loan). The buyer signs the note and a trust

deed, which permits its holder (the trustee) to sell the property and pay off the loan if the buyer fails to pay. If a homeowner takes out a second loan that is secured by the property, that trust deed is called a "second deed of trust." (See Mortgages, below.)

Preparing a Deed

Fill-in-the-blank deed forms are available from form books and office supply stores, online, and in law libraries. A deed must contain the name of the grantor (person transferring the property), the grantee (the new owner), and a legal description of the property (copied from the old deed). It must be signed in the presence of a notary public, who verifies the signatures. The notary will also take a thumbprint or a fingerprint, under a law designed to help prevent you from becoming the victim of a real estate scam. (Gov't. Code § 8206.)

Recording a Deed

All deeds should be recorded—that is, put on file at the county recorder's office. Recording creates a public record of who owns every inch of land in the state. It allows a prospective buyer to look up a parcel of property and find out who owns it, how much it is mortgaged for, and whether it is subject to any other encumbrances or restrictions—a lien or easement, for example.

To record a deed, take the original signed deed to the recorder's office in the county where the property is located. The clerk will make a copy and file it in the public records. Recording costs a few dollars per page. You will also have to fill out a change of ownership form, which notifies the county tax assessor that the property has changed hands.

EARTHQUAKE INSURANCE

Whenever an insurance company issues a homeowner's insurance policy, it must offer earthquake insurance (though the company can offer state-sponsored insurance). (Ins. Code § 10081.) The offered policy must cover loss or damage to the dwelling and its contents and living expenses for the occupants if the house is temporarily uninhabitable. The offer of earthquake coverage must be printed in at least 10-point bold type. (Ins. Code § 10083.)

If the homeowner decides not to buy earthquake coverage, the insurance company must send the owner written notice that the policy does not include earthquake coverage. The insurance company must continue to offer earthquake insurance every other year, and every policy renewal must include the statement that the policy doesn't contain earthquake coverage. (Ins. Code §§ 10086, 10086.1.)

EASEMENTS

An easement is a legal right to use someone else's land for a particular purpose. The property owner must allow the easement holder to use the property according to the terms of the easement.

Written Easements

Easements are usually in writing and recorded (put on file), like property deeds, at the county recorder's office. They may also be referred to in property deeds or title insurance reports.

Utility easements are the most common kind. For example, the electric company may have the right to string wires across your property, or the water or gas company may have an easement to run pipes under your land. Utility easement holders have the implicit right to enter property (at reasonable times and with reasonable notice) to service their equipment. To find out where utility easements are located on your property, call the company or check the maps at the county planning office or city hall. A survey of the property will also show utility easements.

Property may also be subject to private written easements—easements that allow a neighbor to use a driveway or ensure that a neighbor has sewer or solar access, for example. If your property is subject to private easements, get copies of the easement documents from your neighbor or the county recorder. If you don't know where the easements are and what uses they allow, you could unknowingly interfere with the easement rights and be liable for the damage.

Easements by Necessity

Even if it isn't written down, a legal easement can exist if it's absolutely necessary for one property owner to cross someone else's land for a legitimate purpose. The law grants people a right of access to their homes, for example. So if the only access to a piece of land is by crossing a neighbor's property, the law recognizes an easement allowing access over the neighbor's land. This is called an "easement by necessity."

Easements Acquired by Use of Property

Someone can acquire an easement over another's land for a particular purpose by using the land without permission, openly, and continuously for five years. (Code of Civ. Proc. § 321.) An easement acquired in this way is called a prescriptive easement. Once an easement is created in this way, it's permanent unless purchased back by the land owner or allowed to lapse by the easement owner.

Typically, a prescriptive easement is created when someone uses land for access, such as a driveway or shortcut. But many times, a neighbor simply begins using a part of the adjoining property. He may farm it or even build on it. After five years, he gains a legal right to use the property for that purpose.

Preventing Prescriptive Easements

If you don't mind someone using part of your property, the simplest way to prevent a prescriptive easement is to grant the person permission to use the property. Your permission cancels any claim to a prescriptive easement. You should put the permission in writing. You can cancel the permission at any time (or according to any cancellation term you put in the written permission).

If you don't want someone to use your property, tell the person to stop. If the person doesn't stop, you may have to take more drastic measures, such as calling the police or suing for trespassing.

Public Easements

When members of the public do the trespassing, a public right to use property can be created. For example, if the owners of beachfront property let the county pave a private drive, which is then used by many people for access to the beach, the public would gain a right to use the drive.

When the public is using a private strip, posting signs granting permission at every entrance and at certain intervals protects you from claims of a prescriptive easement. (Civ. Code § 1008.) If possible, also put the permission in writing and record it (file a copy) at the county recorder's office. (Civ. Code § 813.)

Terminating an Easement

Easements don't change when the property changes hands. Subsequent owners must continue to let whoever owns the easement use the property. (Civ. Code § 1104.)

A property owner can, however, buy back an easement from the easement's owner. The document should be recorded, like the original easement, at the county recorder's office. A prescriptive easement that isn't used for five years may be forfeited because it has been legally abandoned. (Civ. Code § 811.)

FENCES

Local laws often regulate fence height and materials and may require you to get a building permit before building a fence. Fences in front yards are often limited to four feet in height; in backyards, six feet is often the maximum allowed. A row of trees that is used as a fence may also be subject to these laws. These laws are often loosely enforced; if no one complains, most cities ignore violations.

Regulations in planned communities and subdivisions (called Covenants, Conditions, and Restrictions, or CC&Rs) may be more detailed.

Cities and homeowners' associations grant exemptions from fence ordinances or rules if the property owner has a good reason—for example, if a tall fence is needed to screen property from a heavily used street.

Boundary Fences

A boundary fence is a fence that is on the line between two properties and is used by both owners. Neither may remove it without the other's permission, and both are responsible for maintaining it. (Civ. Code § 841.) An owner who makes needed repairs can demand that the other neighbor chip in half the cost.

Spite Fences

A spite fence is any fence (or structure that serves as a fence) that is more than ten feet high, was built to annoy a neighbor, and has no reasonable use for its owner—for example, a 12-foot rough wood fence built a foot from a neighbor's windows. (Civ. Code § 841.4.) The affected neighbor can sue the fence builder and ask a court to order the spite fence removed.

Rural Fences

Most California counties follow the "closed range" rule, which means that livestock owners must fence in their animals or be liable for any damage they cause to others' property. Some counties, however, follow the "open range" rule. In those counties, landowners who don't fence their property can't complain about damage caused by others' animals.

HOMESTEAD

A homestead is not the land a settler could get for free in the 1800s from the federal government. Rather, it refers to the portion of an owner's equity interest in a house, condominium, or mobile home that is protected from creditors.

There are two kinds of homestead protection. Every owner with equity in residential property that he or she lives in is entitled to automatic homestead protection—that is, he or she can keep a certain amount of the proceeds if a creditor ever forces a sale of the home. To get greater protection, and to discourage creditors from forcing a sale of the home in the first place, some owners file a Declaration of Homestead. (Code of Civ. Proc. §§ 704.710 and following.)

A creditor can force a sale of a homesteaded home only if there will be sufficient proceeds to:
- pay all existing liens (claims against the property)
- pay off all mortgages and other loans secured by equity in the home, and
- pay the owner the homestead amount.

The creditor will also want to make sure that there is enough money left over to pay for the costs of selling the house and pay the debt owed by the owner. Many creditors find that it isn't worth the trouble to force a sale.

How a Declaration of Homestead Works

A Declaration of Homestead is a legal document that homeowners can file with the County Recorder in the county where they live. The document protects a specified amount of the owners' equity in their home from a forced sale, just like an automatic homestead.

However, a Declaration of Homestead also protects that same amount from creditors if the owners voluntarily sell their home. For six months after the sale, this amount is protected from creditors. If the owners invest the money in a new home and file another Homestead Declaration on that home during the six-month period, the money remains protected. Some title companies, however, refuse to clear title in this situation, despite the clear language of the homestead law. (Code of Civ. Proc. § 704.960.) They insist that owners pay off judgment liens with the equity that is supposed to be protected by the declared homestead.

How Much Equity Is Protected

The amount of equity an owner can keep depends on the owner's circumstances when the home is sold:

- Single owners can exempt $50,000.
- Members of a family (which includes spouses or registered domestic partners living together and most family members) can exempt $75,000.
- Those who are 55 or older and whose income is $15,000 or less (single) or $20,000 or less (married or registered domestic partners) can exempt $150,000.
- Those who are disabled or are over 65 can exempt $150,000.

Debts That Are Unaffected by Homestead

A homestead does not protect the owner's equity in a home against certain kinds of debts. This means that a creditor can force a sale of the home despite the homestead, and can take even that portion of equity that the homestead protects, when the debts are:

- child support or spousal support (alimony)
- mortgage or home equity loans (if you pledge your home as collateral for the loan, the creditor must be able to sell the home to collect on the debt), and
- tax debts.

How to File a Declaration of Homestead

A Declaration of Homestead is a simple one-page form. The owner must fill it out, have it notarized, and send it in to the County Recorder in the county where he or she resides. There is a small filing fee.

MORTGAGES

In California, someone who borrows money from a lender to finance the purchase of a house signs a document called a deed of trust. The deed of trust gives a trustee (often a title company) the right to sell the property (foreclose), with no court approval, if the borrower fails to pay the lender on time. In other words, if the buyer defaults, the lender can request that the trustee sell the house and pay the lender from the proceeds. The foreclosure process usually takes six months or more, and the borrower has several chances to make up missed payments.

The trust deed and the deed that actually transfers ownership of the property to the buyer are both filed (recorded) at the County Recorder's Office. This makes them part of the public record.

Deducting Mortgage Interest Payments

With certain restrictions, the mortgage interest paid on a home is deductible from state and federal income taxes. For mortgages taken out before October 1987, there is no limit on the amount of interest you can deduct. For mortgages taken out after October 1987, the IRS says you can deduct no more than the interest on a mortgage balance of:

- $1 million for mortgages to buy, build, or improve a home, or
- $100,000 for mortgages used for other purposes (for example, a home equity loan to finance a car).

These figures are for married couples who file a joint income tax return. If you're single, cut the figures in half. For more information, see IRS publication 936, *Home Mortgage Interest Deduction*, available at www.irs.gov.

NOISE

Almost every community has an ordinance prohibiting excessive and unreasonable noise. Police enforce these laws; it's up to the investigating officer to decide what is unreasonable under the circumstances.

Many municipal ordinances forbid:

- loud noise during "quiet hours," such as after 11 p.m. and before 8 a.m.
- noise that exceeds certain decibel limits, or
- specific kinds of noise, such as continually barking dogs or loud motorcycles.

If a neighbor's noise is excessive and deliberate, it may also violate state law against disturbing the peace. (Pen. Code § 415.)

NUISANCE

If your neighbor is doing something that is illegal, indecent, offensive, or unsafe and interferes with your enjoyment of your property, that is a nuisance. (Civ. Code § 3479.) Some common examples include making excessive noise, producing offensive fumes, or drug dealing. If the problem affects the entire neighborhood (even if it affects one person the most), it is a public nuisance. (Civ. Code § 3480.)

Even if there's not a specific law banning the activity, you can sue your neighbor to have it stopped. (Civ. Code §§ 3493, 3501.) A lawsuit is rarely necessary, however; disputes can usually be resolved with help from a neighborhood mediation service. If you can't work things out short of legal action, small claims court is usually the best place to bring your dispute.

The law also allows someone affected by a public (but not a private) nuisance to remove or destroy the thing that constitutes the nuisance, as long as he or she gives notice to the neighbor first and doesn't commit a "breach of the peace" or cause unnecessary injury. (Civ. Code § 3495.)

PROPERTY TAXES

California has a unique system of taxing real estate. It's the result of Proposition 13, a ballot measure passed in the mid-1970s that amended the state constitution. (Rev. & Tax Code § 50; Const. Art. XIII-A § 1.)

All property tax assessments are based on the value of the property in the 1975-76 tax year. As long as the property doesn't change hands, the assessment can increase a maximum of 2% each year from that base figure, unless local voters approve a larger increase—for example, to fund local schools.

However, the assessment is raised to the current market value of the property when ownership of the property is transferred (except in certain intrafamily transfers, such as between spouses or from parent to child). That virtually always means a big tax increase for a new owner. Improvements that increase the value of the house can also increase the tax assessment. Property taxes are 1% to 1.25% (depending on the county) annually of the assessed value of the house.

Assessment Exception for Homeowners Over 55 or Disabled

Homeowners who are over age 55 or severely or permanently disabled (only one spouse of a married couple need qualify) who sell one house and purchase another of equal or lesser value within two years in the same county (or in a county that participates in a statewide transfer system) may transfer their old tax assessment rate to the new house. (Rev. & Tax Code § 69.5.)

Deducting Property Taxes

Payments made for property taxes are fully deductible from state and federal income taxes.

Transfers to Living Trusts

When real estate is transferred to a revocable living trust, and the owner of the real estate is the trustee of the trust, the property is not reassessed for property tax purposes. (Rev. & Tax. Code § 62(d).)

SOLAR ENERGY

Solar Energy Systems

No one may unreasonably prohibit or restrict the use or installation of a solar energy system under any deed, contract, covenant, condition, restriction, or other instrument affecting the transfer or sale of real property. Reasonable restrictions are those that do not significantly increase the system's cost or decrease its efficiency or that allow for an alternate system with comparable benefits. Systems that produce hot water and electricity must meet state-mandated standards. (Civ. Code §§ 714, 714.1.)

Solar Easements

California law specifically recognizes solar easements—easements that give a property owner the right to receive sunlight to power a solar energy system that results in heating, space cooling, electric generation, or water heating. The document creating the easement must describe the dimensions of the easement, the restrictions on vegetation or structures that would block sunlight, and the conditions under which the easement can be revised or terminated. (Civ. Code § 801.5.)

TAXES FROM THE SALE OF A HOUSE

Upon selling a home, an individual may exclude up to $250,000 of capital gain from tax. For married couples filing jointly, the exclusion is $500,000. (I.R.C. § 121.) If unmarried co-owners sell a house, each of them may exclude up to $250,000 if they meet the requirements.

To claim the whole exclusion, you must have owned and lived in your residence an aggregate of at least two of five years before the sale (this rule is called the "ownership and use" test). You can claim the exclusion once every two years.

Even if you haven't lived in your home a total of two years out of the last five, you are still eligible for a partial exclusion of capital gains if you sold because of a change in employment, health, or unforeseen circumstances. You get a percentage of the exclusion, based on the portion of the two-year period you lived in the home. To calculate the percentage, take the number of months you lived there before the sale and divide it by 24.

If you expect huge gains from selling a house—more than can be excluded from tax under the new rule—you might consider ways to divide ownership of the house to reduce taxes.

TITLE SEARCHES AND INSURANCE

Title insurance guarantees that someone who's selling a piece of real estate has the legal right to sell it, and that no one else has ownership rights that could surface later and cause problems for the new owner.

Title Searches

A title search is a search of all public records relating to a certain parcel of property. It's routine when real estate is sold; the goal is to find out whether there are any problems (unpaid property taxes, for example) that will interfere with the transfer.

A title search costs a few hundred dollars and is usually done by a title insurance company. A title search tells you whether:

- the property has been pledged as security for a loan (mortgaged)
- a written easement has been granted
- certain liens (legal claims) have been placed on the property
- the property taxes haven't been paid
- a lawsuit has been filed contesting ownership of the property, or

• a prior deed was invalid.

Unrecorded transfers or easements, of course, don't show up in a title search. Community property interests also won't be uncovered in a title search—for example, even if the deed to a house is in one spouse or domestic partner's name alone, it may legally belong to both.

Title Insurance

Title companies guarantee the results of their searches by issuing title insurance policies. Title insurance protects a buyer (or a lender who finances the purchase of the property) against claims that the search overlooked something. A typical title insurance policy would cover an owner's losses if, for example, any of the transfer documents are fraudulent or forged, or there is a lien or easement on the property that the title company didn't find when it searched the records.

Separate policies protect the buyer and the lender. The buyer's policy insures to the amount of the purchase price. If someone (including the seller) is lending money to the buyer, and the loan is secured by a deed of trust on the property, the lender usually buys a policy for the amount of the loan.

TITLE TO REAL ESTATE

Someone who owns property is said to have title to it. If more than one person owns a piece of property, title can be held in different ways. Choosing the right way to hold title is important, because each one has different legal consequences.

Tenancy in Common

To create a tenancy in common, the deed must transfer property to two or more persons either "as tenants in common" or without specifying how title is to be held. Shares of co-owners are presumed to be equal unless unequal shares are specified on the deed.

If you're a co-owner, you may sell or give away your interest, or leave it to someone in a will or living trust. If you want the whole property sold, you can go to court and get a court order (called a partition order) requiring the sale. After the sale, the proceeds will be divided among the co-owners. At your death, your interest passes to your heirs under state law or to the beneficiaries you named in a will or living trust.

Joint Tenancy

The most significant feature of joint tenancy, in most situations, is that when one co-owner dies, the surviving owner(s) automatically own the property, without probate proceedings. This is true even if the deceased owner's will left his share of the property to someone else.

To create a joint tenancy, the deed must transfer property to two or more persons "as joint tenants" or "with right of survivorship." All joint tenants must own equal shares of the property. If you're a joint tenant, you may end the joint tenancy by transferring your interest to yourself or to someone else, or you may get a partition order from the court. (Civ. Code § 683.2.)

Community Property

Community property real estate is a special form of title for married couples and registered domestic partners. Community property is created when a deed transfers property to the couple "as community property" or "as husband and wife." Each person owns a one-half interest in the property. Community property ownership ends when the property is transferred to someone outside the marriage or the spouses or partners change the way they own it—for example, by transferring it to themselves as tenants in common. Both owners must approve transfers of community real estate. (Fam. Code § 1102.) If you hold title this way, you can leave your half of the property to anyone, but if you don't say who should inherit it, it goes to your surviving spouse or partner.

Community Property With Right of Survivorship

Married couples and registered domestic partners can also own community property in a special way, with the "right of survivorship." If you use this form of ownership, when one spouse or partner dies, the other will automatically own the property, without any probate court proceedings. To do this, you must hold title to the property as "community property with right of survivorship." (Civ. Code § 682.1.)

Partnership

Partnership property is created when a deed transfers property to a partnership by name, or partnership money is used to buy the property. (Civ. Code § 684.) The share of each co-owner and the conditions under which the partnership can sell or give away the property are determined by the partnership agreement or the Uniform Partnership Act. (Corp. Code §§ 16101 and following.) When one partner dies, his or her interest in the property usually goes to the partner's heirs under state law or to the beneficiaries named in the will, but the partnership agreement may give the partnership the right to buy in at a certain price.

TREES

A number of state laws affect trees, recognizing their special place in the hearts of those who own them.

Ownership

The location of the trunk determines who owns a tree. If the trunk is entirely on one person's land, that person owns the tree, even though the roots may grow into the other's land. If the trunk is on a boundary line, it belongs to both (or all) landowners. (Civ. Code §§ 833, 834.)

The owners of a boundary tree are jointly responsible for its care and maintenance. Neither owner may harm or remove a healthy boundary tree without the other's permission. (A court might make an exception to this rule if removing the tree were absolutely necessary for one owner to make reasonable use of his or her property.) If the tree is dangerous because it is diseased or dead, either owner may (and should) remove it.

Damage to a Tree

Generally, someone who wrongfully damages or removes a tree is liable to the owner for three times the amount of the actual monetary loss. If, however, the damage was unintentional or the person reasonably believed the tree was on his land, the amount owed is only twice the amount of the actual loss. (Civ. Code § 3346.) If the damage or removal was intentional or malicious, a court might also make the wrongdoer pay an additional amount (called punitive damages) as punishment.

Intentionally or carelessly harming someone's tree is also a crime—a misdemeanor punishable by a fine of up to $1,000, up to six months in the county jail, or both. (Pen. Code § 384a.)

Encroaching Branches and Roots

Property owners have the right to cut off branches and roots that stray onto their property. But the owner may not:

- trim past the property line
- enter the neighbor's property without permission unless the limbs threaten imminent, grave harm
- cut down the tree itself, or
- destroy the tree by the trimming.

A city permit may be required for any significant trimming or for pruning certain species of tree; check with the city clerk's office.

A landowner seriously inconvenienced by the encroaching branches or roots of a neighbor's tree can also sue the neighbor for nuisance.

Dangerous or Diseased Trees

Some cities remove dangerous trees from private property themselves. Others order the owner to do it, pronto; if the owner doesn't do it, the city steps in, takes out the tree, and bills the owner.

A tree owner in a town or city who knows, or should know, that a tree is obviously unsound and likely to cause damage must correct the problem or be liable for any injury or property damage that does occur. In rural areas, owners may not be held liable if they didn't know the tree was dangerous.

Protected and Forbidden Trees

It's increasingly common for cities to restrict removal of certain valuable native species of trees, such as redwoods or certain pine trees. Other species may be designated a nuisance or a danger, and their planting may be prohibited.

VIEWS

Most California landowners have no legal right to an unobstructed view from their property. Neighbors are free to block the view by letting their trees grow or by building useful structures.

Dozens of cities, however, have passed ordinances that give owners the right to sue neighbors whose growing trees block the view they had when they moved in or on a certain date. These laws usually require the person who complains to pay for the tree trimming. Some exempt certain kinds of trees; Oakland, for example, doesn't allow a neighbor to force the cutting of a redwood, California live oak, box elder, bigleaf maple, and other species.

Subdivision restrictions may also protect residents' views. Check your rules, usually called Covenants, Conditions, and Restrictions (CC&Rs).

ZONING

Zoning ordinances regulate how landowners can use their property. A primary goal is to separate incompatible uses, such as residences and industries.

Zoning Ordinances

City and county zoning laws divide an area into districts, which are set aside for particular uses. Usually, there are districts for single-family homes and other districts for apartments or mixed uses. Other zones are earmarked for different types of commercial use. Usually some part of town is reserved for light and heavy manufacturing. Outside of cities, laws allow various types of agriculture.

Within zoning districts, more detailed rules apply. In most places, dwellings must be set back from the street a minimum distance, and only a certain percentage of the lot may be covered by structures and driveways. In most places, however, zoning officials don't go looking for violations; they take their cues from neighbors' complaints.

To check on zoning laws for your city or county, call the local planning or zoning department or read the ordinances themselves online or at the public or law library.

Exceptions to Zoning Laws

Cities and counties sometimes give permission to use land in a way that isn't allowed by the zoning ordinance. These exceptions are called variances or conditional use permits.

Getting an Exception to a Zoning Ordinance

To get an exception, first outline your plans to someone in the zoning or planning department and get some feedback. The staff should be able to refer you to the local ordinance that sets out criteria for granting exceptions.

You'll have to make a formal written request, and the zoning department will probably hold public hearings to give neighbors a chance to object. Get neighbors to speak on your behalf or to write letters or sign a supportive petition. You're very unlikely to get a variance if the neighborhood is against you. If you're turned down, most places have a planning or zoning board you can appeal to. If you lose again, you can probably appeal to a second board, often the city council. If this doesn't work, consider trying to get your property rezoned or even getting the zoning ordinance itself amended. You may also be able to challenge the ordinance, or the city's enforcement practices, in court.

■

Relationships

Federal and state laws enter into even our most private relationships. This section discusses the legalities of marriage and divorce, as well as gay and lesbian relationships and living together when you're not married.

The section also covers federal and state regulations regarding birth control and abortion. Be aware that the law in these areas is volatile and can change along with the political climate.

TOPICS

Abortion

Adultery

Annulment

Bigamy

Birth Control

Common Law Marriage

Community and Separate Property

Divorce

Domestic Partners

Domestic Violence

Gay and Lesbian Couples

Living Together

Marital Debts

Marriage

Separation

Spousal Support (Alimony)

RELATED TOPICS

Children

Adoption

Artificial Insemination

Child Support

ADDITIONAL RESOURCES

Planned Parenthood, 800-230-PLAN, www.plannedparenthood.org, gives information about abortion, birth control, and sexual health, and provides reproductive health services through local clinics.

Annulment: A Step by Step Guide for Divorced Catholics, by Reverend Ronald T. Smith (ACTA Publications), shows you how to get a religious annulment.

How to Do Your Own Divorce in California, by Charles Sherman (Nolo Occidental), contains step-by-step instructions on obtaining a divorce without a lawyer.

Divorce Helpline, 800-359-7004, provides legal information about divorce in California, over the phone, for $10 per call and $5.00 a minute.

Divorce & Money: How to Make the Best Financial Decisions During Divorce, by Violet Woodhouse with Dale Fetherling (Nolo), explains the financial aspects of divorce and property division.

Building a Parenting Agreement That Works: How to Put Your Kids First When Your Marriage Doesn't Last, by Mimi Lyster (Nolo), shows separating or divorcing parents how to create win-win custody agreements.

A Legal Guide for Lesbian & Gay Couples, by Hayden Curry, Denis Clifford, and Frederick Hertz (Nolo), sets out the law and contains sample agreements for couples.

Living Together: A Legal Guide for Unmarried Couples, by Ralph Warner, Toni Ihara, and Frederick Hertz (Nolo), explains the legal rules that apply to unmarried couples and includes sample contracts governing jointly owned property.

Divorce Without Court: A Guide to Mediation & Collaborative Divorce, by Katherine E. Stoner (Nolo), describes two alternatives to a contested divorce in court. The book explains what to expect in mediation or collaborative divorce, and helps you negotiate the best arrangement with your former spouse.

ABORTION

Abortion law is determined by both the state and the federal governments. States are free to allow abortions in any circumstances they choose, but cannot restrict abortions in ways that the U.S. Supreme Court determines would violate the federal constitution. Under the U.S. Supreme Court's 1973 ruling in *Roe v. Wade* (410 U.S. 113 (1973)), states may not restrict a woman's right to an abortion during the first trimester of pregnancy. After the first trimester, a woman's right to choose an abortion must be balanced with the state's right to protect a fetus.

In California, a women's right to an abortion is guaranteed by the California Constitution. Proposed limits on abortions—such as restricting them to pregnancies resulting from rape and incest—have routinely been rejected by state courts. California courts have also ruled that minors may seek abortions for medical reasons (such as when the minor's health is at risk), without first getting parental consent.

ADULTERY

Adultery is sexual intercourse between a married person and someone other than his or her spouse. Adultery is not a crime in California. And because California has a no-fault divorce law, adultery is not legally relevant when a couple divorces and divides marital property.

ANNULMENT

An annulment is a legal proceeding to end a marriage and treat it as though it never happened. In California, a marriage may be annulled if:

- A person under age 18 marries without parental or court permission. The annulment must take place before the minor turns 18.
- A person has remarried, but her first spouse shows up after being missing for at least five years or presumed dead. The second marriage may be annulled.
- A person of "unsound mind" (not capable of consenting to marriage) enters into a marriage. A person who comes to reason and remains in the marriage, however, is not entitled to an annulment.

- A person enters into a marriage after being defrauded by the other spouse. A misled spouse who learns the truth and stays in the marriage, however, can't get an annulment.
- A person agrees to marry after being forced to do so by the other spouse. Again, a person who freely lives with the other after the forced marriage begins won't be granted an annulment.
- A person was, at the time the marriage began, incapable of having children and such incapacity continues and appears to be incurable. (Fam. Code § 2210.)

To file for an annulment, spouses use the same forms they would use if they were filing for divorce. If a marriage is annulled, the couple's property is divided as though they had been married properly, then sought a divorce. If one spouse defrauded or forced the other into the marriage, the noninnocent spouse may be awarded less than 50% of the accumulated property. Children of an annulled marriage are treated like children in divorce—that is, custody and child support will have to be determined, and the children are still considered children of a marriage.

Religious Annulments

Within the Roman Catholic church, a couple may obtain a religious annulment after obtaining a civil divorce. Many people do this so they can remarry within the church. The requirements for a religious annulment are different from those listed above for an annulment under civil law.

BIGAMY

Bigamy is the crime committed when a married person knowingly marries again. However, someone who remarries after his or her spouse has been missing for at least five years or is believed dead is not guilty of bigamy if the first spouse turns up. Prosecution for bigamy is rare, unless the bigamist defrauds one of his spouses financially—for example, by spending the second spouse's income on the first spouse.

Bigamy is punishable by a fine of up to $10,000 or imprisonment for up to one year. A "spouse" who marries a person known to already be married may be punished by a fine of at least $5,000 or a term of imprisonment (no length specified). (Pen. Code §§ 281-284.)

BIRTH CONTROL

The right to decide whether or not to use contraception is an individual privacy right guaranteed by the California and U.S. constitutions. Although the right to privacy has been under recent attack in federal court decisions involving abortion, the right to use contraception is not currently at risk.

Rights of Minors

Federal law requires that public health facilities provide family planning services to all women of childbearing age. However, private doctors and church-affiliated hospitals may refuse to provide these services to minor or unmarried patients.

California law does not require parental notification or consent before a person under 18 can receive contraceptive services from a doctor or health service agency. In addition, no one is legally prevented, because of age, from buying nonprescription contraceptives such as condoms and spermicidal foam.

Birth Control Availability

The right to use birth control and access to birth control are two different things. Availability of birth control often depends more on its cost, and whether or not it requires a doctor's prescription, than on the legal status of contraceptive rights.

The federal Food and Drug Administration is often instrumental in determining whether or not a particular contraceptive can be marketed in the U.S. Because it is responsible for determining the safety and value of products sold in the U.S., the FDA can speed or slow access to new contraceptive technologies.

COMMON LAW MARRIAGE

In some states, couples can become legally married by living together for a long period of time, holding themselves out to others as husband and wife, and intending to be married. These are called common law marriages. Contrary to popular belief, a common law marriage is not obtained simply by living together for a long time, even in the states with common law marriages. The couple also must intend to be married.

California does not permit the establishment of common law marriages. A couple must obtain a marriage license and have a ceremony to get married in this state. If a couple moves to this state after having formed a common law marriage in one of the states listed below, however, California will treat the marriage as valid. (Fam. Code § 308.) This means the parties to a common law marriage can get divorced in California.

If either party to a common law marriage denies that it exists, the other may file an action in superior court to have the validity of the marriage determined. (Fam. Code § 309.) To end a common law marriage, a couple must obtain a divorce or annulment.

States That Allow Common Law Marriages

Alabama	Kansas	Rhode Island
Colorado	Montana	South Carolina
Georgia*	Ohio*	Texas
Idaho*	Oklahoma	Utah
Iowa	Pennsylvania*	Washington, DC

New Hampshire recognizes common law marriages only when one partner dies without a will or other estate plan.

*These states recognize common law marriages created prior to a certain date only (January 1, 1997 in Georgia; January 1, 1996 in Idaho; October 10, 1991 in Ohio; and September, 2003 in Pennsylvania).

COMMUNITY AND SEPARATE PROPERTY

In California, property owned by a married person is classified as either community property or separate property. Community property belongs equally to both spouses; separate property legally belongs to just one spouse. Whether property is community or separate depends on when it was acquired, what kind of property it is, and how it has been used during the marriage.

Classifying Property

Here are the general rules on classifying property that belongs to a married person.

Property acquired before marriage. All property that each spouse owned before marriage is that spouse's separate property.

Property acquired during marriage. Generally, all property acquired by either spouse during marriage is community property, except for gifts and inheritances, which remain the separate property of the recipient. (Fam. Code § 770.) Also, any property purchased by a spouse during marriage entirely with money acquired before marriage is that spouse's separate property, as is property acquired by a spouse during marriage with the proceeds of or income from that spouse's separate property. (Fam. Code § 770.) Here are the specific rules:

- **Wages, salaries, and tips** earned during marriage are community property.
- **Pensions.** The portion of a pension earned during the marriage is community property; the remainder is the separate property of the pension earner.
- **Social Security** benefits are the separate property of the earning spouse.
- **Employment benefits** (such as stock options or profit-sharing plans) are community property if they are based on the spouse's work during the marriage, even if they will not be distributed until after the marriage has ended. Benefits based on the spouse's work before marriage or after separation are separate property, even if they are distributed during the marriage.
- **Copyrights, patents, artwork, and royalties** are community property if they are created, invented, or generated during marriage. If created before marriage or after separation, they are separate property, even if they are sold during the marriage.
- **Personal injury recoveries** (lawsuit settlements, for example) that either spouse receives during marriage from a third party are community property during the marriage. At divorce, however, these

funds become the separate property of the injured spouse, unless the money has been combined with community property. (Fam. Code §§ 2603, 781.)

- **Businesses existing before marriage** are the separate property of the owner spouse, but if either spouse contributes community money or expends efforts to run or improve the business during the marriage, the value of this contribution is community property. Businesses created during marriage are community property, unless they are created entirely from separate property.

- **Property held in joint title** (joint tenancy, tenancy in common, community property, husband and wife) is presumed to be community property.

- **Revenues and profits** (such as rent or interest) earned on community property are community property. Profits from separate property are the separate property of the owner spouse. And if a particular item is purchased with community property money (for example, from the sale of real estate bought with the couples' wages), that item is community property. The same rule applies for separate property: If one spouse uses his or her own separate property to buy something, the item purchased is separate property. (This is referred to as the "source rule.")

Property acquired after separation. If the separation is permanent—that is, the couple intends to divorce—all property acquired afterward is separate property. If it is a trial separation, and they may reunite, all property acquired is community property. (Fam. Code § 771.)

Property acquired outside California. If a couple acquires property while living outside of California that would have been community property if the couple had been living in California, that property is treated as community property when the couple moves to California. It is referred to as quasi-community property. (Fam. Code § 125.)

Making Your Own Decisions About Property

These legal rules are only presumptions. If you and your spouse decide, for example, that your pension will be entirely your own separate property, you need only sign an agreement to that effect. (You'll need a lawyer to help you prepare such an agreement, which must comply with specific state laws.)

Similarly, you may make a gift of your separate property to the community if you wish; the separate property then becomes community property. Only a written agreement expressly changing separate property to community or community property to separate can change the characterization of marital property.

Beware, however, of unintended transfers. When separate and community property are combined in a bank account, the resulting mixture is presumed to be community property. The only way a spouse can claim that a particular item purchased with the combined money is really that spouse's separate property is to trace all deposits and withdrawals. When spouses combine community and separate property to make a purchase such as a house or car, the property is considered community. However, if the couple splits up, each spouse will be entitled to be reimbursed for separate property contributions. Similarly, if one spouse spends separate property on a community property asset or on a separate property asset of the other spouse, the spouse will be entitled to a reimbursement at divorce.

Dividing Property at Divorce

Spouses can divide their property at divorce any way they like. If they cannot reach an agreement, the judge will generally award all separate property to the owner-spouse and divide the community property equally.

DIVORCE

Technically called "dissolution of a marriage," divorce is the legal procedure necessary to end a marriage or a registered domestic partnership. In California, divorce may be granted based on irreconcilable differences between the spouses or incurable insanity of one spouse. (Fam. Code § 2310.) There is no need to allege fault on the part of either spouse; if one spouse wants a divorce, there is nothing the other one can do, legally, to block it.

California Residency Requirement

One spouse must live in California for at least six months, and in the county where the case is filed for three months, immediately before filing for divorce. (Fam. Code § 2320.) As long as this residency requirement is met, it makes no difference where the marriage occurred. Once the case is filed, it doesn't matter if one or both spouses move out of state; the California court still has authority to grant the divorce.

Divorce Proceedings

There are two ways to get a divorce in California. A "summary dissolution" requires very little paperwork and no court appearance. (Fam. Code §§ 2400-2406.) It is limited to couples who:

- wish to divorce based on irreconcilable differences
- have been married fewer than five years
- have no children, and the wife is not currently pregnant
- own no real estate
- have less than $4,000 in community debts (not counting car loans)
- own less than $25,000 in community property (not counting cars), and
- have less than $25,000 in separate property (not counting cars) each.

Both spouses must sign a property agreement (unless there is no property) when the divorce is filed. They must also give up the right to seek spousal support. The divorce becomes final six months after filing. During this period, either spouse can revoke the summary dissolution and insist on a regular dissolution. Once the divorce is final, neither spouse can appeal or ask for a new proceeding.

Couples who don't meet the requirements for a summary dissolution must get a regular dissolution. A regular dissolution can be handled by mail in some cases, but sometimes requires a court appearance and extensive paperwork. The divorce will not be final until at least six months from the date one spouse was served with (received) the summons and other legal papers.

Restraining Orders

Certain restraining orders are automatic in every divorce. Neither spouse can:

- take the couple's children out of state without written permission from the other spouse and the court
- borrow against, transfer, or sell any property except in the normal course of business or with the written consent of the other party or a court order, or

- cash in, borrow against, or cancel any insurance policy (health, auto, life, disability) held for the benefit of the divorcing couple or their minor children. (Fam. Code § 2040.)

A spouse who needs a restraining order for physical protection from the other spouse must request it from the court. (See Domestic Violence, below.)

DOMESTIC PARTNERS

California's new domestic partnership law, AB 205, went into effect in January of 2005. The new law greatly expands the rights of registered domestic partners, offering many of the benefits and obligations of marriage. Domestic partnership registration with the State of California is limited to same-sex couples and couples of the opposite sex in which one or both partners are over 62 (the law does not apply to couples of the opposite sex in which both partners are under 62). In addition, to register as domestic partners, both members of the couple must:

- share a common residence
- agree to be jointly responsible for each other's basic living expenses during the partnership
- be neither married nor in a domestic partnership with another person
- not be close blood relatives, and
- be at least 18 years of age.

Both members of the couple must file a Declaration of Domestic Partnership, available from the clerk of each county, stating that they fulfill these requirements. (Fam. Code §§ 297-299.6.)

Under AB 205, registered domestic partners are treated like spouses for all purposes under California law. This means that registered domestic partners have community property rights, rights to seek spousal support, and obligations for debts incurred during the domestic partnership by the other party. Each partner has an equal right to manage and control community property, and must handle that property to benefit both partners. A child born into the partnership is considered the child of both parents, although because other states and the federal government won't recognize the domestic partnership, it's still a good idea for the non-birth parent to do an adoption. Domestic partners have the same privilege as spouses to refuse to testify against each other in court, and the same rights as married couples to family student housing, senior citizen housing, and other housing benefits. Each partner has the right to inherit from the other's estate, to make anatomical gifts upon the death of the other partner, and to make health care decisions if the other partner becomes incapacitated. For more information about domestic partnership in California, see the websites of the National Center for Lesbian Rights at www.nclrights.org and Lambda Legal Defense and Education Fund at www.lambdalegal.org.

All of these benefits are available under state law. California's domestic partnership laws do not affect federal laws, so registered domestic partners still cannot file joint tax returns or collect Social Security benefits if one partner dies, or take advantage of any other federal laws governing married people.

The State of California offers domestic partner benefits to all state employees. Some California cities and counties also offer domestic partner benefits to unmarried (gay, lesbian, and heterosexual) employees. A few of these cities and counties allow all resident unmarried adult couples to register. However, none of these domestic partner relationships carry the same rights and responsibilities as registration under AB 205.

In Laguna Beach, Sacramento, San Francisco, and West Hollywood, registered couples are currently entitled to certain public benefits, such as family health benefits, family leave, and hospital and jail visiting privileges normally reserved for married couples.

All insurers doing business in California must provide identical coverage to domestic partners and heterosexual spouses. The same goes for an auto insurance company that gives lower rates to spouses who jointly own their cars and share the same insurance policy.

DOMESTIC VIOLENCE

There is domestic violence in many California households. Those who are abused range in age from children to the elderly, from all backgrounds and income levels. The majority of those subjected to domestic violence are women abused by men, but women also abuse other women, men abuse men, and women abuse men.

Many forms of abuse are considered domestic violence, including:
- physical behavior such as slapping, punching, pulling hair, or shoving
- forced or coerced sexual acts or behavior such as unwanted fondling or intercourse, jokes, and insults aimed at sexuality, and
- threats of abuse—threatening to hit, harm, or use a weapon on another.

Recent changes to domestic violence laws have focused on strengthening police officers' responses to calls from victims. Officers are encouraged by law to arrest offenders if a restraining order has been issued. (See below.) And they must file written reports of domestic violence investigations that include notations of whether the officers who responded:
- observed any signs that the alleged abuser was under the influence of drugs or alcohol, and
- determined whether any law enforcement agency previously responded to a call at the same address involving the same people. (Penal Code §§ 13701, 13730.)

Temporary Restraining Orders

The most powerful legal tool to stop domestic violence is a temporary restraining order: a decree from the court, tailored to the particular circumstances of the relationship, requiring that the perpetrator stop the abuse. To get a restraining order, an abused person must testify or show a court evidence of the abuse (hospital or police records, for example). Police are also authorized to issue restraining orders under some circumstances, but they rarely do so.

Typical restraining orders require that the abuser must:
- stop the striking, bothering, molesting, telephoning, sexually assaulting, or other harassment
- stay a certain distance away from the person who was being abused, the family household, or other specific places such as work, school, or a residence
- leave a residence where he or she was living
- not take or sell any of the property of the person he or she was harassing or any of their community property if there is a marriage
- not take the parties' minor child out of California or a local area

without written permission from the abused parent
- not use any of the property jointly owned with the abused person, and
- adhere to a specific visitation schedule for minor children.

A person who is being abused can get a restraining order against a:
- spouse or former spouse
- cohabitant or former cohabitant
- adult blood relative, or
- person with whom he or she has had a dating or engagement relationship.

Once a restraining order is in effect, police are encouraged to arrest an abuser who violates it.

Getting Help

The most important step you can take if you have experienced domestic violence is to find out what your options are. A number of groups provide counseling, transportation, shelter, interpreting services, legal help, and referrals. Look in the telephone book under "Crisis Intervention Service" or "Women's Organizations" or contact WOMAN, Inc. (Women Organized to Make Abuse Nonexistent) at 415-864-4722, 877-384-3578, or www.womaninc.org.

GAY AND LESBIAN COUPLES

Same-sex couples cannot legally marry in California. However, a new law, AB 205, provides that same-sex couples who are registered domestic partners are subject to many of the same rights and responsibilities as married couples. See the section on Domestic Partnership, above, for more information. Even with the new law, because the federal government does not recognize state domestic partnerships and recognition by other states is also in question, it is always a good idea for same-sex partners to sign documents like durable powers of attorney and to prepare wills and living together contracts to make clear their intentions and protect their relationship.

LIVING TOGETHER

Unmarried couples can live together (cohabit) legally in California. It is illegal for someone selling or renting a house, apartment, or condominium to discriminate against unmarried couples.

Contracts

Contracts between unmarried couples to share income, purchase property, and provide for support are legal as long as they are not based on the performance of sexual services. (*Marvin v. Marvin*, 18 Cal. 3d 660 (1976).) In theory, oral and implied contracts are just as valid as written ones; in practice, however, it is difficult to get a court to enforce any contract not in writing.

Inheritance

Unlike married couples, unmarried couples do not automatically inherit from each other if there is no will. You can, however, leave property to anyone you wish, including your living together partner, by will or living trust. Or you can own property in joint tenancy with your partner, which gives the survivor an automatic right to inherit the deceased person's share.

Credit Discrimination

The federal Equal Credit Opportunity Act forbids discrimination on the basis of marital status and requires creditors to treat unmarried and married couples equally. (15 U.S.C. § 1691.)

Employment Discrimination

State law prohibits employers from discriminating against their workers on the basis of marital status. (Gov't. Code § 12940(a).) An employer cannot provide parental leave only to its married workers, for example, or hire only unmarried workers, believing they will be more willing to travel and work late hours.

MARITAL DEBTS

For a married or divorced couple, responsibility for paying a debt depends on when the debt was incurred, who incurred it, and what it was for. A debt is treated like a form of property for legal purposes: It can be a separate debt of only one spouse or a community debt owed by both spouses. Most debts incurred during marriage are community debts. Generally, only the spouse who incurred a separate debt is legally responsible for repaying it, but both spouses are liable for repayment of a community debt.

Debts Incurred Before Marriage

Generally, a spouse is not responsible for repaying the debts his or her mate incurred before marriage. (Fam. Code § 913.) Creditors, however, are entitled to seize the debtor spouse's half of the couple's community property, as well as the debtor spouse's separate property, to repay the debt.

Debts Incurred During Marriage

Both spouses are generally liable for all debts incurred during marriage, with a few exceptions, including:

- If the debt is of no benefit to the marriage (rent payments for an apartment one spouse keeps for meeting his or her lover, for example), the spouse who benefits from the debt may be solely responsible for paying it. (Fam. Code § 2625.)
- If a spouse agrees to pay certain community debts as part of a divorce settlement, this agreement is binding only on the two spouses. The creditors can still seek repayment from both spouses. (Fam. Code §§ 916, 2024.)

If one spouse incurred debts during marriage that are considered separate under these rules, the separate property of the other spouse can be taken by creditors to pay the debt only if it is for the "necessaries of life" (food, clothing, shelter, or medical care) and the debtor spouse has no separate or community property left to pay the creditor. (Fam. Code §§ 914, 2623.)

Educational Debts

After divorce, debts for education must be paid by the spouse who incurred them. The theory is that it is unfair to penalize the spouse who not only didn't receive the benefit of the education, but more than likely supported the other during the schooling. (Fam. Code § 2641.) In some cases, depending on how much time has passed since the debts were incurred, the community must reimburse the spouse who did not receive the benefits of the educational expenses.

Tax Debts

Tax debts owed by a couple for filings during the marriage belong to the community; both spouses are responsible for paying the IRS. However, a spouse may be able to escape liability for the bill if she qualifies as an "innocent spouse" under the IRS guidelines.

Under these rules, the innocent spouse can avoid (or at least minimize) liability for tax debts if the following are true:

- The couple did not file a joint return.
- The innocent spouse did not know, and had no reason to know, that the other spouse did not report certain income.
- The unreported income belongs solely to the other spouse (in other words, it is not community property).
- The innocent spouse received no benefit from the unreported income.
- It would be unfair to include the unreported income in the innocent spouse's income.

These rules went into effect on July 22, 1998. For returns filed or debts incurred prior to that date, different requirements must be met. Check the IRS's website at www.irs.gov for more details.

Debts Incurred Between Separation and Divorce

Debts incurred after permanent separation and before divorce are jointly owed by both spouses only if they are for necessaries of life (food, shelter, and clothing) for a spouse or children, and the debt has not been assigned to only one spouse under the provisions of a child support order. A creditor may obtain payment from either spouse. (Fam. Code §§ 916, 2623.)

A spouse, however, is generally not liable for other debts incurred by his or her mate after permanent separation. (Fam. Code § 2623.)

MARRIAGE

California requires that people who want to marry be:

- **Of the opposite sex.** Some lesbian and gay couples go through religious marriage or commitment ceremonies, but the resulting relationship is not recognized by the state. (But see Domestic Partners, above.)

- **At least 18 years old.** People under 18 need the consent of a parent or guardian and of a superior court judge, who may require marriage counseling. (Fam. Code §§ 301–304.)
- **Sufficiently unrelated to each other.** Parents and children, grandparents and grandchildren, brothers and sisters (including half siblings), and uncles and nieces or aunts and nephews cannot marry each other. (Fam. Code § 2200.) First cousins can marry each other in California, although these marriages are banned in many states.
- **Sane and mentally capable of consent.** Insane and severely mentally retarded persons can't marry. Because it is difficult to tell when someone is or isn't insane, a person experiencing a lucid interval between periods of insanity can legally marry. That a person has been mentally ill in the past is no bar to marriage.
- **Sober.** The county clerk can deny a marriage license to a person who has been drinking or is obviously under the influence of a drug. (Fam. Code § 352.)
- **Physically able to consummate the marriage.** In theory, each party to a marriage must have the physical ability to have sexual intercourse, even if the woman is past child-bearing age. (This requirement is not enforced.)
- **Unmarried.** You can be married to only one person at a time. (Fam. Code § 301.)

To get married, you must have the following:

- **A license.** Both spouses must visit the county clerk's office to buy a license before marrying. (Fam. Code § 350.)
- **A ceremony.** You must participate in some form of ceremony, performed by an active or retired judge, commissioner, or assistant commissioner, or by a priest, minister, or rabbi of any religion. (Fam. Code §§ 400, 420.)
- **A witness.** You need one witness other than the person conducting the ceremony. (Fam. Code § 422.)

Confidential Marriages

Couples who wish to avoid the licensing requirement may choose a confidential marriage. (Fam. Code §§ 500-511.) To be eligible, a couple must have lived together for a period of time established by the county and must both be 18 or older. You can get a confidential marriage from the county clerk or from a notary public who is licensed to perform such marriages. In either case, you must pay a fee and file a marriage certificate. Ask the county clerk for details.

SEPARATION

Separation can be formal (legal) or informal.

Formal separation is a substitute for divorce. The couple divides their property and debts, decides custody and visitation, and arranges child and spousal support, just as in a divorce. Legal separation often occurs when a couple will not divorce for religious reasons, or if a dependent spouse needs medical care and cannot afford it alone.

Informal separation can be either:

- trial separation—living apart for a test period to decide whether to go your separate ways or to get back together, or
- permanent separation, in which the couple has decided to split up for good.

Assets received and debts incurred by the spouses during a trial separation are considered community property—that is, the spouses are entitled to equal shares of the property and are equally obligated to pay the debts.

Assets received and debts incurred after permanent separation are the separate property or responsibility of the spouse obtaining or incurring them. A court, however, can order that debts for necessities (food, clothing, and shelter) incurred after permanent separation for the benefit of either spouse or the minor children be paid by the spouse who was better able to pay the debt when it was incurred. (Fam. Code § 2623.)

SPOUSAL SUPPORT (ALIMONY)

Spousal support (also referred to as alimony) is a series of payments made to one spouse by the other for a specified period of time after divorce. Spousal support is not granted in all, or even half, of divorce cases. When deciding whether or not to award support, the court must consider these factors:

- the age and health of each spouse
- whether the earning capacity of each spouse is sufficient to maintain the standard of living established during the marriage

- the supported spouse's marketable skills
- any limitations on the supported spouse's employability due to periods of unemployment to take care of the children or house
- the degree to which one spouse contributed to the education, training, or career of the other
- the needs of each spouse
- the ability of the supporting spouse to pay
- the obligations and assets of each party (including separate property)
- the duration of the marriage—there is a presumption that spousal support is appropriate in marriages that lasted more than ten years
- the ability of the supported spouse to work without an adverse effect on the children
- the tax consequences to each party, and
- the goal that the supported spouse be self-supporting within a reasonable period of time whether there is documented evidence of domestic violence, or a criminal conviction of abuse. (Fam. Code §§ 4320, 4330.)

In addition, many judges now consider whether and how much child support the paying spouse is obligated to pay. As a general rule, if child support obligations are large, spousal support will be granted in a reduced amount.

Tax Rules

Spousal support payments made under the terms of a written court order or separation agreement are tax-deductible to the person paying. They are taxable income to the recipient.

Modifying Spousal Support

Unless a court order expressly prohibits it, a court can change the terms of a spousal support order—both amount and duration of support—as long as the order is in effect. In marriages lasting more than ten years, the court retains the power to modify spousal support indefinitely, unless both spouses sign a written waiver. (Fam. Code § 4336.)

To modify spousal support, a spouse must file papers with the court that granted the divorce. The spouse must show that there has been a material change of circumstances since the last spousal support order, which could include an increase or decrease in either party's income.

Spousal support may be reduced if the payer can show inability to pay or that the recipient's need for support has decreased. The court will presume that the recipient's need for support has diminished if he or she is living with someone of the opposite sex, but this presumption can be rebutted by evidence that the need has not changed. (Fam. Code § 4323.)

Ending Spousal Support

Unless otherwise agreed by the parties, spousal support ends:

- when the recipient remarries or dies, or
- after the period of time established in the court order has passed.
  (Fam. Code §§ 4335, 4337.) ■

Serious Illness

Many of us are concerned about what will happen to us if a serious accident or illness strikes and we are unable to make our own medical and financial decisions. This section covers the legal options we have if we become incapacitated, as well as some other legal issues raised by serious illness.

TOPICS

Advance Health Care Directives (Living Wills and Powers of Attorney)
Conservatorships
Durable Powers of Attorney for Finances
Emergency Medical Treatment
Organ and Body Donation

RELATED TOPICS

Government Benefits
  Disability Insurance
  Medi-Cal
  Medicare
Inheritance and Wills

ADDITIONAL RESOURCES

Quicken WillMaker Plus (software for Windows by Nolo), lets you use your computer to create a valid will, living trust, durable power of attorney for finances, health care directive, and other important legal documents.

Living Wills & Powers of Attorney for California, by Shae Irving (Nolo), provides official California forms and detailed instructions to help you prepare your own advance health care directive and durable power of attorney for finances.

The California Courts Self-Help Center offers free publications and forms for California conservators. You can find the Self-Help Center online at www.courtinfo.ca.gov/selfhelp. Click "Seniors" to find the information for conservators.

Long-Term Care: How to Plan and Pay for It, by Joseph L. Matthews (Nolo), explains options for people who must find long-term care for themselves or a family member.

ADVANCE HEALTH CARE DIRECTIVES
(LIVING WILLS AND POWERS OF ATTORNEY)

The right to die with dignity, and without the tremendous agony and expense for both patient and family caused by prolonging lives artificially, has been supported by the U.S. Supreme Court, the federal government, and the state legislature.

This individual right also protects someone who wants more extensive care than doctors wish to provide. For example, a doctor may be unwilling to try experimental treatments or maintain long-term treatments on a patient who has only a slim chance of recovering.

In California, you can direct your medical care with a document called an advance health care directive. (Probate Code § 4701.) California's advance directive form permits you to do several important things:

Name someone to carry out your health care wishes and make other medical decisions for you. The first part of the advance directive form is called a "durable power of attorney for health care." A power of attorney is simply a legal document that you use to name someone to make decisions for you or to take action on your behalf. The words "attorney" here means anyone authorized to act for you; that person definitely doesn't have to be a lawyer.

A power of attorney is considered "durable" if it stays in effect even after you are incapacitated. Powers of attorney that aren't durable are not valid if you are no longer able to make your own decisions.

You use this durable power of attorney to name the person who will make sure your health care preferences are honored and who will make any other necessary medical decisions for you. This person is called your health care agent. Most people name their spouse, partner, or a grown child as agent. It's best to appoint just one agent and name a backup in case that person is unable to serve. California's advance directive allows you to name up to two alternate agents.

The advance directive gives your agent broad authority to make health care decisions on your behalf, though if you choose, you can limit your agent's authority when you complete your document.

State your health care wishes. You can use the advance directive form to state your preferences for medical treatment in as little or as much detail as you like. For example, you can indicate whether or not your want to receive life-prolonging treatment—such as a respirator or CPR—if you are close to death from a terminal illness, you are in a permanent coma, or your agent (after consulting your doctor) determines that treatment would be more likely to put you at risk than to help you. You can choose from general statements about your wishes, or you can provide more specific instructions about the kinds of treatments you do or do not wish to receive under various circumstances.

To make informed choices about which medical procedures you do and do not want, it may be a good idea to discuss your advance directive with your doctor, if you have one. He or she can more fully explain your options and answer any questions you may have. You will also find out whether your doctor has any medical or moral objections to following your wishes. If he or she will not agree to follow your wishes, consider changing doctors.

Once you've written out your wishes and presented your document to your health care providers, it becomes a part of your official medical record and all medical care providers are required to follow your directions. If a treating physician is not willing to honor your wishes, the physician must transfer you to another doctor or facility that will. If a health care provider improperly refuses to honor your wishes or transfer you to another care facility, your agent or any other concerned person can seek help from a court. A judge can compel the health care provider to comply with your instructions and to recognize the authority of your agent. (Probate Code § 4766(e).)

Specify whether you wish to donate organs, tissues, or body parts after your death. If you want to donate any of your organs or body parts after death, the advance directive form contains a place for you to say so. (See Organ and Body Donation, below, for more information on this topic.)

Name the primary physician who will be responsible for your care. If you have an established relationship with a doctor whom you trust, you may want to specify that this doctor supervise your care, working with your health care agent. The advance directive form allows you to do so.

Unless you indicate otherwise, your advance directive becomes effective only if your doctor determines that you are incapacitated and unable to communicate your wishes for care. If you prefer, however, you can allow your health care agent—not a doctor—to decide when to put your document into effect, by checking a box that makes your document effective as soon as you sign it.

To make your advance directive valid, you must sign it in the presence of two qualified witnesses or a notary public. When you obtain your form (see the resources listed below), it should be accompanied by instructions that explain exactly how to complete it and who is qualified to act as a witness.

In most instances, you do not need to consult a lawyer to prepare an advance directive. The form is quite simple and can be obtained, free or for a nominal fee, from a number of sources. Here are a few good ones:

- *Living Wills & Powers of Attorney for California*, by Shae Irving (Nolo), guides you step-by-step through the process of completing California's official advance health care directive form. Forms are available as tear-outs and on a CD-ROM that comes with the book.

- The National Hospice and Palliative Care Organization provides advance directive forms and a basic set of instructions for completing them. You can download a form for free from the organization's website or order it over the phone. Call 800-658-8898 or visit the website at www.caringinfo.org.

- Local hospitals may be a good source for advance directive forms. Ask to speak with the patient representative. By law, any hospital that receives federal funds must provide patients with appropriate forms for directing health care; the patient representative may also be able to help you fill them out.

CONSERVATORSHIPS

A conservatorship is a legal arrangement in which an adult appointed by a court oversees the personal care or property of another adult considered incapable of managing alone. The person who takes over is the "conservator." The incapacitated person is the "conservatee." Often conservatees suffer from advanced stages of Alzheimer's disease, are in comas, or have other serious illnesses.

Depending on the circumstances, the conservatee might not be permitted to make decisions about how his or her money is managed or spent. The conservatee could be denied the right to make his or her own medical decisions, vote, or have access to a car. Conservatorships are also used to prevent other people from taking financial advantage of a person who is unable to manage their own financial affairs.

A conservatorship lasts until the conservatee dies or can resume caring for his or her own daily needs or finances. The court will monitor a conservatorship to ensure that it remains necessary and that the conservator is doing a good job. A conservator who is harming the conservatee or taking unauthorized actions regarding the conservatee's property can be removed from his job. A court must approve the ending of a conservatorship.

Types of Conservatorships

There are several kinds of conservatorships:

- **Conservator of the person.** A conservator of the person is responsible for attending to the conservatee's personal needs. Depending on the court's findings, the conservator may need to make important medical choices. Before permanently moving the conservatee out of California, the conservator first must obtain a court order. (Probate Code §§ 2350 and following.)

- **Conservator of the estate.** A conservator of the estate is responsible for using the conservatee's money and other assets to support and educate the conservatee and any dependents (Probate Code § 2420), as well as investing and handling the conservatee's funds carefully. The conservator must obtain court approval before undertaking any serious transactions, such as selling the conservatee's house, and must prepare periodic accounting reports for the court.

- **Conservator of the person and estate.** A conservator of both the person and the estate must attend to the conservatee's personal needs and manage the conservatee's assets.

- **Limited conservatorship for developmentally disabled adult.** This type of conservatorship is specially tailored to encourage developmentally disabled adults to be self-reliant and independent. Examples of developmental disabilities include mental retardation, cerebral palsy, epilepsy, and autism.

- **Mental health (LPS) conservatorship.** LPS conservatorships may be established to provide individualized mental health treatment and services for someone who has a mental disorder or other impairment, such as alcoholism, and who is either a danger to himself or others or is "gravely disabled"—unable to take care of basic personal needs such as food, shelter, and clothing. (Welf. & Inst. Code §§ 5000 and following.) LPS conservatees, who can be either adults or minors, are sometimes hospitalized in mental health treatment facilities or placed in board and care homes. LPS conservatorships are initiated by professionals in mental health facilities.

How to Create a Conservatorship

To set up a conservatorship, an adult must file documents with a court and have copies given to the proposed conservatee and mailed to the proposed conservatee's close relatives. A court investigator will talk to the proposed conservatee and others who are familiar with the situation. A hearing date will be set up, and the judge will decide whether or not to appoint a conservator.

The proposed conservatee may nominate someone to serve as conservator. If there's no nomination, the Probate Code sets a priority of who may be appointed as conservator, starting with the proposed conservatee's spouse or domestic partner. The court has the ultimate authority on whom to appoint as conservator according to its determination of what is in the best interests of the conservatee. (Probate Code §§ 1810-1812.)

DURABLE POWER OF ATTORNEY FOR FINANCES

With a durable power of attorney for finances, you can arrange for someone to take care of your financial matters if you become unable to do so yourself. If you are older or face an upcoming operation or life-threatening illness, preparing a durable power of attorney is a simple, very inexpensive, and reliable way to ensure that your finances stay in the hands of someone you trust. Durable powers of attorney are also critically important for members of unmarried couples—straight or gay—who want to be certain that their partner is easily able to make important decisions on their behalf.

The person you name to make decisions for you is called your agent, or sometimes your "attorney-in-fact." (Here, the word "attorney" means anyone authorized to act for another person; it's definitely not restricted to lawyers.) You can give your agent authority to pay bills, make bank deposits, collect insurance and government benefits, manage property and investments, and handle other aspects of your financial affairs.

You can make your durable power of attorney for finances effective as soon as you sign it. Or you can specify that it will take effect only if you become incapacitated, as stated in writing by a doctor or other person that you appoint to make that decision.

Creating a Durable Power of Attorney

It's easy to create a durable power of attorney for finances. California has a statutory fill-in-the-blanks form. (Probate Code § 4401.) You can find the form and detailed instructions for filling it out in *Living Wills & Powers of Attorney for California*, by Shae Irving (Nolo). If you use the California statutory form, you must be sure to complete it properly and sign it in front of a notary public.

If you give your agent power over your real estate, you must put a copy of your document on file in the land records office of any county where you own property. This is called "recording" the document. It is not necessary to file your power of attorney with any other government agency or court.

If You Don't Make a Durable Power of Attorney

If you don't prepare a durable power of attorney for finances and you become unable to handle your financial affairs, a court will probably have to hold a hearing and appoint someone, called a conservator, to manage your finances. For more information, see Conservatorships, above.

EMERGENCY MEDICAL TREATMENT

Hospitals routinely provide necessary emergency care to patients who are unconscious and unable to consent to treatment. Although hospitals prefer to have at least the consent of a family member (a parent or spouse, for example), emergency treatment can be provided without this consent.

DNR Orders

In addition to the advance health care directives discussed above, you may want to secure a Do Not Resuscitate (DNR) order to make sure your wishes for emergency care are clear to medical personnel. A DNR order documents the wish that you not be administered cardiopulmonary resuscitation (CPR) in an emergency. (DNR orders, also called "Requests to Forgo Resuscitative Measures," are authorized by Probate Code §§ 4780 to 86.)

You may want to consider a DNR order if you:

- have a terminal illness
- have a high risk for cardiac or respiratory arrest, or
- have strong feelings against the use of CPR under any circumstances.

Because emergency response teams must act quickly in a medical crisis, they often do not have the time to determine whether you have a valid health care directive explaining treatments you want provided or withheld. If they don't know your wishes, they must provide you with all possible life-saving measures. But if emergency care providers see that you have a valid DNR order—which is often made apparent by an easily identifiable bracelet, anklet, or necklace—they will not administer CPR.

If you ask to have CPR withheld, you will not be provided with:

- chest compression
- electric shock treatments to the chest
- tubes placed in the airway to assist breathing
- artificial ventilation, or
- cardiac drugs.

If you want a DNR order, or if you'd like to find out more about them, talk with a doctor. A doctor's signature is required to make the DNR valid—and he or she will probably help by obtaining and completing the necessary paperwork. If the doctor doesn't have the form or other information you need, contact the California Medical Association, 916-444-5532.

ORGAN AND BODY DONATION

After you die, you may want to donate some or all of your organs or tissues for transplant, or give your entire body to a medical school to aid in research and education. Most people who are not afflicted with cancer; AIDS; hepatitis; venereal, heart, or bone disease; or other infectious diseases are eligible to donate organs. Whether or not to do so is, of course, a very personal matter. Here's some information that may help you decide whether or not you want to be a donor and some suggestions for carrying out your wishes.

The Need for Donated Organs

Many Californians are in dire need of organ transplants. More than 18,000 people in this state (and more than 90,000 nationwide) are currently waiting for life-saving organ transplant surgery—and based on current rates of donation, one in three of them will die before receiving a transplant. Although the number of organ donations in California has been slowly and steadily on the rise, the need for organs still far exceeds the number of organs donated.

Costs of Organ Donation

It will not cost your family anything if you want to donate your organs. The recipient pays the expenses, usually through insurance, Medicare, or Medicaid.

The Organ Donation Procedure

Before an organ is removed from a donor, two doctors who are not involved in the transplantation must declare that the patient is "irretrievably deceased" and brain dead. Then the body is kept on a respirator to keep blood flowing though the organ until it can be removed and given to a waiting recipient. All of this usually takes about 24 hours.

Donation does not disfigure the body and does not interfere with having a funeral, even an open-casket service.

Specifying Your Wishes

The best way to indicate your preference that your organs be donated is to obtain a donor card from the local Department of Motor Vehicles. You simply fill out the card and keep it with your driver's license; there's also a small sticker that you can attach to the front of your license to show that you are a donor. This can alert others to your wishes in the event of an accident, when your advance directive may not be immediately available.

In addition, if you prepare an advance health care directive (see above), you can use part of that form to state that you wish to donate organs at death. You may specify which organs, tissues, or body parts you will donate and the purposes for which they may be used—for example, transplant, research, or education.

Finally, and most important, you should discuss your views about organ donation with those who are close to you. Even if you complete a donor card from the DMV and put your wishes in an advance directive, it's possible that an objection by a close relative could defeat your wishes after your death. The best thing you can do is let those close to you know that you feel strongly about donating your organs.

To learn more about organ donation, see the Health and Human Services Department's website at www.organdonor.gov or call 800-55-DONOR (800-553-667).

The California Organ and Tissue Donor Registry

To encourage people to become organ donors, and to facilitate matches between organ donors and recipients, California has recently created a statewide organ and tissue registry. In addition to using the methods discussed above, Californians who want to be organ donors can list themselves in the state's central database. You can register to be a donor online at www.donatelifecalifornia.org. To date, more than 200,000 Californians have signed up.

Whole Body Donation

Most medical schools need donations of bodies for medical research and instruction. There is no age limit on body donations, but the donation may be rejected if any of the organs have been removed or for various other reasons. It is important to choose a mortuary to handle your final arrangements in case the institution has to reject your donation.

After using a donated body for study or instruction, a medial institution will usually cremate it—and bury or scatter the cremated remains in a specified plot. However, the remains can usually be returned to family members for burial—usually within a year or two. Those who want the body or remains returned to a friend or family member for final disposition should specify this when arranging for the donation.

For more information on body donation, contact the University of California, San Francisco at 415-476-1981. ■

Small Businesses

This section covers basic material for business people, including legal rules for forming different kinds of businesses and choosing a business name.

Many laws that affect businesses are made on a local level. We do not cover these laws—including license and permit requirements and specific zoning regulations—here. Check local ordinances for more information.

TOPICS

Corporations
Fictitious Business Names
Limited Liability Companies (LLCs)
Nonprofit Corporations
Partnerships
Professional Corporations
Responsibility to Employees
Sole Proprietorships
Trademarks and Service Marks
Trade Secrets

RELATED TOPICS

Consumers' Rights
  Sales Tax
Copyrights and Patents
Employees' Rights
Landlords and Tenants
  Leases and Rental Agreements

ADDITIONAL RESOURCES

The Small Business Start-Up Kit for California: A Step-by-Step Legal Guide, by Peri H. Pakroo (Nolo), explains how to get a California business started quickly, easily, and cheaply.

How to Write a Business Plan, by Mike McKeever (Nolo), shows new business owners how to write a business plan and secure financing.

Legal Guide for Starting & Running a Small Business and *Legal Forms for Starting & Running a Small Business,* by Fred S. Steingold (Nolo), both of which contain all the information and forms you need to start and run your small business. Both books are available on the *Quicken Lawyer Business Pro* Software CD.

Business Buyout Agreements: A Step-by-Step Guide for Co-Owners, by Anthony Mancuso and Bethany K. Laurence (Nolo), explains how to protect your business interests by drawing up an agreement between you and your business co-owners setting out what will happen if you or a co-owner leaves the company. A must for any new business with more than one owner.

Trademark: Legal Care for Your Business & Product Name, by Stephen Elias (Nolo), tells small business owners how to choose a name that competitors can't use.

The U.S. Patent and Trademark Office, Washington, DC 20231, www.uspto. gov, offers information about acquiring federal trademark rights.

Form a Partnership: The Complete Legal Guide, by Denis Clifford and Ralph Warner (Nolo), provides step-by-step instructions for writing a partnership agreement that will prevent problems later.

How to Form a Nonprofit Corporation in California, by Anthony Mancuso (Nolo), shows how to form a nonprofit corporation and includes all necessary forms on CD-ROM (also available in a corporate records binder edition with all incorporation forms on CD-ROM).

How to Form Your Own California Corporation, by Anthony Mancuso (Nolo), is the definitive guide to incorporating a California business without a lawyer. All forms are available on CD-ROM and as tear-outs (also available in a corporate records binder edition with all incorporation forms on CD-ROM).

The Corporate Records Handbook: Meetings, Minutes & Resolutions, by Anthony Mancuso (Nolo), shows how to prepare standard minutes of annual and special director and shareholder meetings for an existing corporation. It also contains resolutions to approve the various legal, tax, financial, and business transactions that commonly occur during the life of a small corporation. All forms and resolutions are provided as tear-out forms and on CD-ROM.

Nolo's Quick LLC: All You Need to Know About Limited Liability Companies, by Anthony Mancuso (Nolo), explains the basics of limited liability companies in easy-to-understand language and helps you quickly determine whether structuring your business as an LLC is the right way to go.

Form Your Own Limited Liability Company, by Anthony Mancuso (Nolo), provides step-by-step instructions and all forms necessary to set up a limited liability company.

Tax Savvy for Small Business, by Frederick W. Daily (Nolo), tells small business owners what they need to know about federal taxes and shows them how to make good tax decisions.

The Employer's Legal Handbook, by Fred S. Steingold (Nolo), answers employers' questions about hiring, firing, and everything in between.

Working With Independent Contractors, by Stephen Fishman (Nolo), explains who qualifies as an independent contractor, describes applicable tax rules, and shows employers how to set up effective working agreements with independent contractors (agreements are included on disk).

Working for Yourself: Law & Taxes for Independent Contractors, Freelancers & Consultants, by Stephen Fishman (Nolo), is a guide for consultants and other independent contractors. It covers all business start-up requirements with a focus on meeting IRS rules to qualify for independent contractor tax status.

Whoops! I'm in Business: A Crash Course in Business Basics, by Attorneys Richard Stim & Lisa Guerin (Nolo) includes practical tips and resources explaining every step of the business lifecycle.

CORPORATIONS

Unlike a sole proprietorship or a partnership, a corporation is a legal entity separate from its creators and owners. The corporation itself can own property, owe money, and pay taxes. Doing business as a corporation offers distinct advantages, particularly limitation of the business owners' (shareholders') liability for normal corporate debts and, sometimes, tax savings. For many new small businesses, however, the expense and paperwork required to incorporate outweigh the possible benefits, at least until the business is more established.

Limited Liability

One of the main advantages of incorporating is that in most cases, it limits the personal liability of the people who own the business. (Limited liability companies—LLCs—also provide business owners with this advantage.) If the corporation loses a lawsuit, for example, the owners' personal property cannot be seized to pay the judgment unless the individual owners have personally guaranteed the debt or obligation. They stand to lose only the money that they have invested in the corporation. An owner who personally guarantees business loans or contracts, however, loses this limited liability.

To preserve limited liability, the business owners must keep their finances and the corporation's finances separate. If a court concludes that they have mingled personal and corporate funds to the extent that the corporation isn't really a separate entity, or that the owners have significantly underfunded the corporation, the court might hold the owners personally liable for the corporation's debts, especially if they engaged in fraud.

Taxes

A corporation is a separate tax-paying entity from the individuals who own it. This allows corporate shareholders who also work as corporate employees to split business income between themselves as individuals, and their corporation. By splitting income, they can take advantage of lower corporate tax rates on business income. For example, the first $50,000 of taxable corporate income is taxed at 15%. Taxable income above that amount is taxed at the next higher corporate tax rate tier of 25%, and then 34% for income above $75,000. These corporate tax rates are all below the top individual marginal tax rate of 39%. However, because the corporate

rate goes up to 39% on retained income between $100,000 and $335,000, it sometimes makes sense to pay this income to yourself to avoid these higher rates.

Income splitting works as follows: Salaries, payments for benefits, bonuses, and other income paid to shareholder-employees are all deductible expenses for the corporation. The employees report their income on their personal tax returns, and the corporation pays taxes only on profits left in the corporation. The real trick to making incorporation work for you is finding the right mix of personal and business income that lowers your overall tax bill yet still channels enough cash to you personally and to your business to keep both comfortable.

Income splitting is now also possible for sole proprietorships, partnerships, and limited liability companies. Any of these businesses can check the "corporation" box on IRS Form 8832, "Entity Classification Election," and file the form with the IRS. The IRS will then treat the unincorporated business as a corporation. Because of the added record keeping and tax return complexity that accompanies corporate tax treatment, most unincorporated business owners do not make this election. With a corporation, however, this additional complexity and its associated potential for tax savings are built into the business structure.

The IRS allows a corporation to retain a significant amount of earnings (for most businesses, a maximum of $250,000) without paying it to the shareholders as dividends, which are taxable at both the corporate and individual level. Additional earnings can be kept in the corporation without penalty to meet the legitimate future needs of the business.

In California, a corporation must pay an annual corporate franchise tax, based on its net income in the previous year. The tax rate is 8.84% of annual taxable corporate income, with a minimum of $800 per year. However, corporations formed after January 1, 2000 don't have to pay this minimum during their first tax year (although they will have to pay income taxes based on their actual net income).

How to Incorporate

Here are the steps to incorporate a small, privately held corporation in California (that is, a corporation in which stock will not be sold publicly, but will instead be held by a small group of people who know each other):

- Choose a president, secretary, and treasurer. One person can hold all of these positions, as well as being the entire board of directors and the sole stockholder. (In other words, in California, you can form a one-person corporation.)
- Choose a name for your corporation that is not the same or confusingly similar to that of an existing California corporation. If you choose a name that is already on the books, the secretary of state will reject your articles of incorporation. Your business name must not violate anyone's trademark or service mark, either. (For more information, see Trademarks and Service Marks, below.)
- File the articles of incorporation, the document that creates and describes the corporation, with the California Secretary of State's office. In this document, you must give your corporate name, along with the names of the corporate directors or incorporators and the number of shares in your company. After these are filed with the secretary of state, you should write bylaws. These specify the dates for corporate meetings and restate the most significant provisions of state law that will apply to your corporation.
- Pay a filing fee of $100.
- Comply with California's securities laws. For most small business corporations, this simply means filing a one-page form with the Department of Corporations and paying a $25 fee. Publicly held corporations are subject to more complicated stock issuance regulations promulgated by the U.S. Securities and Exchange Commission.

S Corporations

"S corporation" status is a special corporate tax election that provides the legal benefits of a corporation (limited personal liability) and the tax status of a partnership. Because a newer business form—the limited liability company—achieves this dual result more efficiently (see Limited Liability Companies, below), S corporation status is no longer as popular as it once was. But S corporation tax status may still make sense in two situations:

- when an existing corporation wants to have profits passing through the business taxed at the shareholder level only, or

- to save on self-employment taxes, because S corporation shareholders are not subject to these taxes on profits allocated to them by their corporation. (By contrast, limited liability owners active in the business are generally subject to self-employment taxes on their shares of LLC profits.)

FICTITIOUS BUSINESS NAMES

Most businesses use a name—Speedy Printers, King Street Market—made up by the owners. A fictitious business name is any name that is different from the name of the individual, partnership, LLC, or corporate name of the business owners. Any business name that includes the name of the business owner and suggests the existence of additional owners (for example, Smith & Company or Jones & Sons) is also a fictitious business name.

A business using a fictitious business name must register the name within 40 days of starting to regularly transact business in California. A business that doesn't register its fictitious name cannot use the courts to bring a lawsuit. Also, banks usually won't open an account in the name of the business without proof of registration.

Nonprofit corporations and real estate investment trusts are not required by law to register their fictitious business names in California.

How to File a Fictitious Business Name Statement

File a fictitious business name statement with the clerk of the county where the business will have its principal place of business in California. Businesses that have no place of business in the state, or that do business in many counties, can file with the clerk's office in Sacramento County.

The clerk can provide a blank form for the statement, or owners can make their own. The statement must include:
- the fictitious business name
- the street address of the primary place of business, in or out of state
- the names of the business owners, partnership, LLC, or corporation using the name, and what form of business it is (for example, limited partnership or sole proprietorship)
- the date the business began doing business using the name, and
- the signatures of the business owners.

Within 30 days of filing the statement, the business owners must publish it in a newspaper of general circulation in the California county that is the principal place of business, or in Sacramento County if there is no place of business in California. The statement must run at least once a week for four successive weeks. Within 30 days of completing publication, the owners must file an affidavit (a sworn statement that the business statement was published), including the publication itself, with the county clerk.

A fictitious business name statement expires after five years and must be filed again at expiration. In addition, a new statement must be filed within 40 days after any required information in the old statement changes, or that statement expires. (Bus. & Prof. Code §§ 17900 and following.)

LIMITED LIABILITY COMPANIES (LLCS)

The limited liability company (LLC) is a relatively new form of business organization. It allows people to conduct business without taking on personal liability for business debts and judgments, and without having to incorporate. Limited liability companies are particularly useful for groups of people whose businesses engage in potentially risky activities, and who can't find reasonably priced liability insurance. A limited liability company can be organized with just one member or multiple members.

Taxes

For federal and state income tax purposes, a one-person limited liability company is taxed like a sole proprietorship and a multi-owner limited liability company is automatically taxed like a partnership. Owners, called members, report their share of the business income on their individual tax returns. The limited liability company must also file an informational tax return so the IRS can check to see that members are reporting all income.

California limited liability companies must pay a minimum franchise tax of $800 each year. In addition, companies with more than $250,000 in gross annual receipts must pay additional taxes that range from $900 to $11,000 per year, depending on the amount of gross receipts.

Tax Note: The IRS lets LLCs choose how they will be treated for federal tax purposes. By default, an LLC with two or more members is treated as a partnership, and a one-member LLC is automatically taxed as a sole proprietorship. But an LLC can elect to be taxed as a corporation, meaning that initial business profits will be taxed at the lower corporate tax rates of 15% and 25%. To arrange this, you must file IRS Form 8832, "Entity Classification Election."

While an LLC can elect to be taxed as a corporation for state tax purposes as well, if it fails to make this election, the state will tax it as a partnership or sole proprietorship, depending on how many members it has.

How to Form an LLC

- Choose an available business name (one that is not the same or confusingly similar to that of an existing California LLC) that complies with California's naming rules. (Your LLC's name must not violate another company's trademark. For more information, see Trademarks and Service Marks, below.)
- File articles of organization, the document that sets up the LLC, with the secretary of state's office. You must provide only your LLC's name and the name and address of a person—usually one of the LLC members—who will act as your LLC's "agent for service of process," to receive legal papers in any future lawsuit involving your LLC.
- Pay a filing fee of $70 to the Secretary of State when you file your articles of organization.
- Pay the annual minimum tax of $800 to the Franchise Tax Board.
- Create an LLC operating agreement, setting out the rights and responsibilities of the LLC members.

Note for Professionals: California is in the minority of states that do not allow licensed professionals to form an LLC. However, lawyers, accountants, and architects can form a registered limited liability partnership (RLLP), a business form similar to an LLC. An RLLP is basically a partnership that relieves professional partners from personal liability for debts, contracts and claims against the partnership, including claims against another partner for professional malpractice. However, a professional in an RLLP remains personally liable for his own professional malpractice. If you are a member of a profession that requires a state license (other than a lawyer, accountant, and architect), you must form a regular California corporation or a professional corporation, depending on your type of business, to get the kind of legal protection afforded by LLCs and RLLPs. (See Professional Corporations, below.) It's also the opinion of the California Attorney General (AG) that businesses that render services under nonprofessional, occupational licenses may form limited liability companies (LLCs) in California. An occupational licenses is one based on character, responsibility, good faith, and financial requirements and is distinguished from a professional license, which is based on education, training, and testing prerequisites.. California LLC and tax rules can change at any time—be on the lookout for new laws for professionals.

NONPROFIT CORPORATIONS

Certain types of organizations can become nonprofit corporations. Most nonprofit groups elect nonprofit corporate status primarily to attract tax-exempt and tax-deductible support for worthy causes. Nonprofit corporations get the benefits granted to all corporations, such as limited personal liability for shareholders and directors.

Requirements

In California, a nonprofit corporation must fit into one of these three categories:

- **Public benefit corporation.** A business formed for a public or charitable purpose, such as building a local library or raising money to help AIDS patients.
- **Religious corporation.** A business formed for religious purposes. This can include an organized religion, a group formed to promote the study of a certain religion, or even a group to promote better understanding between people of different religions.
- **Mutual benefit corporation.** A business formed to benefit its own members, such as a trade association, rotary club, or automobile association. Because mutual benefit corporations are regulated under separate rules, they are not covered here.

The articles of incorporation (the papers filed with the California Secretary of State to create the corporation) must state which type of nonprofit is being formed. They must also state that the corporation is not organized for any person's private gain (unless it is a mutual benefit corporation).

Tax-Exempt Status

Unlike regular corporations, nonprofit corporations can apply for tax-exempt status and avoid paying federal income taxes altogether. The rules for tax-exempt status can be found in Section 501(c)(3) of the Internal Revenue Code; because of this, tax-exempt corporations are often called 501(c)(3) corporations. Tax-exempt status is not an automatic benefit of organizing as a nonprofit corporation; you must apply for tax exemption separately. (Many organizations that might be eligible for 501(c)(3) status prefer to operate as commercial enterprises because they do not want to be subject to the moneymaking, profit distribution, and other restrictions applicable to nonprofits.)

To qualify for tax-exempt status, a nonprofit corporation:

- Must be organized and operated exclusively for charitable, religious, scientific, literary, and/or educational purposes.
- Cannot substantially engage in activities that are unrelated to the group's tax-exempt purpose, for example, a corporation formed to promote literacy should not spend too much time running a for-profit book sales operation.
- Cannot be organized to benefit individuals associated with the corporation. No corporate earnings can be distributed to the individuals who run the corporation, except for salaries paid to staff workers. Any corporate profits must be used to benefit the public interest, and any corporate assets remaining when the corporation liquidates must be given to another tax-exempt nonprofit organization.
- Is forbidden from participating in political campaigns involving candidates for public office and cannot substantially engage in other political activities, such as attempting to influence the outcome of legislation.

If a corporation qualifies as tax-exempt under these federal tests, it will also qualify as tax-exempt in California, because California's tax-exempt statutes mirror the IRS rules. This means that the corporation does not have to pay an annual franchise tax to the state as regular corporations do.

Unrelated business tax. Nonprofit corporations must pay tax on money made from activities unrelated to their tax-exempt purposes. The first $1,000 of unrelated business income is not taxed, but normal corporate tax rates apply to any income beyond that. This is true both for federal and state taxes.

California welfare exemption. Nonprofit corporations that own or lease property to use for their tax-exempt purpose can avoid paying property taxes by qualifying for this exemption. Other state property exemptions exist for nonprofit corporations as well. Contact your county tax assessor for an application and information.

Public Charity or Private Foundation?

There are two types of 501(c)(3) tax-exempt nonprofit corporations: public charities and private foundations. The IRS presumes that a 501(c)(3) corporation is a private foundation unless it meets the requirements to be classified as a public charity. Some of these rules are very technical; we only summarize them here.

Most 501(c)(3) nonprofits formed in California can qualify as public charities. Public charity status is extremely valuable. Private foundations are burdened by numerous operating restrictions, including limitations on holdings in private businesses and the requirement that the corporation annually distribute its net income for charitable purposes; public charities are not similarly limited. In addition, those who contribute to private foundations can deduct only up to 30% of their adjusted gross income, but contributors to public charities can deduct up to 50% of their adjusted gross income. Also, as a practical matter, a 501(c)(3) nonprofit corporation must be classified as a public charity to obtain public and private support; grants to private foundations are less common.

To qualify as a public charity, a corporation must meet one of the following three tests:

- **Automatic qualification.** Some types of corporations automatically qualify as public charities: churches, schools, hospitals and medical research organizations, public safety organizations (generally, groups that test products to determine whether or not they are fit for use by consumers), and government organizations. In addition, any corporation operated solely in connection with one of these groups qualifies automatically.

- **Public support.** A corporation can qualify as a public charity if it regularly solicits funds from the general public and receives money from government agencies as well as private contributors and agencies. A corporation that relies primarily on a few large grants or donors will probably not qualify as a public charity under this test.

Two tests are used by the IRS to determine whether a corporation receives enough public support to qualify:

— A corporation will qualify if it receives at least one-third of its total support from government sources, contributions made by the general public, or other publicly supported organizations.

— A corporation will qualify if it receives at least one-tenth of its total support from the sources listed above and attracts additional public support using a program to continuously solicit funds from the public.

Note that these one-third and one-tenth calculations are made based on the cumulative figures from the four prior tax years. The corporation does not have to meet this standard every year; if average public support over the four years is one-third or one-tenth of total support, that is sufficient.

• **Gross receipts support test.** Groups that plan to generate income from performing tax-exempt services may qualify under this third public charity classification. The corporation must:

— Receive more than one-third of its total support from gifts, grants, contributions, membership fees, and gross receipts from admissions, performing services, or providing facilities in an activity related to the group's tax-exempt purpose—for example, a dance troupe could count money made from ticket sales for public performances and tuition fees for dance classes.

— Not make more than one-third of its annual support from business or investment income unrelated to its tax-exempt purpose. For example, if a corporation formed to run a school also operated a moving business, income from this profit-making side business would count as unrelated income.

Tax Deductions for Donors

Individuals may deduct up to 50% of their adjusted gross income for contributions to tax-exempt public charities. Corporations may deduct charitable contributions up to 10% of their annual taxable income.

Contributions that can be deducted include donations of cash or property. The deductibility rules are the same for federal and state income tax.

PARTNERSHIPS

A partnership consists of two or more people doing business together, sharing duties, expenses, and profits in a manner they've agreed on. It is relatively easy to set up, and partners can tailor their arrangements to meet their needs with a written partnership agreement.

Creating a Partnership

No special legal paperwork is necessary to create a partnership. However, the partnership must complete the paperwork required of any California business, such as registering a fictitious business name and getting necessary permits and licenses.

If you don't make a written partnership agreement, many aspects of your partnership will be determined by a law called the Uniform Partnership Act (Corp. Code §§ 15001 and following) or the Uniform Partnership Act of 1994 (Corp. Code §§ 16101 and following), national laws that have been adopted in California. (The formation date of your partnership determines which Act you are governed by.) However, by writing an agreement, partners can fashion many details of their partnership to meet their specific needs. For example, partners can agree to own unequal shares of the business, agree to particular buy-out procedures, or agree that one partner will be in charge of day-to-day management of the business. Written partnership agreements are private and don't have to be filed with any state agency.

Liability

Any partner can obligate the partnership—for example, incur a debt, sign a contract, or enter a business agreement for the partnership. In addition, partners are personally liable for partnership debts. If the partnership loses a lawsuit, the judgment can be collected not only from the property of the partnership, but also from the personal property of all the partners. However, most sensible businesses purchase insurance to guard against this risk.

Taxes

Partnerships are not a separate entity for tax purposes like corporations are. Partners pay taxes on their share of partnership profits on their personal income tax returns, in the year in which the partnership made the money. This means that partners can use partnership losses to offset profits made from other sources in the same tax year as long as the losses and profits come from similar types of income-producing activity—for example, active business pursuits, investments, or businesses run by other people.

Limited Partnerships

A limited partnership is a hybrid business form that combines aspects of corporations and partnerships. A limited partnership must have at least one general partner, who is responsible for running the business and is personally liable for partnership debts, as explained above. The general partner can be either a person or a corporation. In addition, the business has limited partners: passive investors who do not actually participate in running the partnership business. The liability of limited partners for partnership debts is limited to the amount that they invested. Limited partnerships are often created to invest in real estate or when other types of partnership businesses need capital but don't want to take on new general partners or incorporate.

Limited partnerships are more heavily regulated than general partnerships. A limited partnership must register with the California Secretary of State. (Corp. Code § 15621.) It must also comply with complicated federal securities regulations, unless the limited partnership interests are all sold in one state or are sold privately to a few people (often 35 or less) who have close business or personal ties or are sophisticated investors. Note that the legal and tax characteristics of a limited partnership are similar to those of a limited liability company; the difference is that the latter does not require a general partner—all investors in a limited liability company can manage the business.

PROFESSIONAL CORPORATIONS

Traditionally, licensed professionals such as physicians, lawyers, and veterinarians were not allowed to incorporate, because it was thought that incorporation would distance the usually close relationship between professionals and their clients. Today, professionals are allowed to incorporate, but in many cases must form a professional corporation with different (and, in many cases, more stringent) rules than regular corporations. In addition to the general principles stated here, each profession has its own regulations and requirements; consult the agency that oversees your profession for more details.

Who May Form Professional Corporations

Members of the following professions are authorized to incorporate as professional corporations :

- accountants
- acupuncturists
- architects
- chiropractors
- clinical social workers
- dentists
- doctors
- lawyers
- marriage, family, and child counselors
- nurses
- optometrists
- pharmacists
- physical therapists
- podiatrists
- psychologists
- shorthand reporters
- speech pathologists and audiologists, and
- veterinarians (Moscone-Knox Professional Corporations Act, Corp. Code §§ 13400 and following.)

A "professional corporation" renders professional services in a single profession and must have a registration certificate issued by the agency regulating the profession. However, professional corporations rendering services by persons licensed by the following California boards are not required to obtain certificates: Medical Board, Osteopathic Medical Board, Dental Board, Board of Pharmacy, Veterinary Medical Board, Architects Board, Court Reporters Board, Board of Behavioral Sciences, Speech-Language Pathology and Audiology Board, or Board of Registered Nursing.

Limited Liability

Professional corporations don't provide the same measure of protection against personal liability as regular corporations do. Shareholders of a regular corporation are not personally liable for the corporation's debts. However, in a professional corporation, a professional shareholder is always personally liable for his or her own malpractice. However, the professional is insulated from personal liability for the malpractice of other professionals in the corporation. The professionals in the corporation must carry the minimum insurance set out in the regulations for that profession.

Just like shareholders of a regular corporation, professionals are not personally liable for nonmalpractice work incidents, business claims against the corporation, or other corporate debts.

Taxes

Professional corporations must pay the California corporate franchise tax, just like a regular corporation. This tax is 8.84% of the corporation's annual taxable income, with a minimum of $800 (although there is no minimum franchise tax charged for the corporation's first year).

Professional corporations also must pay federal income tax. A professional corporation pays the regular corporate tax rate unless it meets both of the following criteria for the definition of a personal service corporation:

- All stock in the corporation is held by employees performing professional services for the corporation.
- All activities of the corporation involve performing services in the field of health, law, engineering, architecture, accounting, actuarial science, performing arts, or consulting.

These personal service corporations must pay a 35% flat federal corporate tax rate on all taxable income. However, most personal service corporations rarely pay corporate taxes—instead, they pay out most of the corporation's income in the form of salaries and benefits (and the shareholder employees pay personal income taxes on this money).

Requirements for Incorporation

In addition to the requirements to form a regular corporation and the requirements specific to the profession, professional corporations:

- Must be licensed by the appropriate state board.
- Must choose a proper name. Some are required to indicate that they are a professional corporation. In addition, some professions may not use fictitious business names, but must use the names of one or more shareholders as their corporate name.
- May only have shareholders, directors, and officers who are licensed in that profession. Some professions allow people who are licensed in specified related professions to hold these positions.
- May be required to get a minimum amount of liability insurance.
- May be required to file annual reports with the agency that oversees that profession.

Limited Liability Partnerships for Professionals

California law allows lawyers, accountants, and architects to obtain the same insulation from lawsuits enjoyed by incorporated professionals by forming a special type of partnership, called a registered limited liability partnership (RLLP). As long as the RLLP practitioners obtain adequate insurance, each will be immune from personal liability for the malpractice of other professionals in the firm who are not under the professional's supervision. Limited liability partnerships are taxed as partnerships, not corporations, so they don't owe the 35% flat tax that applies to personal service corporations under federal tax law. (Of course, they must pay taxes on business income at their individual tax rates.) (Corp. Code §§ 15047 and following.)

RESPONSIBILITY TO EMPLOYEES

Employers must know the legal rights of their employees. These rights, protected by both federal and California law, include:

- the right not to be discriminated against or harassed because of race, sex, age, religion, or other protected characteristics
- the right to reasonable privacy in interviews and on the job

- the right to a safe workplace, as determined by both the state and federal Occupational Safety and Health Agencies, and
- the right to a certain amount of income security, in the form of workers' compensation, unemployment benefits, and minimum wage protections.

All of these subjects are covered, from the employee's perspective, in the chapter on Employees' Rights.

Taxes and Withholding

Employers are responsible for withholding a certain percentage of their employees' paychecks for federal and California income tax and another portion for Social Security tax and state disability insurance. In addition, the employer must pay a share of Social Security tax and federal unemployment tax for each employee.

SOLE PROPRIETORSHIPS

A sole proprietorship is a business that is owned by one person (the sole proprietor) and is not structured as a corporation or limited liability company. Sole proprietors include freelance writers and photographers, craftspeople who work on a contract basis, salespeople who are paid only by commission, and independent contractors who are not on any employer's regular payroll.

If spouses co-own and run a business, they can still operate it as a sole proprietorship (and not as a partnership) and report their business income as part of their joint tax return. This is true in California and all other community property states. If one spouse owns the business and the other works for it for pay, the owner will have to declare the spouse as an employee or independent contractor. If one spouse owns the business and the other spouse occasionally volunteers to help the business without pay, the owner won't have to declare the spouse as an employee or independent contractor.

If you own your business as a sole proprietor, you have unlimited personal liability for business debts and other legal obligations of your business (lawsuits over negligence or breach of contract, for example). If your business can't meet its financial obligations, creditors can come after your nonbusiness property.

For income tax purposes, you and your business are a single entity. You report business profits and losses on your personal income tax return. This means that you can use business losses to offset income from other sources, such as investments, other business pursuits, or salary earned at a job. Also, the income of your business is taxed to you in the year that the business receives it, whether or not you remove the money from the business.

There are no registration requirements to become a sole proprietor. Sole proprietors must simply meet the general requirements that apply to businesses in California, including:

- filing a fictitious business name certificate with your county (unless you use your own name)
- getting a California seller's permit if you plan to sell things (not services) to customers, and
- getting any additional licenses and permits necessary to do business in your chosen field and region. (For example, a restaurant needs a permit from local health officials and, if it serves beer and wine, a permit from the State of California.)

TRADEMARKS AND SERVICE MARKS

A trademark is a word, phrase, logo, color, sound, smell, or other symbol used by a business to distinguish its products from those of its competitors. If a business uses the name or logo to identify a service (providing fast food, for example), it is called a service mark. In practice, legal protections for trademarks and service marks are identical; we refer to both as trademarks. Domain names can also function as trademarks when the website is used to sell goods or offer services.

The value of a trademark lies in its ability to distinguish the products of the company, and so to attract customers. As a general rule, the first business to use a protectable mark has the exclusive right to continue using it. That business can sue others to prevent them from using it, or any name or graphic that is similar enough to cause customer confusion.

What Trademarks Can Be Protected

Not all names are entitled to trademark protection. Words used in their usual descriptive context, (called "weak" marks), are difficult to protect under trademark law because no single company is allowed to monopolize their use. Examples include descriptive terms, such as "Dependable Tires" (for a tire store) ; and surnames or geographic names, such as "Smith's Barber Shop" or "California Cleaners". However, names using descriptive words, surnames or geographic terms, may become protectable (or "strong") if, through long use and extensive public familiarity, they become associated exclusively with one company. "McDonald's" and "Bank of America" are well-known examples.

Strong trademarks receive a higher level of protection; they can be exclusively used by the company that created them. A strong mark could be a name made up by the company, such as "Exxon" or "Reebok," or it can be a word used in an arbitrary or surprising way, such as "Apple" for computers or "Penguin" for books. Finally, names that are creatively suggestive of the product's qualities, without being merely descriptive, are also strong marks. Examples include the "Roach Motel" and "Chicken of the Sea" tuna.

Trademark Searches

Once a business chooses a trademark, it should conduct a search to make sure no other business is already using it. If the mark is already in use, using it means risking a lawsuit. Businesses can conduct trademark searches themselves, either manually, on the Internet (www.uspto.gov), or by hiring a search firm.

Registration

Once a mark is in use in California, it can be registered with the California Secretary of State. (Bus. & Prof. Code §§ 14200 and following.) The secretary of state provides the application form and charges $70. Registration lasts for ten years; when it expires, it can be renewed for another ten.

If a mark is used—or affects commerce—across state, territorial, or national lines, it can be registered with the U.S. Patent and Trademark Office. You can reserve a mark for registration if you plan to use it within six months, but you cannot complete the registration until you actually use your mark in commerce. The U.S. Patent and Trademark Office website (www.uspto.gov) is the place to go for information about federal trademark registration. This site offers three useful online programs: TESS, TARR, and TEAS. TESS is a searchable database of federally registered trademarks, TARR provides information on the status of pending registrations, and TEAS is a system for electronic filing of trademark registrations.

Registration is not required to get the protection of trademark laws. Registration, however, gives notice to all would-be copiers that the trademark is in use. Also, federal registration makes it easier for a trademark owner to get large money damages if a dispute over a mark ends up in court. (15 U.S.C. §§ 1050 and following.)

Infringement

In California, if someone uses another's trademark without permission, the business that owns the trademark can sue for a court order (an injunction) stopping the use. If the trademark is very well known, it may not even be necessary to show that customers might be confused by the similarity between the two marks; it is enough that the strength of the mark is "diluted" by another company's unauthorized use. The use of another's trademark can also be enjoined if the unauthorized use would tend to tarnish the trademark owner's business reputation for providing quality goods or services.

If the trademark is registered in California, and another business uses it to advertise or sell counterfeit goods or services, the trademark owner can sue for a court order seizing the counterfeit goods. The infringing business may also have to pay up to three times the loss caused by the counterfeiting.

Domain Names

To do business on the web, most companies acquire at least one domain name, which may be the same as the business's name or something completely different.

Domain names can be protected as trademarks when the website they identify sells goods or services. Domain names that describe a product or service, however, such as coffee.com, drugs.com, and business.com, are difficult to protect as trademarks because they are considered generic terms. On the other hand, distinctive or fanciful names such as yahoo.com and amazon.com are entitled to a high level of trademark protection. Between these two poles are domain names that merely suggest the underlying product or service, such as medscape.com or inc.com. These domain names are also entitled to protection as trademarks and are easy to remember and associate with the products or services available at the website.

Many good domain names have already been taken. A business can go to any domain name registry to search for and register domain names. A domain name registry is a company that sells and renews domain names. After you buy a domain name (for $35 or less a month, depending on the registry), the registry will deal with the technical aspects of ensuring that your site is displayed when someone types in your domain name. For an alphabetical list of approved registries, go to www.internic.net or www.icann.org. You'll need to provide some information to the registry and pay a fee (approximately $35 per domain name). To check on name availability, go to any domain name registry and use the search feature. If the name is taken, you can learn who owns it by checking at www.whois.net.

TRADE SECRETS

A trade secret is any confidential information that gives a business a competitive advantage and that the business takes reasonable precautions to keep others from learning about. A trade secret can be a formula, process, or device, or even a unique compilation of information such as a marketing list. If information is entitled to trade secret status, the owner of the information is entitled to have a court prevent use or disclosure of the information by anyone who has wrongfully acquired it.

Reasonable precautions include:

- restricting access to the secrets through the use of passwords, codes, and restricted locations
- posting warnings and telling all employees that the information is considered a trade secret and must be kept confidential
- using nondisclosure agreements, which require persons to whom trade secrets must be disclosed for business purposes to get proper authorization before disclosing the trade secret
- using confidentiality agreements, by which employees agree not to disclose trade secrets, and
- using covenants not to compete, by which an employee who leaves the company, or a former employee of a company that is sold, agrees not to use the information.

If a trade secret is stolen through corporate espionage or used by another in violation of a nondisclosure agreement or as a result of a breach of an employee's duty of trust, the trade secret owner can sue both the thief and the ultimate user of the information—usually a new employer—for trade secret infringement. The trade secret owner can ask the court to issue an injunction (court order) preventing use of the trade secret. In some cases, the court may also award money to compensate for profits improperly made by use of the protected information, money lost as a result of the theft, or royalty payments. If the theft was willful and malicious, the court may double the monetary award. (Civ. Code §§ 3426.1-3426.10.) Finally, under the Economic Espionage Act of 1996, trade secret theft is now a federal crime. ■

Traffic and Vehicle Laws

Although traffic offenses are technically criminal violations (except parking tickets), we have included them in this book because they are part of our everyday dealings with the law. Here, you will find explanations of the most common offenses and the penalties for committing them, as well as the basic laws that govern driving and registering your vehicle.

TOPICS

Alcohol and Drug Related Offenses

Car Insurance Requirements

Equipment, License, and Registration Violations

License Suspensions and Revocations

Moving Violations

Parking Tickets

Registration and Smog Tests

Seat Belt and Child Restraint Requirements

Young Drivers

RELATED TOPICS

Consumers' Rights

Car Rentals

Car Repairs

Car Sales

ADDITIONAL RESOURCES

Beat Your Ticket: Go to Court & Win, by David Brown (Nolo), shows how to contest a parking or traffic ticket anywhere.

Fight Your Ticket & Win in California, by David Brown (Nolo), shows how to contest a parking or traffic ticket in California.

How to Insure Your Car: A Step-By-Step Guide to Buying the Coverage You Need at Prices You Can Afford, by the Merritt Editors (Silver Lake Publishing), includes standard policy forms, case studies, and worksheets to prepare for meetings with agents, brokers, and adjusters.

The Bureau of Automotive Repair, 800-952-5210, provides information about compliance with emission laws.

ALCOHOL AND DRUG RELATED OFFENSES

Several traffic violations involve alcohol or drugs, but are not as serious as drunk driving. Most are infractions, which means the driver will get a ticket and will have to send in the fine or appear in court. These violations include:

- **Open container on person of driver.** You can be cited for this offense if, while driving a car, you had an open (unsealed) container holding any amount of alcohol on your person (that is, in your hand, your pocket, or your purse). If the container was not on your person, but rather was in the car or on a passenger, you have not committed this offense. (Veh. Code § 23222(a).)

- **Open container kept in vehicle by driver or owner.** You can be cited for this offense if you are in a car or own it, and there is an open container holding any amount of alcohol anywhere in the car other than the trunk or the living quarters of a camper. You do not have to be driving the car to commit this offense; if the car is parked and you are in it, that is sufficient. (Veh. Code § 23225.)

- **Driver drinking in vehicle.** An officer who sees you drink alcohol while driving will cite you for this offense. (Veh. Code § 23220.)

- **Marijuana in vehicle.** You can be cited for a misdemeanor if you are driving with up to one ounce of marijuana in your car. (Veh. Code § 23222(b).)

Drunk Driving

The following offenses are misdemeanors, and carry fairly stiff penalties. In certain circumstances—for instance, a fourth conviction within seven years or a serious injury accident—these offenses can be charged as felonies. (Veh. Code §§ 23152, 23153, 23566.)

- **Driving under the influence.** It's illegal to drive while your ability to drive safely is significantly affected by alcohol or drugs. Your blood alcohol level is immaterial: If alcohol or drugs are impairing your driving, you have committed this offense, even if you are taking legal prescription drugs or over-the-counter medication. (Veh. Code § 23152(a).) You can be cited for driving under the influence even if the officer did not personally observe you drive the car, but there must be some evidence (even circumstantial evidence) that you did at some point move the car while intoxicated.

- **Driving with blood alcohol above a certain level.** It's illegal to drive a passenger vehicle when the concentration of alcohol in your blood is 0.08% or greater. (Veh. Code § 23152(b).) If an officer wants to test your blood alcohol level, you must be given a choice of blood or breath tests. If you do not submit to a test, your license can be suspended. (Veh. Code § 13353.) If this occurs, you have the right to a DMV hearing within a specified time.
- **Attempted drunk driving.** If you are drunk and attempt to start or drive a vehicle, you can be charged with a misdemeanor. (*People v. Garcia*, 214 Cal. App. 3d Supp. 1 (1989).) The penalties are half those for driving under the influence. (Pen. Code § 664.)

Young Drivers and Alcohol

The police may seize the driver's license of a driver under the age of 21 on the spot if they suspect the young motorist of drinking and the youth refuses to take, fails to complete, or fails to pass a breath test. (Veh. Code § 23136.) The law limits blood alcohol levels for drivers under 21 to 0.01%, which means that any amount of alcohol in a young driver's blood is illegal. (Veh. Code §§ 23136, 13353.2.)

If a police officer submits a sworn statement to the DMV reporting, among other facts, the officer's grounds for believing a young driver violated Veh. Code § 23136, the driver may lose his or her license for one to three years. The driver can appeal the action within ten days of receiving the notice of the order of suspension or revocation, or can ask the DMV for a restricted license if there is a critical need to drive. When the license is reinstated, the young driver must pay an additional $100 to cover the expense of implementing the law.

Penalties

For a first conviction of driving under the influence or with a blood alcohol level of 0.08% or more, you must be fined a minimum of $1,053, and you may spend up to 48 hours in jail if probation is not granted. The maximum penalty is a $2,700 fine and six months in jail. Penalties for subsequent convictions are much more severe; you may sentenced to up to a year in jail, and your license may be revoked. For a fourth offense, you can be sent to state prison for up to three years.

CAR INSURANCE REQUIREMENTS

All California drivers are required to have insurance that covers damage caused by a car that they own or drive. The minimum coverage allowed is:

- **Bodily injury.** $15,000 per person/$30,000 per accident.
- **Property damage.** $5,000 per accident. (Veh. Code § 16056.)

Drivers must also carry liability insurance to protect against the following risks:

- injuries the driver causes to someone else while operating a motor vehicle, and
- damage the driver causes to someone else's property, including another car, a street light, a telephone pole, or a building, while operating a motor vehicle. (Veh. Code § 16451.)

If the police ask you for proof of insurance, you must give the name and number of your insurance policy. A very few drivers are "self-insurers"; this means that they keep a sum of money sufficient to cover the minimum insurance requirement on deposit with the state. These people must provide their deposit number. If the vehicle you are driving is owned by the United States government, you need only show proof of its ownership, not proof of insurance.

The penalty for a first offense of driving without proper insurance is a $200 fine plus $351 in penalty assessments. The maximum penalties: are a $500 fine plus $861 in assessments.

Proof of Insurance

When you renew your car registration, you must be able to prove to the DMV that you are insured according to law or that you are self-insured. (Veh. Code § 4000.37.) In addition, you're required to carry proof of "financial responsibility" at all times in your car, such as a card from your insurance company. You must show this documentation to a police officer if asked—but an officer may not stop you solely in order to determine whether you are in compliance with the law. (Veh. Code §§ 16020, 16028.) Giving false information about financial responsibility is a misdemeanor, punishable by a fine of up to $750, up to 30 days' imprisonment, and mandatory suspension of your license for one year. (Veh. Code § 16030.)

Insurance Policies and Rates

A company can change the rate it charges for insurance within 60 days of verifying the rate and underwriting a new policy. After that time it cannot change the premium during the policy period. A company that originally insured you may reject your application for coverage within the first 60 days, but it must give you at least ten days' notice. After 60 days, an insurance company can cancel your policy only if any of the following are true:

- You fail to pay premiums.
- Your license (or the license of someone else in your household) is suspended.
- You gave false information on your application or otherwise commit fraud.
- There is a major change in your risk to the insurance company after your policy is issued—for example, your safety record suffers or you greatly increase the number of miles you drive each year.

The company must mail you a notice of cancellation at least 20 days before cancelling. Only ten days' notice of cancellation is required if you didn't pay the premium. (Ins. Code § 661.)

At renewal time, an insurance company will examine your claims record. If you have made too many claims or have been cited for two or more moving violations over the previous three years, your premium will probably be increased. If your driving record has deteriorated, the company may choose not to renew your policy. If the company refuses to renew your policy, they must let you know at least 30 days before your policy expires. Then they must give you the reason for nonrenewal within 15 days of the policy's expiration. (Ins. Code §§ 663, 666.) Your premiums cannot be increased, however, because of an accident in which you were not at fault. (Ins. Code § 491.)

EQUIPMENT, LICENSE, AND REGISTRATION VIOLATIONS

Violations of rules regarding equipment, license, and registration are correctable. If you fix the condition for which you got the ticket, you are entitled to have the violation erased, meaning it won't go on your record.

Equipment Violations

If your car has a minor problem, such as a broken tail light or missing mirror, you can be cited for an equipment violation. You should be given up to 30 days to correct the problem and have the charges against you dismissed, unless the problem:

- was caused by persistent neglect (bald tires, for example)
- shows evidence of fraud (such as a forged registration sticker), or
- is an immediate safety hazard (such as a broken windshield).

After you repair the condition for which you were ticketed, you can get any highway patrolman or police officer to certify that you have made the correction. (Call the sheriff or police department to arrange an appointment.) This certification can be provided on the back of the ticket. Then, send the signed ticket to the traffic court, along with a $10 administrative fee, and the charges will be dismissed. (Veh. Code §§ 40610, 40611.) You may be charged with a misdemeanor if you intentionally fail to correct an equipment violation. (Veh. Code § 40616.)

License and Registration Violations

You are legally required to have your driver's license and proof of valid registration with you when driving. If you don't, an officer will usually cite you with a correctable violation. You can have any highway patrolman, police officer, or DMV employee certify (on the back of the citation) that you have a valid current license or registration. Send this certification and a $10 fee to the court address on the notice, and the violation will be dismissed. (Veh. Code § 40611.)

If your license is not current or your vehicle is unregistered when you are stopped, you have committed a different offense. This is not correctable, because you cannot show proof that you were properly licensed or registered. You must get a license or proper registration and pay a substantial fine.

LICENSE SUSPENSIONS AND REVOCATIONS

The California Department of Motor Vehicles (DMV) is authorized to take away your driver's license under certain circumstances. If your license is taken for up to three years, this is considered a suspension. A revocation lasts more than three years. During the time your license is suspended or revoked, you are not legally allowed to drive a vehicle.

Suspension or Revocation Following a Hearing

If you commit any of the following acts, the DMV will hold a hearing to determine if your license should be suspended:

- **Negligent driving.** The DMV uses a point system to identify negligent drivers. A moving violation or accident that is your fault, as reported by an officer, counts as one point. Serious violations, such as reckless driving, hit-and-run, driving over 100 mph, and driving under the influence of alcohol or drugs, count as two points. If you accumulate four points over any 12-month period, six points in a 24-month period, or eight points in a 36-month period, you are considered a negligent driver, and your license can be taken away. (Veh. Code § 12810.5.)

  Even if your point count isn't high enough to be considered negligent under this formula, your license can be taken away if you:

  — are involved in an accident involving death, injury, or serious damage to property (Veh. Code § 13800)

  — are involved in three or more accidents in a 12-month period (Veh. Code § 13800)

  — are convicted of reckless driving two or more times (Veh. Code § 13361)

  — are convicted of hit-and-run driving (Veh. Code § 13361)

  — are convicted of vehicular manslaughter (Veh. Code § 13361)

  — are convicted of possession of certain controlled substances when a vehicle was involved with or incidental to the offense (Veh. Code § 13202(a)), or

  — violate driving restrictions imposed on your license (Veh. Code § 13800).

- **Driving under the influence.** Your license can be suspended for four months for driving with a blood alcohol level of 0.08% or above. (Veh. Code §§ 13353.2-13353.5.) The DMV can impose a one-year or 16-month license suspension for a second or third offense, respectively.

- **Refusing to take a blood, breath, or urine test.** If you are stopped by an officer who suspects you of driving under the influence, you must submit to a test or lose your license for a year. You are entitled to a choice of tests, and the officer must inform you that your failure to take any test will result in a license suspension. If you have already had a suspension or conviction for driving under the influence, your license can be suspended for an additional two years. (Veh. Code § 13353.)

The DMV Hearing

The DMV will notify you of your right to a hearing before your license is suspended. If you don't request such a hearing, in writing, within ten days from the date this notice was sent to you, the DMV is allowed to take action on your case without holding a hearing. If it does so, you may later ask it to reopen the matter. (Veh. Code § 14103.)

Defending Yourself at a DMV Hearing

You may bring witnesses and other evidence to the hearing if you wish. The referee will let you tell your side of the story, and will probably ask some questions about the violations. You will need to convince the referee that there are good reasons why your license should not be suspended. Evidence you should consider presenting includes:

- anything about the violations that is in your favor
- proof that an accident was not your fault
- testimony that you were not offered a choice of blood alcohol tests, or that the officer did not have reasonable cause to believe you were driving under the influence
- proof that you drive many miles a year
- evidence that your livelihood depends on your ability to drive
- statements by witnesses that you are a careful and good driver
- physician's reports of your physical condition and ability to drive, and
- evidence that you have recently completed a driver's training class.

The hearing will be conducted by a DMV "referee," who acts as a judge. The referee can suspend or revoke your license or put you on probation. The terms of probation may include a restricted license (one that allows you to drive only to work, for example) or a requirement that you take a driving class. You can ask the DMV to review the referee's decision within 15 days; you will receive information on how to appeal when you are sent the referee's decision.

Automatic Suspensions

The DMV will take away your license without a hearing if you are convicted of any of the following:

- a felony in which a vehicle was used (Veh. Code § 13350(2))
- causing injury or death while driving under the influence (Veh. Code § 13352)
- misdemeanor driving under the influence, unless the court imposed probation for a first offense and ordered a 90-day driving restriction (Veh. Code § 13352)
- reckless driving, hit-and-run involving bodily injury, or three convictions of hit-and-run or reckless driving within one year (Veh. Code §§ 13350, 13351, 13355)
- possession and possession for sale of certain controlled substances when a motor vehicle was involved in or incidental to the commission of the offense, or
- any drug use or possession offense. (Veh. Code §§ 13202(b).)

Forfeiture and Driving Without a License

Your car may be impounded if you are caught driving without a valid license. If your license expired up to 30 days before you were caught and you can show that you would otherwise have been properly licensed, you should be able to keep your car.

If you are caught a second time for driving without a valid license, your car may be confiscated and sold, and you may even face jail time. (Veh. Code § 14607.6.)

MOVING VIOLATIONS

Many traffic offenses are infractions, which means that you cannot be sentenced to jail if you are convicted. The maximum fine (including penalty assessments) for a first offense is $281. Most of these offenses are reported to the DMV and go on your driving record; this may affect your insurance rates. Your license may also be suspended if you get numerous violations.

Speeding

It is always illegal to exceed 65 mph, or 55 mph on an undivided two-lane road, unless a higher speed limit is posted. (Veh. Code §§ 22349, 22356.)

A speeding citation can also be given if you exceed a safe speed. This is called the basic speed law. The basic speed law requires that drivers use extreme caution in hazardous conditions such as weather, visibility, traffic, and the condition and size of the roadway; or driving at a speed that endangers people or property. Surprisingly, under the basic speed law, it is not necessarily illegal to exceed the posted limit on a street. The posted limit is presumed to be the fastest speed at which you can drive safely, but if the conditions merit, you may be speeding while driving beneath the posted limit, or driving safely above the limit. (Veh. Code § 22351. *Weaver v. Chavez*, 133 Cal. App. 4th 1350.)

Not Stopping

You can be cited if you fail to come to a complete stop at a stop sign. You must stop at the limit line, crosswalk, or entrance to the intersection. You can also be cited for failure to stop if you enter an intersection while a stop light is red. (But as long as your front bumper enters the intersection while the light is yellow, you have not committed this offense.) (Veh. Code §§ 22450, 21453.)

Blocking the Intersection

It is illegal to enter an intersection unless there is enough room to get across without blocking traffic from either side. This is known as the Anti-Gridlock Act. It is most often enforced when traffic is heavy or stopped, and vehicles are stuck in the intersection after the light changes. (Veh. Code § 22526.)

Improper Turning

Several offenses are related to turning. (Veh. Code §§ 22100-22113.)

- **Staying to the right or left edge of the road.** You must stay as close as practicable to the right or left edge of the street (in the lane that is travelling in your direction) when turning right or left.
- **Prohibited U-turns.** You may not make a U-turn if a sign prohibits it. In a business district, you can make a U-turn only at an intersection or opening in a divided highway. In a residential district, you can make a U-turn at any intersection that has a stop sign or light, or anywhere else as long as no car is approaching within 200 feet.
- **Unsafe turning and lane changes.** You must pull out and back up from a stopped position safely. You must signal turns for 100 feet before turning, and you must signal lane changes similarly if there is anyone behind you in any lane traveling in your direction.

Failure to Yield to Pedestrians

Drivers must yield the right of way to pedestrians who are crossing the street in a marked crosswalk or who are crossing at an intersection in an unmarked crosswalk. An unmarked crosswalk is the part of the street that would connect sidewalks on either side of an intersection. (Veh. Code § 21950(a).)

Miscellaneous Violations

A number of moving violations can be fairly lumped together under the category of rudeness. These include failure to yield the right of way, driving too slowly, blocking traffic, tailgating, driving improperly in a carpool lane, and improper passing.

Dealing With an Infraction Citation

You have several options for dealing with infraction citations. You can:

- pay the fine
- go to traffic school and pay the fine (if you do this, the offense won't go on your record)
- plead "guilty with an explanation" at an informal hearing or arraignment and hope that the judge will give you a smaller fine, or
- plead not guilty and fight the ticket.

If you decide to fight the ticket, you will appear before a judge at a trial. You may bring witnesses or evidence if you wish, and you will have the opportunity to cross-examine the officer who cited you. If the officer does not show up, you will be found innocent: The law requires that you be proven guilty, and only the officer's testimony can do that. At some "informal" hearings without the officer present, the officer's notes may be used. However, you do not have to agree to an informal hearing and can insist on a formal trial.

PARKING TICKETS

Parking tickets are big business for the cities and towns that issue them.

If You Don't Pay

Parking tickets won't affect your driving record, as long as you take care of them by either paying the fine or fighting the ticket. But if you accumulate too many parking tickets or wait too long to pay them, the penalties can be severe. The city or county will notify the DMV, which will refuse to renew your registration until you have paid your fines plus an administrative fee.

How to Fight a Parking Ticket

Parking tickets are no longer processed by the courts (except for appeals). Instead, they are handled by the city or county that issued the ticket, or by a private business that handles tickets for the city or county. To contest a parking ticket, you must contact the office listed on the ticket and explain why you don't think you should have to pay. The office will investigate your citation and will mail you the results of the investigation. The office will either cancel your parking ticket (and you are home free) or refuse to dismiss the ticket. If the office won't dismiss the ticket, you can request a hearing within 15 days of the mailing of the written denial by mailing the fine with a letter requesting a hearing as soon as possible. You will then be notified by mail of a hearing date. If you win, the fine will be refunded to you. (Veh. Code § 40215.)

REGISTRATION AND SMOG TESTS

Every year, you must renew the registration on your car. (Veh. Code § 4601.) If you bring a car here from another state, you must register it here within 20 days. (Veh. Code § 4152.5.)

The state may require your car to pass a smog test before you can renew your registration. Except for cars four or less model-years old, all cars made after 1966 are required to have a smog check inspection every two years. If your car doesn't pass on the first try, there is a cap on the amount you must spend to bring it into compliance, depending on the car's year.

Model Year	Allowed Charge
1966-71	$50
1972-74	$90
1975-79	$125
1980-89	$175
1990-95	$300
1996 and newer	$450

(H & S Code § 44017.)

Cars manufactured before 1966 are exempt from the smog check rules unless your registration renewal form says "Smog Check Required." If you qualify as a low-income owner, the repair cost may be lowered to $200. If your emissions control equipment (smog equipment) has been removed, modified, or disconnected, the cost limits do not apply—you must pay whatever it takes to get your car to comply.

If your vehicle cannot be brought into compliance within the cost limit, call the Bureau of Automotive Repair at 800-952-5210. BAR may refer you to a referee station to issue you a waiver.

- **New cars.** If your car is still under warranty, you are entitled to have defects that cause it to fail a smog test corrected for free by the dealer.
- **Used cars.** The seller is required to give the buyer an original smog certificate, not more than 60 days old. If the vehicle is being transferred to a person's grandparent, parent, spouse, child, or grandchild, the old owner does not have to supply a smog certificate.
- **Diesel vehicles.** Diesel vehicles are exempt from smog checks. (H & S Code §§ 44011, 44012.) Owners can fill out the back of their auto renewal registration exempting themselves if the vehicle registration

indicates the vehicle is a diesel. If the registration says "gasoline fueled," the owner must have the car examined by a BAR referee station to get an exemption.

SEAT BELT AND CHILD RESTRAINT REQUIREMENTS

California requires all passengers to wear a seat belt or other safety restraint.

Seat Belts

Every passenger over the age of four must wear a seat belt, unless a disability prevents it. If any passenger is not wearing a seat belt when the car is pulled over, the driver may get a ticket. In addition, any passenger over the age of 16 who is not wearing a seat belt may be personally cited. The fine for a first offense is $20.

The owner of a vehicle is personally responsible for maintaining seat belts in working order. If a car is pulled over and the seat belts are not in usable condition, the owner may be cited, even if she is not in the car at the time. (Veh. Code § 27315.)

People riding in the back of open pickup or flatbed trucks must wear safety belts. This restriction does not apply on farms, if the back of the truck is enclosed, or if the vehicle is being used in a parade that is supervised by law enforcement and the vehicle travels 8 mph or less. (Veh. Code § 23116.)

The law used to prohibit officers from stopping cars only for suspected seat belt violations; only if the driver was pulled over for another suspected offense could the officer issue a seat belt citation. However, police and highway patrolmen are now allowed to stop drivers for seat belt violations alone. (Veh. Code § 27315.)

Car Seats for Children

While riding in a vehicle, every child under the age of six or weighing less than 60 pounds must be in a "child passenger restraint system"—a government-approved child car seat, usually with a harness. The person who gets the ticket is the child's parent or, if no parent is in the car, the driver. The fine for a first offense is $100.

The police can stop a car if they suspect that a child in the car is not in a proper car seat. (Veh. Code §§ 27360, 27360.5, 27361.)

YOUNG DRIVERS

There are a handful of California laws that govern how, where, and when young people can drive.

Instruction Permits

Drivers who are under the age of 18 must obtain instruction permits before applying for a license. A young person must be at least 15 to obtain a permit, and must comply with the following requirements and restrictions pertaining to its use:

- **Education.** A young driver must hold an instruction permit for six months before applying for a provisional driver's license. Permits are issued by the Department of Motor Vehicles when the applicant has completed a required course in driver education (classroom training) and is taking a required course in driver training (behind-the-wheel).
- **Duration.** The instruction permit is valid for only one year.
- **Supervision.** Young drivers holding instruction permits must be supervised by a licensed driver who is at least 18 years old.

Provisional Driver's License

After holding an instruction permit for at least six months, a driver under the age of 18 may apply for a provisional driver's license, which must be renewed every year until the driver turns 21. The following requirements and restrictions apply:

- **Training.** The driver must complete 50 hours of supervised driving practice; at least ten of them must be after dark.
- **Restricted driving times.** During the first year of the provisional license, the driver may not drive between midnight and 5 AM unless accompanied by a licensed parent or guardian, licensed adult over 25 years old, or certified driving instructor.
- **Restricted passengers.** During the first six months, the driver may not transport passengers who are under the age of 20 unless supervised by a licensed parent or guardian, licensed adult over 25 years old, or certified driving instructor. After that time, the driver may, without supervision, transport passengers who are under the age of 20, but only between the hours of 5 AM and 12 AM.

Exceptions to the Rules

A young driver who has a provisional driver's license may drive during the hours of midnight to 5 AM, or transport an immediate family member without the presence of a parent, guardian, licensed driver over 25 years of age, or certified instructor, in the following circumstances:

- **Medical necessity.** The driver has a medical condition that makes the use of alternative transportation unreasonable. The driver must carry a signed statement by his or her doctor containing a diagnosis and probable recovery date.
- **Employment necessity.** The driver has a job that involves driving and other transportation is inadequate. The driver must have a signed statement from the employer, including a probable date when the employment will be completed. For example, teenagers leaving a late-night babysitting job ought to have a note from their employer, verifying that they were working and have no other reasonable way home.
- **School or school activity necessity.** Students may drive during otherwise prohibited times if they are engaged in school activities and there is no reasonable alternative transportation. Students must carry a statement signed by the principal, the dean, or a staff member attesting to the student's participation and estimating when the activity ends. For example, a student driving to early-morning water polo practice should have a note from the coach verifying the student's participation and indicating when the season will be over.
- **Family necessity.** Young drivers may drive during otherwise prohibited hours if it is necessary to transport the driver or a member of the driver's immediate family. The driver must carry a statement signed by the driver's parent or guardian, verifying the reason and stating when the necessity will cease. For example, a young driver who must transport a nondriving sibling to or from work should carry a signed statement from his parent explaining the situation.

Law enforcement officers may not stop a vehicle solely in order to determine whether the driver is in compliance with this law. (Veh. Code § 12814.6.) ■

Index

Remember:
Little publishers have big ears.
We really listen to you.

Take 2 Minutes & Give Us Your 2 cents

Your comments make a big difference in the development and revision of Nolo books and software. Please take a few minutes and register your Nolo product—and your comments—with us. Not only will your input make a difference, you'll receive special offers available only to registered owners of Nolo products on our newest books and software. Register now by:

PHONE
1-800-728-3555

FAX
1-800-645-0895

EMAIL
cs@nolo.com

or **MAIL** us
this registration card

fold here

- -

NOLO

Registration Card

NAME _____ DATE _____

ADDRESS _____

_____

CITY _____ STATE _____ ZIP _____

PHONE _____ EMAIL _____

WHERE DID YOU HEAR ABOUT THIS PRODUCT? _____

WHERE DID YOU PURCHASE THIS PRODUCT? _____

DID YOU CONSULT A LAWYER? (PLEASE CIRCLE ONE)   YES   NO   NOT APPLICABLE

DID YOU FIND THIS BOOK HELPFUL?   (VERY)   5   4   3   2   1   (NOT AT ALL)

COMMENTS _____

WAS IT EASY TO USE?   (VERY EASY)   5   4   3   2   1   (VERY DIFFICULT)

We occasionally make our mailing list available to carefully selected companies whose products may be of interest to you.

❑ If you do not wish to receive mailings from these companies, please check this box.

❑ You can quote me in future Nolo promotional materials.
   Daytime phone number _____.

CLAW 9.0

Nolo *in the* NEWS

"Nolo helps lay people perform legal tasks without the aid—or fees—of lawyers."

—USA TODAY

Nolo books are ..."written in plain language, free of legal mumbo jumbo, and spiced with witty personal observations."

—ASSOCIATED PRESS

"...Nolo publications...guide people simply through the how, when, where and why of law."

—WASHINGTON POST

"Increasingly, people who are not lawyers are performing tasks usually regarded as legal work... And consumers, using books like Nolo's, do routine legal work themselves."

—NEW YORK TIMES

"...All of [Nolo's] books are easy-to-understand, are updated regularly, provide pull-out forms...and are often quite moving in their sense of compassion for the struggles of the lay reader."

—SAN FRANCISCO CHRONICLE

fold here

- -

Nolo
950 Parker Street
Berkeley, CA 94710-9867

Attn: CLAW 9.0